BEYOND A JOKE

BEYOND A JOKE

Inside the Dark World of Stand-up Comedy

BRUCE DESSAU

preface
publishing

Published by Preface 2011

10 9 8 7 6 5 4 3 2 1

Copyright © Bruce Dessau 2011

Bruce Dessau has asserted his right to be identified as the author of this work under the Copyright,
Designs and Patents Act 1988

First published in Great Britain in 2011 by Preface Publishing
20 Vauxhall Bridge Road
London, SW1V 2SA

An imprint of The Random House Group Limited

www.randomhouse.co.uk
www.prefacepublishing.co.uk

Addresses for companies within The Random House Group Limited
can be found at www.randomhouse.co.uk

The Random House Group Limited Reg. No. 954009

A CIP catalogue record for this book is available from the British Library

ISBN 978 1 84809 3201

The Random House Group Limited supports The Forest Stewardship Council (FSC®),
the leading international forest certification organisation. Our books carrying the FSC label are
printed on FSC® certified paper. FSC is the only forest certification scheme endorsed by the leading
environmental organisations, including Greenpeace. Our paper procurement
policy can be found at www.randomhouse.co.uk/environment

Typeset in Dante MT by Palimpsest Book Production Limited,
Falkirk, Stirlingshire
Printed and bound in Great Britain by Clays Ltd, St Ives PLC

Contents

Introduction

It is all Russell Brand's fault. There were a number of reasons why this felt like the right time to write a book about stand-up comedy, but the loon-haired superstar was at the top of every list.

Thanks to Russell Brand – his lifestyle, his hairstyle, Sachsgate, where, as we shall see, a brief, inappropriate answerphone message changed the face and tone of broadcasting – comedy has changed forever. It is now covered on the front pages as well as the arts pages. Dissected by broadsheet postmodernists and used to brighten up tabloids on quiet news days. Barely a week goes by without another scandal examined down to every last scurrilous detail. Another comedian saying the unsayable and getting broadcasters into hot water.

But what goes on behind the scenes and in the heads of the people that make us all laugh? And, more importantly, what makes someone want to be a stand-up comedian? Once again it's that man Russell Brand. A shameless attention-seeker, a man who has behaved in a certain way and led a life that was hardly 'normal'.

In this book I set out to look at the way comedians behave. The extraordinary extremes they go to offstage, the extraordinary lengths they go to onstage to get a laugh. I will be asking what kind of person becomes a comedian. What makes someone want to stand up and make people laugh for a living. It is something absolutely primal yet also one of the strangest things imaginable. To put it bluntly, comedians are not normal. If they were they would not feel compelled to spend their evenings talking to strangers. No wonder they often lead excessive lives when not working. This is the story of sex, drugs, alcohol and living life to the limit. This is about comedians who are not just funny onstage, they are often also funny in the head. The state of mind that can drive them to the brink of insanity and sometimes beyond also appears to drive their comic creativity.

I cannot help thinking that there must be a link between the strain stand-up comedy puts on a performer and their longevity as well as their sanity. I'm not saying you don't get geriatric comedians – George Burns cigar-chomped his way to a ripe old century, Bob Hope wisecracked his way there with the help of an army of scriptwriters – but there must be something deadly in the comedy performance waters.

As I write in the summer of 2011 I've been looking back at pictures of classic comedians. Peter Cook and Dudley Moore, both dead. Eric Morecambe, Tommy Cooper, Tony Hancock and Peter Sellers, long gone, too soon. Lenny Bruce, dead way too young. George Formby, dead in his fifties but looked ten years older. If touring and being constantly creative don't get you, the drink or drugs will. Yet the back-room boys seem to have the ability to soldier on. Hancock's Galton and Simpson are still around as I write, David Croft, Jimmy Perry and Jeremy Lloyd, who in various permutations created *Dad's Army*, *Are You Being Served?* and *It Ain't 'alf Hot Mum* are all around. Most of the Carry On team, apart from Barbara Windsor, are dead, as is producer Peter Rogers – but he was ninety-five when he popped his clogs in 2009. OK, there is Eric Sykes, still going strong at eighty-eight, but he doesn't have many people to reminisce with about the bygone Goon days apart from eighty-nine-year-old Denis Norden. Performing comedy on stage, night after night, takes its toll. As the deathbed saying goes, dying is easy, comedy is hard.

Some greats, such as Lenny Bruce and John Belushi, do not come back from the brink. Others – hello again, Russell – come back and conquer the world. This is a place where light entertainment can get very dark. Sometimes no amount of laughter is ever enough. However big the gig gets they have to seek further thrills offstage, with antics that would make the most Dionysian of rock stars blush.

Comedians go out to work when others go out to play. They do not lead ordinary lives. As Jimmy Carr once said, 'There are 500 people in the room and I'm the only one in the room facing the wrong way.' *Beyond a Joke* is about the people facing the wrong way. In fact it is a bit like a Jimmy Carr gig. There are things here that might make you wince, but you won't be able to look in a different direction.

This journey through comedy's dark side will set out to explore the question of the links between comedy and depression. From the days of the first clown superstar Joseph Grimaldi, gloom and gags have gone hand in hand, prompting an enduring puzzle. Are dysfunctional people drawn to stand-up comedy or does comedy draw out the dysfunctional side of people? Ruby Wax once told me that she had had builders working on her house who were every bit as unstable as comedians she had worked with. On the other hand Jo Brand, a former psychiatric nurse turned national treasure, has seen comedians backstage exhibiting behavioural traits that have prompted her to suggest they seek professional help. More recently Wax has done an entire show, entitled *Losing It*, at London's Menier Chocolate Factory and then in the West End – plus special gigs at The Priory – to attempt to break the taboo surrounding mental illness. Wax was brutally candid when talking about her own highs and lows, but was not angling for the sympathy vote: 'Please don't feel sorry for me, because I got a show out of it.'

Comedians, put in the crudest terms, are a bunch of oddbods. Stand-up comedy is a not a maths exam in which one can score full marks if one works hard enough. It is far too abstract for that. Yet comedians are always looking for that elusive perfect gig. That 100 per cent performance. Or they are looking to stretch themselves. The proverbial clowns who yearn to play Hamlet. A few years ago I interviewed Rob Brydon, a brilliant, instinctive comedian with the ability to really get under the skin of the most intimate of material while also possessing the skill to be a major mainstream comedy star. This was in 2007, when he was invited to appear in the Old Vic's annual charity event, the *24 Hour Plays*, along with a galaxy of luminaries from the worlds of both theatre and light entertainment. The event was named thus because everything is done from devising to performing in one frantic day. During the interview Brydon expressed the desire to have a chance to do something he had not done before and not just his trademark Ronnie Corbett impression. Maybe, he hinted, casting directors would spot this hitherto unheralded skill and give him a new big break.

On the night Brydon was very fortunate. He was privileged to star opposite one of the country's finest leading female actors, Fiona Shaw, in a piece set in a restaurant about a date that fails to go to plan. I thought Brydon was marvellous as the hapless potential boyfriend, and as well as offering his trademark Corbett impression, which brought the house down, he was given the chance to do a spot of serious drama, with plenty of pathos and considerable depth. A few months later I bumped into Brydon on the set of *Gavin and Stacey* in a house near Barry Island. In the intervening months I'd been reading the second volume of Frank Skinner's autobiography. On meeting comedians all they want to hear is that they've been brilliant, advised the Bard of West Bromwich. So I took this on board, and as we queued outside the catering van for lunch (lasagne and crumble, not on the same plate, BBC budgets aren't that tight) I approached Brydon, who was immediately his friendly self, and I said how much I'd enjoyed him at the Old Vic. I was rebuffed with a harrumphing reply that he had ended up doing his brilliant Ronnie Corbett impression as per usual. So much for Skinner's tip that all a comedian wants is a compliment. They naturally want that, but they also want much more.

Whatever their social or economic background, comedians seem to have a positively Rottweiler-powered drive to be noticed. Stephen Fry grew up well educated, surrounded by comfort, money, books and a stable family background. Russell Brand grew up with plenty of love but also in an environment where his relationship with his biological father was less than conventional. Both seemed to crave the spotlight. There is no doubt that some people do it because they have been deprived in some way. Eddie Izzard's ferocious pursuit of the love of an audience appears to have its roots in the fact that his mother died when he was seven. Joan Rivers has said that her mother never told her she loved her. As a result she has been looking for validation ever since. Despite her success it still seems to be about self-esteem. Even in her mid-seventies she is still searching. In her 2010 autobiographical film, *A Piece of Work*, Rivers confessed that her biggest horror was not death but an empty diary page – 'the thought that nobody wants me'.

It takes a particularly odd person to want to tackle the high-wire act of stand-up comedy without a safety net, but maybe that experience once they are there makes them even odder. This is not a book just about scandalous behaviour, but there is certainly plenty of that here. Comedians are statistically highly intelligent, self-obsessed, ego-driven, free-thinking, often solitary, with too much time on their hands – is it any surprise that they might have difficulty finding room for normality in their lives? Oh, and they are at the narcissistic end of the self-obsession scale too. I remember being at a gig and afterwards someone complaining about the act, 'All he did was talk about himself.' That's what stand-up comedians usually do. If they were not that self-obsessed they would probably not have become stand-up comedians. It goes with the territory. Tunnel vision and neediness is part of the job description.

This may be a story that ends with Russell Brand and the new comedy boom that has seen comedians such as Michael McIntyre and John Bishop explode into our consciousness and become unlikely arena-filling deities, but it certainly doesn't start there. As we shall see, modern comedy has its roots in ancient pagan rites and pre-showbusiness religious festivals that go back so far they even predate Ken Dodd telling his first gag about the Inland Revenue. Never mind BBC newsreaders dressing up in leather hot pants and garish make-up for charity, clowns were the true Lords of Misrule, turning convention upside down. Crooked-backed jesters were society's original escape valve, allowing the people to vent their spleen against the Establishment long before Peter Cook and *Beyond the Fringe* poked fun at the prime minister. Comedy has been with us for ever and will be with us for ever.

And some things never change. The story of the excessive, depressive clown goes right back to Joseph Grimaldi, a superstar two centuries ago who died in penury – unable to walk after so many crowd-pleasing pratfalls had broken his body, he had to be carried to the local tavern every night. Lugubriousness and laughter, comedy and tragedy, seem to be two sides of the very same coin. Comedians really do have to grin and bear it in the truest sense.

Beyond a Joke is also a personal memoir. I'm far too young to have seen Joseph Grimaldi in his pomp – he peaked in the 1800s so there is nothing to download either – but I've been a committed comedy enthusiast for over thirty years. Some people chase twisters, I chase punsters. I go to comedy gigs every week for my work. I go to comedy gigs every week when I'm not working. As the book reaches the present day, I've drawn on interviews, off-the-record chats and backstage encounters with some of modern comedy's biggest names. I've gone marathon running with Eddie Izzard. I gave Matt Lucas a lift after a gig in south London when he was starting out. I've encountered Michael McIntyre when he couldn't get arrested and seen Russell Brand close-up at his most arrestingly outrageous.

I wanted to write this book at this point in time because comedy has changed so much in recent years. It is no longer a fringe activity, enjoyed by a minority. It is on prime-time television. It fills arenas more used to housing major sporting events and rock gigs. Adverts, TV columns, talent-show panels, the Internet – comedians are simply everywhere, bestriding the world like smirking colossi. And yet fundamentally comedy has not changed. It is still one man – I'm afraid that yes, it is still usually a man – getting up in front of an audience and talking in exchange for chuckles. Except that now that audience might be 15,000 devoted fans hanging on their every snappy bon mot rather than a couple of boozers and their dog in the back room of a pub.

This book is, most of all, a celebration of live comedy, the lengths people will go to for success and the toll it takes on those involved. Which is why although complicated geniuses such as Peter Sellers, Spike Milligan, Tony Hancock and the Carry On team get much-deserved mentions, the meat of the narrative lurks elsewhere. While for some stand-up is a stepping stone, this is largely about the people who are drawn to it like the proverbial moth to a flame. And like those moths they can get burned. I have concentrated mainly on those comedians whose careers may have inevitably moved on to the screen, but who really excelled in the seething bear pit of the live performance. For me Russell Brand has lost something of his sparkle and danger since he went to Hollywood. Not that you can completely sanitise a talent such as Brand's. A quick glance at his performance in *Forgetting Sarah Marshall* and you can see that his spirit is still there in the decadent, existentialist rock star dialogue. The question, no pun intended, is how long can he keep this up? Will Hollywood eventually iron out all of his lovely creases?

Stand-up comedy is a discipline that is both exquisitely pure and spectacularly complex, from jesters to wandering minstrels, clowns to music hall, from 1960s satirists to the current crop. From the clean-cut to the controversial. It is what Jack Dee called 'the bastard art form', and there are certainly a lot of performers with no fixed parentage in it. I take my humour very seriously, but I also can't stop laughing when I hear a cracking joke. And along with the tears, the pain, the scandal, the shame, there are plenty of cracking gags in here too.

1

The Crying Clown

From Grimaldi to music hall

Today's comedians do not have a monopoly on spectacular mood swings. Or the disruptive, disturbing, dysfunctional behaviour that frequently goes with them. Long before Sigmund Freud made his pronouncement on the nature of comedy, that jokes bear the traces of repressed desires, often sexual or aggressive, there were comedians who could have benefited from a session on the psychoanalyst's couch. It does not matter how successful you are, there will invariably come a time when the psychological stew that makes you such a mesmerising performer will catch up with you.

Take Joseph Grimaldi, comedy's first true superstar. Born in London on 18 December 1778, Grimaldi went on to become the greatest English clown of his day. Even if his name is forgotten he is still remembered today for creating the red-nosed 'Joey' archetype, one of humour's enduring figures and the source of many people's fear of clowns – coulrophobia. Already we can see in a beloved entertainer a juxtaposition between fun and fear, happiness and terror, magic and misery.

I

Yet while Grimaldi's career was a sequence of grand successes onstage, life offstage was much more of a struggle from his very beginnings. Not for nothing did he adopt the punning catchphrase, 'I make you laugh all night, but am Grim-All-Day.'[1] It neatly encapsulated every clown's problem of reconciling the travails of often tedious, frequently harsh reality, when the brightly coloured costume or 'motley' and make-up comes off, with the pretence of their laugh-a-minute stage life. As Bill Hicks used to say sardonically at the start of his gigs nearly two centuries later, 'Good evening. My name is Bill Hicks. I've been on the road now doing comedy for twelve years, so, uh, bear with me while I plaster on a fake smile and plough through this shit one more time.'

Joseph Grimaldi was the biggest star of the day, a friend of the dashing poet Lord Byron and revered Shakespearean actor Edmund Kean. Looking back, it was obvious that he was always destined for the stage. His father Giuseppe, who had had a hard life himself, was also a panto clown. He was a strict disciplinarian known as 'Iron Legs' after his own performing father and prone to violent rages. In the same way later stand-ups would use comedy to avoid bullying, so young Joseph used it to avoid a beating. As with umpteen comedians down the centuries, humour was a way of coping with life's more malevolent whims. Comedy is, perversely, a rational response to a random universe.

This was certainly the case with Joseph Grimaldi, the first great hell-raising funny man, Grimaldi created the template for the modern comedy superstar. But behind the greasepaint he also set out the template for

---

1 Andrew McConnell Stott, *The Pantomime Life of Joseph Grimaldi*, Canongate, 2009, p.200.

the troubled, dysfunctional personality of the modern comedy superstar.[2] According to his biographer, Andrew McConnell Stott, madness probably ran in his family, and he suffered from bouts of paranoia and that almost mandatory stage staple, chronic insecurity. Grimaldi was loved and worshipped by his fans, who would hang on his every quip, but he was also tortured inside. Grimaldi would make and lose fortunes, be the greatest star and also hit rock bottom. He would abuse his body and pay a heavy price. His attitude to women left something to be desired. In his way he was a forerunner and prototype of the modern dysfunctional entertainer, whose life only really made sense when he was in front of an audience.

Joseph Grimaldi inherited his talent from his father and also his prodigious sexual appetite. Giuseppe slept with most of the dancers in the productions he starred in, eventually marrying one, Mary Blagden, at the time little more than sixteen. But the marriage didn't last, and Grimaldi Senior continued to work his way through a number of women, fathering numerous children including Joseph in the run-up to Christmas 1778. Joseph's mother was Rebecca Brooker, another of Giuseppe's teenage mistresses and over forty years his junior.

'Iron Legs' was a larger-than-life figure who had a huge influence on his son. Home life was chaotic and unstable, depending on how the bookings were going. It was feast or famine in the Grimaldi household. Some weeks there would be a banquet on the table, other weeks just scraps. Young Joseph stood out from his peers from an early age. Not

---

2 Troubled souls attract troubled souls. Rock and roll poet Peter Doherty, a big fan of Tony Hancock, penned a song with fellow Libertine Carl Barat entitled 'The Ballad of Grimaldi' about a doomed, destructive love affair.

difficult considering that on Sundays his father dressed him in emerald green with a laced shirt and a jewelled cane. Young Joe was already attracting crowds as he walked down the street before he was a professional performer. He liked the attention, even though his audience was laughing at him, rather than with him.

It was only a matter of time before he joined the family business on a regular basis. According to Grimaldi's memoirs, edited by the young Charles Dickens, he 'made his first bow and his first tumble' at the theatre in Drury Lane at the age of one year and eleven months. But there is some debate about both his age and the location. He may have been older, and it may have been at Sadler's Wells. Not for the first time in showbusiness the truth did not get in the way of an eye-catching story. His unconventional life and parenting gave him an unconventional outlook on the world which would both stand him in good stead but also become a burden. His schooling was lax, but his stage education was strict, with rehearsals starting early in the morning and ending late in the evening. Reading and writing had to be fitted in around learning to dance and pratfall, and young Joseph struggled. He had particular difficulties with his spelling. Like a number of modern freewheeling comedians such as Eddie Izzard and Ross Noble, he may have been dyslexic, but he swiftly developed a sense of humour and in class would joke his way out of any embarrassment when he had difficulty with words.

He learned his real trade performing with his father, but it was not always a happy time. Legend has it that his father once beat him onstage and the watching critics all applauded, impressed by such a convincing performance. Thus the mythology that behind every great performance there is great pain was born. And sometimes it was indeed true that the two were not very far apart. As he grew up and established himself, Joseph Grimaldi would push his body to the limit, doing his slapstick tricks to thunderous applause. He was in agony, but the adrenaline generated by being onstage meant that he barely noticed the pain he was inflicting upon himself at the time. It would in the end, however, catch up with him.

But tragedy was already just around the corner. Giuseppe died suddenly in 1788, when Joseph was only nine. He left money, but in a pattern that would repeat itself, one of the executors spent it and fled the country. Joseph had to become the main breadwinner of the family. It was a devastating blow to lose a parent, but to be forced to work to support his family was a double whammy. There was no time for mourning, but Joseph soon started to suffer from the bouts of depression that would haunt him for the rest of his life, snapping out of a black mood when it was his cue to go onstage.

Things started to look up though, as he learned his craft. Throughout his teenage years he worked hard and in May 1799 married his girlfriend Maria. Soon after she announced that she was pregnant. Joseph Grimaldi was overcoming his setbacks and would soon be playing to packed houses at Sadler's Wells and Drury Lane Theatre. The slapstick character that first made his name was Guzzle the Drinking Clown, which he performed at Sadler's Wells at Easter 1800. He was twenty-one and a star, but in October his wife Maria unexpectedly died in labour and the baby died too. It was an event that broke the clown's heart. There were fears that he might take his own life and concerns for his sanity.

Grimaldi hurled himself into his work, appearing in London and all over England. It is fascinating to see how the comedy circuit today had its parallels over two centuries ago. Acts have always gone wherever the cash was, and Grimaldi was already starting to make a huge amount – £160 in two nights during a tour of Kent, an absolutely enormous sum for the day. He even seemed to be getting over the loss of his wife and child. In 1802 he married Mary Bristow, who had nursed him through a stage injury. She would stay with him through his dramatic highs and lows for nearly thirty years.

As a performer the young in-demand star was constantly developing his act. Soon he created an entirely new character, moving away from the characters of the *commedia dell'arte*, such as the cat-masked Harlequin and the hunchbacked Punch-like Pulcinella. 'Joey' became his instantly recognisable trademark. The white greasepainted face and large red-lipsticked gash of a mouth tapped into something primal. It could be hilarious and haunting, childlike and disturbing. The playful miscreant who would cause havoc onstage, stealing people's wine and starting fights, was a sensation, resulting in standing-room-only sell-outs. It made people laugh, but it was an outer personification of Grimaldi's inner demons. Like many comedians that came after him, Grimaldi was a human game of two halves, whose triumphs onstage were often cancelled out by his disasters off. Even when it came to simple financial matters he was prone to make bad decisions. At one point he amassed £599 – a small fortune which he wanted to invest – but gave it to a man called Newland, who promptly disappeared with it.

The rollercoaster career of Joseph Grimaldi clearly demonstrates that the comedy world has often been an unstable environment. Gigs today – with smoking not allowed and bouncers on the doors – can be relatively sober, sedate affairs, although that has not always been the case. The late lamented Malcolm Hardee ran the similarly late and similarly lamented Tunnel Club in Greenwich in the 1980s, where audiences would often be noisily and anarchically inebriated. Hardee himself was not averse to urinating into a punter's beer glass if the mood took him. Grimaldi also had to deal with riotous gin-fuelled fans and could trump Hardee's hardest night. At Sadler's Wells in 1807 drunks caused some trouble, and during the melée the shout went up of 'Fight, fight.' But it was misheard, and people thought the cry was 'Fire, fire.' In the stampede to escape the imaginary blaze eighteen people died.

Grimaldi consolidated his reputation in shows that have become pantomime staples such as *Mother Goose*, but there was a downside to the merriment. He was acutely aware of himself and coined what would become his 'Grim-All-Day' catchphrase. While it was smiles in public, off duty depression hung over him like a storm cloud, and the contrast fascinated his fans. How could this ebullient figure who seemed to be having so much fun ever be down? One probably apocryphal story that did the rounds concerned him going to see a physician about his melancholia long before the age of psychoanalysis. The physician offered him what he thought would be the perfect prescription, as recalled by performer-turned-librarian Thomas Goodwin in *Sketches and Impressions: Musical, Theatrical and Social (1799–1885)*: 'Go and see Grimaldi.' 'Alas!' replied the patient. 'That is of no avail to me. I am Grimaldi.'[3]

A century and a half later this tale would do the rounds again, only this time it was told about legendary Swiss clown Grock, born Charles Adrien Wettach in 1880. Grock was a huge sensation all over Europe

---

3 R. Osgood Mason, G. P. Putnam's Sons, 1887, p.200.

after World War I. Crowds would flock to see him at the circus and later in music halls, where he made his fortune. The story is that in Hamburg in 1950 a man went to see a psychiatrist and explained how the woes of the world were getting him down, that all he saw around him was sadness and suffering. The psychiatrist said that the world-famous clown Grock was performing in Hamburg that night and that he should go and see him and cheer up. 'Doctor,' came the inevitable reply like the punchline to existentialism's darkest joke, 'I am Grock.'[4]

Comedian Arthur Smith, the self-appointed Mayor of Balham, who once stood naked in his high street and sang the Moldovan national anthem as a forfeit for losing a bet, likes to quote Friedrich Nietzsche's remark that laughter is 'the one true metaphysical consolation'. But it didn't seem to help Grimaldi. Success didn't make him any happier when the curtain fell. Reading accounts of his life suggests that he may have been an early example of a bipolar performer, manic periods inspiring his onstage flights of fancy, but the low points without the buzz of the audience to feed upon being desperately hard to cope with. Grimaldi was certainly the first clown to be associated with depression. He is comedy's first troubled personality. The archetypal lonely figure who entertains thousands but cannot entertain the prospect of being alone. For the origins of the tears of a clown look no further.

There is one theory, proposed by Cesare Lombroso in his 1891 book *The Man of Genius*, that 'what society recognised as brilliance was in fact the fruit of a split personality. Of these personalities one is the inverse of the other, the lack of moderation in either field providing the relative

---

4 26 June 2011, Soho Theatre, London. American comedian Jeff Garlin, told yet another version, citing 'Coco the Clown' as the source.

component with its exceptional force.'[5] A persuasive case for this theory could be made for many comedians from Grimaldi onwards – depressed offstage, hugely creative once at work. Freud later went on to take this further, suggesting in his 1927 essay *Humour* that 'a person adopts a humorous attitude toward himself in order to ward off possible suffering'. Though there was a haunting payback to this theory. That this kind of avoidance technique, repressing darker thoughts and impulses, could lead ultimately to madness.

The best modern comedy certainly seems to hark back to Grimaldi in its fondness for transgression. From drag artistes to improvisers to Russell Brand, there is darkness as well as levity in each act and in each performer's life. It is the legacy of Grimaldi that we wonder what traumatic thing may have happened in the lives of great modern entertainers, from Frankie Howerd to Tommy Cooper, to have made them what they were. We should note that the world of the stage back then was every bit as wild as it is today. Grimaldi was not the only one whose behaviour could be over the top. Grimaldi's contemporary Edmund Kean was a huge drinker and womaniser and once offered 'I always take a shag before the play begins' as an explanation for being late for a performance.[6]

It was not just Grimaldi's mood that drove him on, however. The world of clowning in the early nineteenth century was every bit as fiercely competitive as the world of stand-up today. Rivals would surreptitiously watch each other's box office receipts or look to see who was being written about most favourably in the newspapers of the day.

---

5 Stott, p.321.
6 Ibid., p.262.

Grimaldi worked hard to see off the many contenders for his crown, such as the influential Jean-Baptiste Laurent, who was responsible for incorporating elongated shoes into the clown's sartorial repertoire. Underhand tricks were far from unknown. One contemporary tried to damage Grimaldi's reputation by billing him in the line-up of a London show when he knew Joseph was working in Birmingham. Grimaldi got wind of the plot and after a breathless hundred-mile nineteen-hour journey by stagecoach made it onstage in the nick of time, pushing past the understudy who was about to go on. Arguments about performances in bars and hostelries were also every bit as heated as they are today on Twitter. When ticket prices went up there were audience riots, with protesters waving banners saying 'OP' – old prices.

One of Grimaldi's strengths was his versatility. He received praise for his straight acting in Sheridan's *The Rivals* and was a satirist too, commenting on class and culture and donning coal scuttles for boots to impersonate a hussar in the middle of the Napoleonic Wars. His favourite type of eccentric outfit involved crafting costumes from vegetables and fruit, most notably in *Harlequin Asmodeus* in 1810, in which he created a 'monster' who then 'attacked' him. According to writers Dalton and Mary Gross this edible fellow may have been part of the inspiration for that other DIY human, *Frankenstein*, written by Mary Shelley and first published later that decade.

In these respects the clown whose name sounds like a particularly bleak supermarket was a prototype for a very contemporary type of celebrity: someone with marketable talents and a name that shifts tickets, which means he can just as easily appear in a drama as a comedy. These days we call it stunt casting; back then it was what stars did. If there had been television in the early 1800s Grimaldi would no doubt have been a chat-show regular too. But he did have his flops, and the consequences were not merely bad reviews. In 1818 he played Grimalkin the Cat in *Puss in Boots* and purred his way through a performance that was greeted initially with cheers. But then a fight broke out in the audience, seats were smashed and a hole was ripped in the curtain when some of the audience objected to the sight of Grimaldi tricking the ogre into turning into a mouse and eating him.

Success could not last for ever though. In his forties Grimaldi's work began to take its toll. Numerous falls had caused his muscles to creak; he had breathing problems and was unable to perform. Sometimes his son Joseph Samuel stood in for him, but the end was on the cards. When he made his last appearance on 27 June 1828 aged only forty-nine, he was too ill to stand and sang sitting down. He had effectively retired from the stage four years earlier. 'I now stand worse on my legs than I used to on my head,' he said in an emotional speech at Drury Lane. The audience demanded an encore, but Grimaldi was simply all laughed out and was unable to give them one. And despite his huge reputation he was shocked to discover that he did not have much in the way of money. By the time of his last performance he was broke. Only benefit shows kept him from destitution.

While he may not have had any money, he remained as popular as ever. When he visited theatres the audiences would call for him to perform his classic song 'Hot Codlins' (toffee apples). In the end this became so disruptive producers were faced with a choice: ban Grimaldi or ban the audience from calling for him to sing. They cannily opted for the latter, knowing that Grimaldi's presence even offstage helped to sell tickets. Without income from shows, however, he was forced to downsize to a small residence in Islington. After his wife Mary died he became increasingly weak, his legs gave out and he had to be carried to the pub every night. On 1 June 1837 he was carried to the pub as usual, then went home to bed. In the morning his housekeeper found him dead. He was fifty-eight.

The death of Grimaldi marked the end of an era. Clowns in pantomime started to fade as pantomimes featured more dialogue and less mime. This is why today clowns are more associated with circuses than the stage. But as clowns drifted towards the fringes in the Victorian era, live comedy became stronger than ever. Following the Theatre Act of 1843 that allowed drinking and smoking in music halls, tavern-owners started to open performance rooms to increase trade. Music halls offering entertainment alongside alcohol began to flourish, much to the horror of the temperance movement, which was trying to keep people away from alcohol, not drive them to it.

By the late 1800s music hall stars were huge celebrities, loved by everyone from the working classes to the aristocracy. Every city high street was peppered with music halls and every bill was peppered with comedians. Dan Leno, born George Galvin, was arguably the first music hall megastar of the late nineteenth century. Dubbed 'the funniest man on Earth', he started life in extreme poverty, in a tenement at the back of King's Cross in 1860, and made his stage debut when still a child at the Cosmotheca Music Hall in Paddington, where he was billed as 'Little George, the Infant Wonder, Contortionist and Posturer'. He went on to be the highest-paid performer of his day.

Leno was actually one of the few stars of the era whose career was not touched by scandal, though even he was rumoured to have one skeleton in the closet. It was claimed that he had married Birmingham-born singer Sarah Lydia Reynolds in 1883 rather than the actual date of 1884 so that fans would not realise that their daughter Georgina was illegitimate. Leno's parents were said to have been absent from the wedding ceremony because they were preparing the food. The real reason, some speculated, was that they were embarrassed about their granddaughter being born out of wedlock. Or perhaps they were just babysitting.

He made his name creating songs and characters, and was in such demand that he would go from theatre to theatre doing his act umpteen times in one night. He was a hugely energetic physical comedian who at his peak was earning a phenomenal £230 a week. Leno was very much a forerunner of the modern character comedian, creating instantly recognisable characters tinged with pathos that everyone could relate to – a beefeater with a fondness for alcohol, the chatty old lady who would never stop talking. He told proper jokes rather than merely trot out patter, and was so successful he was the subject of an early form of merchandising. An inkwell was made in his image, with the top of his hinged head titling back so that one could dip one's pen into him.

Leno performed in front of Queen Victoria and then later Edward VII at Sandringham in 1901. He became a bastion of the Establishment, being given a diamond tiepin by King Edward and nicknamed the 'king's jester'. But at his death aged forty-three in October 1904 his death certificate stated that he had died of 'General Paralysis of the Insane', a euphemism for syphilis, although he may have had a brain tumour. Some said he died of a nervous breakdown, having performed every day for thirty-five years, sometimes up to twenty gigs a night. Whatever the cause of his death, he spent his last months surrounded by mad men in Baldwyn's Park lunatic asylum in Bexley, south-east London. Maybe his near-contemporary Marie Lloyd had a sense of some inner pain when she remarked, 'Ever seen his eyes? The saddest eyes in the whole world. That's why we all laughed at Dear Danny. Because if we hadn't laughed we should have cried ourselves sick. I believe that's what real comedy is, you know, it's almost like crying.'[7]

Leno's ghost is said to haunt the Theatre Royal Drury Lane. He used to use lavender water, and if the scent of lavender is smelt at a production today it is assumed that Dan Leno has been nearby. Leno lived on in another way too. Peter Sellers was convinced that he had spoken to him via the Ouija board, and during some performances felt as if he was possessed by the spirit of Dan Leno.

Music hall spawned many stars who were celebrated and condemned by different sections of society. Marie Lloyd seemed to spend as much time dealing with controversy as she did dealing with fans. Lloyd was born Victoria Alice Matilda Wood in 1870 and after singing with her sisters often in mission halls about the evils of alcohol branched out on her own, changing her name first to Bella Delamare and then to Marie Lloyd, reputedly after seeing the surname in the title of a weekly newspaper and thinking it sounded posh. Success came swiftly with the hit song 'The Boy I Love Is Up in the Gallery'. But that was one of her more clean-cut ditties. Many of her songs were filled with innuendo and

---

7 Stephen Weissman, *Chaplin, A Life*, 2008, Arcade, p.87.

double entendres. On the page there was nothing smutty about the lyrics, but when Lloyd sang the line 'She'd never had her ticket punched before' from 'Oh Mr Porter' and added a sly wink, the audience all knew that she was not necessarily singing about train travel. Lloyd performed in pantomime with Dan Leno at Drury Lane, but preferred performances where she could address the audience directly and form a real relationship with them.

The intimate, subversive style of songs such as 'A Little of What You Fancy Does You Good' and 'I Sits Among the Cabbages and Peas' – about gardening of course – made Lloyd hugely popular. But it also made her a target for moralisers who wanted the music halls closed down, considering them dens of iniquity. After protests Lloyd had to defend herself in front of one of the grandly titled vigilance committees. She demonstrated that any song could be filthy and any song clean by doing 'Oh Mr Porter' without any risqué asides and the traditional, twee 'Come into the Garden Maud' as if it was the bawdiest song in Christendom. When the theatre censor the Lord Chamberlain objected to her singing 'I sits among the cabbages and peas' she helpfully changed the lyrics to 'I sits among the cabbages and leeks'. When challenged she turned on the innocent charm: 'I can't help it if people want to turn and twist my meanings.'

She was a powerful figure in the entertainment world. In 1907, when the music halls tried to make lesser performers do extra shows for no extra pay, she was instrumental in organising a strike. She was generous with both her time and her money, holding meetings in her Hampstead home, but this was to rebound on her. The strike was successful but the theatre owners had their revenge. In 1912 the Royal Command

Performance had a music hall theme and yet Lloyd was not invited. Instead she performed around the corner at the Pavilion Theatre and announced, 'Every Performance by Marie Lloyd is a Command Performance' and 'By Order of the British Public'.

Her private life was equally controversial. She was married three times. Percy Charles Courtenay was a racetrack tout who contrived to meet her backstage after taking a shine to her. She was already pregnant with their daughter Marie, who also went onstage, when they married, but it was a stormy, violent relationship. They split up in 1893, but he used to hang around the stage door and harass her until she took out a warrant to keep him away, fearing for her life. In 1905 when her divorce was granted she married the singer Alexander Hurley.

Lloyd separated from Hurley in 1910, when she fell for jockey Bernard Dillon – she was forty, he was twenty-two. In 1913 they arrived in America calling themselves Mr and Mrs Dillon and were refused entry on the grounds of 'moral turpitude'. They were due to be deported but at the eleventh hour were allowed to stay as long as they slept in separate accommodation. They eventually married in 1914 – Lloyd knocked some years off her age, saying she was thirty-seven not forty-six to make the union sound more respectable – but it was not a happy marriage. Bernard Dillon was violent and abusive and both became heavy drinkers. In 1920 Dillon was charged with assaulting Marie's father, John Wood. They separated and Lloyd continued with her career, but the years had taken their toll on both her voice and her reliability. On 4 October 1922 at the Empire in Edmonton she was singing 'One of the Ruins That Cromwell Knocked About a Bit' and staggered all over the stage before falling over. The audience thought this was part of the act – as they would when Tommy Cooper had a heart attack onstage in 1984 – and laughed, but Lloyd was seriously ill. She died three days later aged only fifty-two.

The comedian has of course roots even further back than the 1800s. He – and it was usually a he – would take the form in different societies of a trickster who operated outside society's norms. Native Americans believed in a fertility character known as Kokopelli, a hunchbacked figure carrying a bag of seeds with a huge erection. Frank Skinner used to wear a Kokopelli ring on tour as a lucky charm. Kokopelli would go around playing pranks on villagers, who would laugh so much they would not notice him ravishing their women, before moving on to another village the following night and doing the same thing. Much in the same way, in fact, that Russell Brand used to operate before he met Katy Perry. Then there is Loki, the Norse god of mischief. Loki also happens to be the first name of Loki Mackay, the current manager of the Comedy Store in Piccadilly Circus, where the modern comedy boom started in 1979.

In European medieval history there was the Lord of Misrule, who was crowned during the Feast of Fools every winter. Inspired by the Roman festival of Saturnalia, society's normal rules would be turned upside down. Masters became servants, servants became masters. As with the jester who was granted licence to speak out in the king's court, this was paradoxically a way of confirming the natural order. The jester was society's safety valve, a controlled way of expressing discontent. In pre-Christian times the original Saturnalia fool kings, however, were sometimes sacrificed at the end of their fleeting reign at the top. Modern-day comedians just end up on *I'm a Celebrity Get Me Out of Here*.

The clown has always had tacit permission to break boundaries, whether a special group of Pueblo indians mocking sacred ceremonies or the modern circus clown tipping water over his chums. In the circus the clown performs within a ring. Anything goes within this line. Stewart Lee would start his 2005 show *'90s Comedian* by drawing a chalk circle on the stage to stand in. This, he explained, was what medieval clowns used to do outside churches to protect themselves from being persecuted for heresy.

Comedy has always had a habit of drawing in the alienated misfits of society, people who set their own moral compass, people who have difficulty conforming, who would struggle to slot into conventional, everyday life due to their physical or psychological make-up, or both. People who craved love and attention that they felt they lacked. Like sport, pop stardom or comedy today, music-hall success in the late 1800s and early twentieth century offered a means of escape from the quotidian grind of daily life. Tolerance and acceptance too. And also financial rewards. Take the tale of male impersonator Vesta Tilley, who started dressing as a man onstage when she was just five years old in the late 1860s. Later in her career she created a series of male characters, including the enduring would-be gent Burlington Bertie and Algy, 'the Piccadilly Johnny with the Little Glass Eye'. In return Tilley earned up to £500 a week. Then there was El Nino Farini, who came from a long line of performers and whose speciality was hanging from a trapeze by the neck while playing the drums. These people had particular talents that drew them inexorably towards the stage. Little

Tich, real name Harry Relph, was only four feet tall and had six fingers on each hand. He was internationally famous for his 'big foot' dance in which he cavorted around the stage in shoes that were two feet long. Tich would balance on them, strut around on them and even hide behind them. Monty Python's Ministry of Silly Walks had nothing on Little Tich.

But there was often a downside to success. George Leybourne, born in the Gateshead slums in 1842, wrote the lyrics to 'The Daring Young Man on the Flying Trapeze' and co-wrote the song 'Champagne Charlie' – in an early example of product sponsorship he had a lucrative deal with Moët and Chandon to sing its praises and in return be seen in public drinking it. Leybourne had a rival, The Great Vance, who had a similar deal with Veuve Clicquot champagne. The two performers were the Oasis and Blur of their day, constantly challenging each other. Vance had a hit with 'Walking in the Zoo', Leybourne responded with the rather less catchily titled 'Lounging at the Aq', about the London Aquarium. But there was a dark side to this lucrative line in product placement. Leybourne developed a taste for alcohol and the excess killed him. Despite his huge success he died broke at the age of forty-two.

The entertainment game can be ruthless. Duplicity and doublethink became a way of life in the early twentieth century. Willie Hammerstein was the son of original American theatrical impresario Oscar Hammerstein and the father of Oscar Hammerstein II, the composer who went on to write *The King and I, Oklahoma!* and numerous other Broadway smashes with Richard Rodgers. Willie Hammerstein has a place in comedy history as the man who brought vaudeville to the masses with shows that were unashamedly populist and often sensationalist. He managed the Victoria Theatre on the corner of West 42nd Street and Seventh Avenue in New York and was always coming up with publicity stunts and novel ways to attract an audience. 'Anything's a good act that will make 'em talk,' he used to say. In a foreshadowing of today's obsession with celebrity in all its manifold guises, he would often simply book members of the public who had appeared in sensational tabloid stories. If pressed he would claim that they had some showbiz talent, and would bill them as something like The Singing Murderess.

Willie was a truly great showman, with a very modern fondness for pithy sound bites, such as his motto 'The best seats in a theatre for a producer are seats with asses in them.' He booked freak acts, sensationalist acts and, legend has it, he once arranged for one of his own acts, Gertrude Hoffman, to be arrested for indecency when she did her Salome-style dance of the seven veils. After the court case the judge ordered Hoffman to wear tights and sent a representative to check up on her. Long before Frank Bruno did panto, Hammerstein booked sports stars such as baseball's Babe Ruth and boxing's John L. Sullivan. He cannily realised that their names were enough to put those asses on those seats. Each time he made the papers with a new story the Victoria box office went into a frenzy.

In 1908 he put a woman dubbed Sober Sue onstage and offered a $100 prize to anyone who could make her smile and $1,000 to anyone who made her laugh – advertising the event with 'You Can't Make Her Laugh – $1,000 If You Can!' In Sober Sue's grim visage comedy and tragedy were supposed to do battle. All the great vaudevillians of the age turned up. All went away unsuccessful. There was understandable outrage across Broadway however, when the truth emerged. Sober Sue was an elderly woman called Susan Kelly who was paid twenty dollars a week to appear, and legend has it she was either blind or deaf or suffered from facial paralysis and was incapable of raising a grin. It was all just a ruse to get those asses on seats by getting stars to appear for peanuts. Hammerstein was the one who was really laughing. His gimmick created a phrase of the day. If a show was genuinely funny, critics would say it 'could make even Sober Sue laugh'. But when the truth emerged the comedy world would never be so innocent again. From sad clowns to unsmiling ladies, the people who banked the box-office receipts were the ones having the last laugh.

Hammerstein was a bona fide colourful character pulling the strings from behind the scenes. As we shall see in the forthcoming pages, a lot of the time comedians have not needed a puppetmaster to get them into the papers, they can do that job for themselves. Sometimes, though, they might need someone to keep them out of the papers. However, Hammerstein's headline-grabbing tactics live on in the tabloid publicists and club-running sensationalists a century later.

2

Booze, Broads and the Painted Penis

Charlie Chaplin and Hollywood's vaudeville hellraisers

The emergence of cinema hammered the first nail into the music hall coffin, before radio and then television slammed the lid. But as one opportunity for bad behaviour closed another opened. Comedians who had cut their teeth on the stage made the transition from vaudeville to celluloid. Many of the stars who went on to become Hollywood institutions had started out treading the boards, a number of them in England, taking their cue from Dan Leno. It is impossible to chart the history of scurrilous stand-ups without a dip into the history of Hollywood.

Cinema's greatest clown Charlie Chaplin was born in south London on 16 April 1889. If a troubled childhood scarred by deprivation is an explanation for success as an adult then it is no surprise that Chaplin became a superstar. His early years were far from easy. His father, Charles Chaplin Senior, was a heavy drinker who died of cirrhosis. His mother, Hannah, suffered from mental illness and spent time in an asylum as well as the workhouse. Her madness might have been due to syphilis. Before she gave birth to Charlie, Hannah may have worked as a prostitute to supplement her meagre income – during this time his older illegitimate half-brother Sydney was born.

Victorian London was a tough place to be born if you were poor. Chaplin's parents moved from digs to digs and split up when he was three. Charlie's father was dead by the time Charlie was ten. Like Grimaldi, Chaplin had to grow up quickly. Shy and quiet when not performing, he worshipped Dan Leno and earned his first few pennies as a dancer as part of the Eight Lancashire Lads. In his early teens, however, he turned to comedy, joining Fred Karno's Army, the gang of British comedians working the theatres, which also included Sydney Chaplin and a young Stan Laurel.

Fred Karno is a hugely important yet often overlooked figure in British comedy history. Later there would be the Carry On team and the Comic Strip ensemble, but in the early years of the twentieth century Karno was comedy king. Operating out of two adjoining houses in Vaughan Road in Camberwell, he sent his acts all over London in special buses. The former performer himself was something of a character, and is said to have invented the custard-pie-in-the-face gag. When acts asked for a pay rise he handed them a large hat and said, 'For big heads.' Like many impresarios before and after him he was decidedly careful with cash – he claimed that he was getting his comics plenty of work, why did they need more money? His personal life had its fair share of hiccups, which he dealt with in his own idiosyncratic style. In 1902, soon after his wife Edith had given birth to a child, she received a package of photographs in the post from Fred, featuring her husband and another woman naked. This was Fred Karno's way of breaking the news that he had a mistress – the Edwardian equivalent of divorce by Facebook. His wife and children moved out and Marie Moore moved in. But Fred was reluctant to pay maintenance and hoped that maybe he could lure his wife back – both for a ménage à trois and to keep his outgoings down.

In 1912 Karno took his troupe to America, where their sketch-based revues were a major hit. In *Mumming Birds* Chaplin played two drunken theatregoers, a well-heeled 'swell' and a lower-class boozer. Both in turn disrupted the performance taking place onstage, the first by being noisy and awkward as he made his way to his seat, the second nearly falling from the boxes onto the stalls. The sketch was well established – Sydney Chaplin had also played the role for Karno. Film-makers realised that this wordless knockabout humour would work perfectly in cinemas, and Chaplin was offered a movie contract with Mack Sennett's Keystone Film Company. Sure enough his talents as a mimic and a silent clown transferred easily to the screen, with his Little Tramp character quickly becoming iconic, making its debut in 1914 in *Kid Auto Races at Venice* and then in *Mabel's Strange Predicament*, which quickly followed. In his autobiography Chaplin claims his outfit was casually put together, the main aim to get laughs out of contrast, so he wore baggy pants, tight jacket, big shoes, cane and hat. The moustache was an afterthought, added because Mack Sennett had expected Chaplin to be much older. *Mumming Birds* itself made it to the screen eventually, as part of a 1915 short, *A Night in the Show*, and also helped to put Chaplin on the movie map.

There has been controversy over the origins of the Little Tramp. It is often accepted that the roots of the idea for the personality came from a Karno sketch character, Jimmy the Fearless, an underdog who would get into sticky situations with authority figures but end up triumphant. In one notable visual gag he would slice up a loaf of bread until it resembled an accordion. Chaplin was said to have been offered the role but was nervous about trying something new and initially turned it down, letting his friend Arthur Stanley Jefferson – better known as Stan Laurel, born in Ulverston in the north of England on 16 June 1890 – do it. When Chaplin saw it was a hit, however, he took the character over, sidelining Laurel. Yet nothing is ever that simple. The Little Tramp may also have been inspired by something specifically American – the homeless hobos who criss-crossed America on trains, scraping by on scraps and the generosity of strangers.

Another version of events casts Chaplin in a more negative light. According to Laurel's biographer Frederick Lawrence Guiles, Stan came up with some of the ideas for the Little Tramp and showed them to Chaplin while they were sharing digs in America. Guiles claimed that Chaplin didn't just purloin the character, he had Laurel sacked from the company. He then started performing it, and the two great British comedians never spoke again. Whatever the truth, the Little Tramp propelled Chaplin ahead of his peers. It would take Laurel a decade to catch him up, after teaming up with Oliver Hardy. In fairness, Chaplin never claimed to be entirely original – pioneering French knockabout star Max Linder was a clear influence, as was Dan Leno. But the similarities with Laurel's early style are very striking indeed

Chaplin, rather like his character, was clearly no fool. He could see he was on to a winner and demonstrated a canny streak by negotiating a better deal for himself with Sennett. Then in 1919 he set up an entirely new company, United Artists, with Douglas Fairbanks, Mary Pickford and D. W. Griffith. It was a move that brought him major fame and enormous wealth. Privately, however, his life was already becoming complicated. In 1918 he married sixteen-year-old actress Mildred Harris, but they separated after little more than a year. After their divorce in 1920 she went on to have a relationship with the Prince of Wales, who would later become King Edward VIII before abdicating.

The 1920s was a truly golden era for Chaplin, but along with bouquets came brickbats. Accusations of control freakery were thrown in his direction, but the success of his films suggested that he was merely a perfectionist with exacting standards. Like many comedians after him, Chaplin may have suffered from a form of obsessive–compulsive disorder, which helped his work but hindered his life. He was said, for instance, to bathe up to a dozen times a day. You don't have to be Sigmund Freud to work out that this may have been an attempt to cleanse himself of his grim slum-dwelling origins.

The 1920s was also a mixed time for Charlie's half-brother Sydney. Having been quite successful as a comic performer himself in the early days of Hollywood, he had been happy to take more of a background role, guiding Charlie's career and helping to negotiate his first million-dollar contract. He was also a successful entrepreneur outside show-business while still acting, helping to set up Syd Chaplin Airlines. In the late 1920s, however, Sydney signed his own lucrative contract with British International Pictures, an ambitious new company based at Elstree. Having made one film, *A Little Bit of Fluff*, which showed that he still shared Charlie's deft gift for physical comedy, things were looking good for Sydney until he was involved in a scandal shortly before the making of *Mumming Birds*, the title harking back directly to the long-running sketch Sydney and then Charlie had starred in when Fred Karno's troupe toured America in the early 1900s. Before filming commenced, actress

Molly Wright claimed that Chaplin had bitten off one of her nipples. Sydney had taken the precaution of leaving the country for Belgium, so she sued British International Pictures for 'assault, libel and slander'. The company paid out to avoid a salacious court case, and Sydney hoped that the gutter press would not have the kind of field day it had enjoyed with his scandal-prone half-sibling. *Mumming Birds* was never made and Sydney turned out not to have been such a great businessman after all. The only thing outstanding about this Chaplin's career was a string of unpaid tax bills. Sydney Chaplin was declared bankrupt in 1930. He still lived well, however, until he died in France on 16 April 1965.

Sydney's more illustrious relative was undoubtedly a creative comic genius, but like so many before and since him, prone to disaster when it came to forming and sustaining relationships. One of his greatest productions, *The Kid* (1921), mixed pathos with sublime slapstick humour as Chaplin's Little Tramp brings up an abandoned baby. It was a film that tugged at the heartstrings and made a star of Chaplin's tiny sidekick, Jackie Gleason. While the movie had a happy ending, Chaplin's private life was less triumphant. Lita Grey, born Lillita Louise MacMurray, had had a part in *The Kid,* and when Chaplin made *The Gold Rush* (1925) he embarked on an affair with his teenage co-star. Grey became pregnant and had to leave the production. Chaplin reputedly offered to pay her to marry someone else, but Grey's mother insisted that they tie the knot despite a twenty-year age gap. Grey and Chaplin had two sons in quick succession, but it was not a cheerful union. By the time he made *The Circus*, in 1928, he was already in the middle of a major divorce battle. Grey's grounds for divorce included miserliness, neglect and, perhaps most damaging, Chaplin's sexual behaviour.

27

The resulting case was viciously fought out in public when the divorce papers were published. Grey seemed hell-bent on ruining Chaplin's career, while Chaplin claimed he was the victim of a 'dastardly plot'. He told the press the stress had caused him to have a nervous breakdown and it was nonsense that Grey had seen him 'necking' fellow performer and mutual friend Merna Kennedy. Chaplin's defence didn't wash, however, which was understandable as he had probably indulged in a lot more than necking with Kennedy. Nor did his pleas of (relative) poverty, in which he claimed that most of his money was being ploughed back into film production, sway the court. Grey was awarded $825,000, then the largest divorce settlement in American history.

One of the allegations in the divorce papers was Chaplin's infidelity. It became clear that he had a libido and ego that powered his sexual engine as much as his creative talents. Before their marriage he had been involved with his early co-star Edna Purviance. They had remained friends and appeared in over thirty films together. In fact she stayed on Chaplin's payroll until her death in 1958. Sometimes his urges bit back – literally. After the release of *The Gold Rush* he was said to have pursued a woman called Blyth Daly at a post-premiere party while his wife and baby were at home, until Daly bit him so hard Chaplin panicked that he was suffering from blood poisoning.

In 1925 Chaplin also found time for an affair with Louise Brooks, a strikingly glamorous bob-haired icon most famous for her appearance in the 1929 melodrama *Pandora's Box*. Brooks revealed an unusual Chaplin habit. He used to paint his penis with iodine, as this was believed to reduce the risk of contracting sexually transmitted diseases. 'Charlie came running at me with his little red sword,' she recalled. It was a party trick that understandably never made it into his movies. Chaplin's fixation on hygiene may well have been linked to memories of his mother's syphilis and his fear of madness. The iodine had another childhood resonance. With their mother in the workhouse, Charlie and Sydney had been sent away to Hanwell School for Orphans and Destitute Children to the west of London. While there Charlie contracted ringworm and had to have his head shaved and painted with iodine to sort out the problem.

Chaplin's career was strong enough to survive the divorce scandal with Grey. He went on to make enduring films with a political edge, such as *Modern Times* in 1936 and *The Great Dictator* in 1940, but even when he was in late middle age his libido got in the way of his movie career. In 1942 he was accused of being the father of actress Joan Barry's baby. Chaplin was impressed by Barry's potential and had given her a film contract, capped teeth and fur coat. In his autobiography Chaplin gives a rather long-winded quasi-medical explanation for her appeal. 'Miss Barry was a big handsome woman of twenty-two, well built, with upper regional domes immensely expansive which . . . evoked my libidinous curiosity.'[8] His curiosity was satisfied when he bedded her following his divorce from his third wife, Paulette Goddard. Barry became pregnant and had a daughter, but blood tests suggested that Chaplin was not the father.

The relationship threw up plenty of ripe details for the gossip columns. Barry was reputedly unstable. Before she met Chaplin she had been known to shoplift, binge-drink and take drugs. The relationship was never going to be a placid one, and perhaps Chaplin was drawn to her volatility because it had echoes of his own mother's mental illness. She

---

8 Chaplin, *My Autobiography*, Penguin, p.408.

was said to have visited him over Christmas 1942 and pointed a gun at him before they ended up in bed together. Despite the negative blood tests the court still ordered him to support the child. Some commentators were not convinced Chaplin was not the father, speculating that he had been able to falsify the paternity test results. The tide of public opinion seemed to have turned against the superstar.

There was no happy ending for either Chaplin or Barry. Chaplin's film career never quite recovered this time. His next film, *Monsieur Verdoux*, about the trial and execution of a ladykiller in the murderous sense, failed to recapture past commercial glories. Barry was institutionalised in 1953 and diagnosed as schizophrenic after she was found walking barefoot in the streets, carrying a pair of baby sandals and a child's ring, and saying, 'This is magic.'

Chaplin had as much influence on comedy as Grimaldi. While he slipped out of favour after World War II and went into exile, his talent has never been forgotten. The Little Tramp's movies live on, and his reputation for excess off the screen also endures. In the 1960s he wrote his autobiography, in which he reflected on the nature of being a comedian and pondered the psychological make-up of clowns. 'Many famous English comedians committed suicide,'[9] he wrote, naming three long-forgotten names – T. E. Dunville, Mark Sheridan and Frank Coyne. Mark Sheridan was a huge music hall star and had been responsible for popularising the song 'I Do Like to Be Beside the Seaside'. Born in County Durham he was a success all over Britain. On the surface he was a jovial joker, nicknamed after one of his hit songs 'one of the b'hoys', but he

---

9 Chaplin, *My Autobiography*, p.46.

was also plagued with insecurities and would sometimes not turn up for scheduled performances because of illness brought on by nerves. In January 1918 he opened in a new show, *Gay Paree,* at the Coliseum in Glasgow. The reviews the next day were not quite as adulatory as Sheridan was used to. Later that afternoon his body was found in Kelvingrove Park with a bullet hole in the forehead and a Browning revolver by his side. T. E. Dunville was a bill-topping eccentric dancer and contortionist. In 1924 his body was found in the Thames near Reading shortly after he heard someone say 'that fellow's through' in a bar.

Chaplin may have anxiously recalled how great comedians he had once seen playing to packed houses eventually drifted out of the spotlight, but it was a mark of his unique genius that even after his death on Christmas Day in 1977 he was never going to be forgotten. No amount of bed-hopping can take away from his comic legacy. In fact you could say Chaplin was still getting around after his death. In 1978 his body was stolen by a Pole, Roman Wardas, and a Bulgarian, Gantscho Ganev, who tried to sell it back for £400,000. Eventually Chaplin's corpse was recovered and reburied, this time surrounded by cement. It took being encased in concrete to keep the priapic prankster down.

After Chaplin's departure for Hollywood Fred Karno's career took some interesting turns. By now he had a houseboat on the Thames and one day had the idea of building a grand hotel-cum-leisure-complex, which he dubbed Karsino, on nearby Tagg's Island. For once no expense was spared, and a hotel, casino, sports facilities, ballroom and bar opened on 18 May 1913. Shows were spectacular with Karno employing the casting-couch technique when it came to finding suitable dancers. It was not a complete success though. Waiters swindled him by serving house wine at vintage prices, pocketing the difference, and someone ran off with the takings. Karsino survived the Great War thanks to partying soldiers and, legend has it, spies with plenty of cash to splash around, but by the 1920s Karno had to go back to putting together live shows for theatres. He kept working until he was nearly seventy, briefly in Hollywood having been introduced to the famous film-maker Hal Roach by Chaplin and Stan Laurel. But Karno didn't like answering to anybody else and returned to England in a huff, where he launched Karno's Krazy Komics. For once his casting couch didn't work. Newcomer Phyllis Dixie turned him down, but when she did become a star she sang a tribute to him: 'I failed my first audition, I couldn't sing in a horizontal position.'

While this story of the dark side of comedy is largely about stand-up comedians there is no avoiding the antics of some of the great comedians who went on to conquer Hollywood. The most notorious is Roscoe 'Fatty' Arbuckle. When Arbuckle was born in Kansas on 24 March 1887, his father had doubts about his paternity and so named him after a local Senator, Roscoe Conkling, who he hated and was a notorious philanderer. Comedians are rarely brought down by scandal. Usually they can find a way back, but Arbuckle is the one who had it all and lost it all. Like Chaplin he had a tough childhood. His mother died when he was twelve and his father refused to support him, forcing him to go onstage. It paid off. In a talent competition he was not doing particularly well when a shepherd's crook appeared from the wings to haul him off. Arbuckle did a somersault into the orchestra pit to avoid it, got cheers from the audience and kicked off his vaudeville career.

By 1909 he was working in films and by 1913 was one of the stars at the Keystone Film Company alongside Chaplin. It is even said that he helped develop the visual style of the Little Tramp, who used Arbuckle's balloon trousers, boots and undersized hat to great comic effect. Arbuckle could afford to help others out. He was one of the highest-paid actors in Hollywood, signing a million-dollar contract in 1918. He made his name in the knockabout Keystone Kops series and had a reputation for clever slapstick that did not just rely on his increasing bulk, which tipped the scales at nearly twenty stone. Arbuckle was actually very light on his feet and so sensitive about his size he refused to succumb to obvious gags such as being stuck in door frames, though he was not averse to getting a pie in the face in the name of comedy. But his weight and heavy drinking increasingly affected his health. At one point 'The Prince of Whales' had a leg infection and it was feared his leg might have to be amputated. He recovered, but in the process became addicted to morphine, which he had taken as a painkiller.

After the end of World War I alcohol was outlawed in America but Prohibition did little to curb the party atmosphere in Hollywood. Actors worked hard but they also partied hard late into the night and between shoots would really let their hair down. It was not difficult to track down a bootlegger and pick up some strong alcohol. Arbuckle was not particularly outgoing off camera, but like his friends he did like to party and in 1921 booked some rooms in the St Francis Hotel in San Francisco. It may not have been the party to end all parties but it was the party that ended Arbuckle's glittering career.

One of the guests, aspiring actress Virginia Rappe, became ill and later died. Arbuckle was accused of raping Rappe and accidentally killing

33

her and was tried three times for manslaughter. The true events may never be known, but what appears to have happened was that Rappe may have recently had an abortion which was not carried out very well, and a knock to her stomach, possibly during some sexual horseplay, injured her internally, causing her subsequent death by peritonitis. In the drunken confusion at the party Rappe's statement, 'Arbuckle hurt me,' was possibly misconstrued. The rumour mill went into overdrive. At first it was suggested his weight burst Rappe's bladder, then that he inserted a bottle inside her.

The legal process was heated but at times took on the character of a stage farce. After two mistrials, in which it was suggested a juror was biased and various witnesses had lied, been bribed or were appearing for the prosecution to reduce their own sentences in other outstanding cases, Arbuckle was unanimously acquitted. But the details of the case, at a time when the press was awash with stories of Hollywood orgies and debauched celebrity behaviour, had a devastating effect on Arbuckle's career. His films were banned and he became a pariah in Hollywood. It was a harsh fate. Compared to some other stars he was believed to be well behaved with women. Even his estranged wife Minta Dufree turned up in court to show her support. Other stars were less helpful. Many did not want to associate with him in case it was assumed that they were prone to similar behaviour. Studio executives instructed their headline acts under contract not to defend him. As it happened Charlie Chaplin was conveniently in Europe at the time so not on the scene to decide whether to back his former mentor.

Arbuckle never truly recovered from the scandal and sank into depression. He worked as a director under the pseudonym of William Goodrich – Buster

Keaton joked that he should have called himself Will B. Good – for a while, and then in the early 1930s, a decade after the court case and following a widespread appeal for his rehabilitation, tentatively started acting again, this time in talkies. But it was too late. Just after Arbuckle signed a new deal with Warner Brothers in 1933 he had a heart attack and died. He was only forty-six.

A chapter on early Hollywood's comedy bad boys who cut their teeth in vaudeville would not be complete without mention of the great W. C. Fields. William Claude Dukenfield, born 29 January 1880 in Darby Pennsylvania, was renowned as comedy's greatest misanthrope, who blessed the world with a number of unforgettable maxims.

Anyone who hates children and animals can't be all bad.
I am free of all prejudices. I hate every one equally.
I cook with wine, sometimes I even add it to the food.
I never drink water because of the disgusting things that fish do
  in it.
'Twas a woman drove me to drink. I never had the courtesy to
  thank her.
If I had to live my life over, I'd live over a saloon.

And perhaps most famously:
Never work with animals or children

Fields based his celluloid persona on a three-pronged persona: hating people in general, children in particular, and being more than partial to imbibing. And you don't get to be that convincing without some truth intruding into your act. Which just goes to show how good a comedian Fields was. He was undoubtedly a loner, who had learned to enjoy his own company in his early days in vaudeville, when he travelled the country as a solo juggler. He was also self-conscious about his skin condition, rosacea, which manifested itself in his large red bulbous nose. People assumed that the redness was alcohol induced, and drink certainly didn't help the condition, but the redness was already there. And in fact bulbous noses ran in his family. The nose was part of his fortune though. Fields had a terrific physical presence in his films, the beak just the icing on the cake.

In real life Fields was not entirely a hater of humanity. He may not have had many friends but was genuinely fond of his wife Hattie and son Claude, even though he eventually divorced Hattie, who had been pressuring him to give up comedy in favour of a more sensible career. After their separation, however, his outlook may have darkened. And he was certainly not keen on fans. He was said to repel any who walked up his Los Angeles drive by hiding in the bushes and firing BB gun pellets at them. Behaving like a drunkard onscreen, however, was less demanding. When he was a star he was always kind to his underage co-stars as long as they didn't upstage him, generous to his own offspring and was understandably devastated when actor Anthony Quinn's three-year-old son drowned in his swimming pool.

After Fields' marriage ended he never wed again but had a number of relationships. In 1917 he had a son, William, with his girlfriend Bessie Poole (a 'large, plump blonde' according to their contemporary, Louise Brooks). Poole had been a dancer with the Ziegfeld Follies at the same time that Fields was a guest performer with them. Poole gave the child up for adoption and was later killed in a bar brawl. Fields had persuaded Poole to sign a document saying that he was not responsible for the child, but undermined his own curmudgeonly reputation by supporting William financially until his graduation. Sometimes, however, reputations do linger. When William was an adult he tracked his biological father down, but Fields reportedly gave strict instructions to his butler: 'Give him an evasive answer. Tell him to go fuck himself.' Though this may have been a standard response for unexpected visitors. It seemed that in later years he did finally conform to the more curmudgeonly image film fans knew and loved.

Fields had never been much of a drinker in his younger years when he was a juggler – he was concerned it would affect his timing – but as his style onstage changed and there was more patter involved he developed a taste for alcohol. Prohibition did little to curb his thirst. As with many of his music hall contemporaries, he made the move from stage to screen, but it took a little longer for his career to take off. Fields' way with words and his distinctive rasping drawl meant that he was more at home with talkies than silent films, which was almost comically ironic given that as a child he had suffered from a stammer. It makes his achievements in the talkies all the more impressive, but it may also have contributed to the development of that much-imitated slow-burn style of monologue. His appearances as card sharps, carnival barkers, con men or hen-pecked husbands made his name. His films also cemented his relationship with alcohol. In 1940's *My Little Chickadee* he summed up his relationship with liquor: 'Once, in the wilds of Afghanistan, I lost my corkscrew . . . and we were forced to live on nothing but food and water for days!' Sometimes even his film names reflected his penchant for a few nips. In *The Bank Dick* his character was called Egbert Sousé, which sounded very French and sophisticated but could also sound like 'soused'.

Once Fields was a star his fondness for a tipple was tolerated. It never seemed to affect his performances however much he drank and he clearly had a huge capacity for booze, making up for his teetotal juggling years. Sometimes when he drank Martinis there was no need for a cocktail shaker. He would simply grasp a bottle of gin in one hand and a bottle of vermouth in the other and take alternate swigs. During other shoots he kept a flask of Martinis on set which he called 'pineapple juice'. On one occasion someone replaced the Martinis in his flask with real juice and he yelled at the top of his voice, 'Who put pineapple juice in my pineapple juice?'

As for soft drinks for his co-stars, legend has it that he made them a bit stronger. He worked with the toddler Baby Le Roy and was concerned that the infant was upstaging him. Eventually during a break he said to Le Roy's mother that he would mind the child for a while. When she was gone he was said to have added a nip of gin to the nipper's fruit juice. By the time the next scene was ready to shoot Le Roy was placid to the point of dozing off on set. There would be no more upstaging. Never work with animals or children indeed. Unless they have been soothed first with a bit of booze.

Nobody could drink as much as Fields, however, without doing themselves long-term damage. By 1936 he was too ill to film and by the late 1930s was suffering from delirium tremens. He made a comeback though and starred in some of his greatest films, particularly two movies released in 1940, *My Little Chickadee* and *The Bank Dick*. In the former he plays Wild West con man Cuthbert J. Twillie opposite Mae West, in the latter a brilliantly boozed-up security guard. He was offered the title role in the *Wizard of Oz*, but reputedly turned it down because it was too small. But by then he had put on a lot of weight and by 1946 was dying in hospital. When a friend visited Fields was reading the Bible. He told his friend he was 'checking for loopholes'. He died soon after of an alcohol-related stomach haemorrhage at the age of sixty-six. Legend has it that he wanted the words 'Here Lies W. C. Fields. I Would Rather Be Living in Philadelphia' on his tombstone but had to make do to with his name and dates of birth and death. A rare straight line from a man who could not resist a joke.

3

He Didn't Know Whether to Block Her Passage or Toss Himself Off

Music hall's mavericks – Max Miller, George Formby and Frank Randle

There have been plenty of cheeky chappies in comedy, but there was only one Cheeky Chappie. It is hard to appreciate now, but at his peak Max Miller was an absolutely enormous household name, dominating live comedy bills for the best part of two decades. He was brash and outrageous, and his suits were so loud they should have had an ASBO slapped on them, but somehow he got away with it by twinkling his dazzling blue eyes, looking into the wings to check the coast was clear, muttering, ''Ere' a funny thing,' and giving his fans a conspiratorial wink. The wily wag took an us-versus-them stance. He and his audience were on the same side against the guardians of morality, who didn't want him to go within touching distance of a taboo, never mind break one. He was so famous that if he was appearing in London and the show ran late the guards at Victoria Station would hold the Brighton Express for him. As comedian Arthur Smith once joked, they've stopped the train for him too, but usually when he is on it and he has been doing something naughty.

Max Miller was born Thomas Henry Sargent in Brighton on 21

November 1894. His parents were constantly short of money and had a nifty habit of moving quickly when the rent was due. By the time Miller was a teenager his schooling had become erratic and effectively non-existent. Instead he earned money working as everything from a golf caddie to a milkman. He was already showing that fondness for extravagant clothes that would later make him stand out on the stage, sporting baggy suits that landed him the nickname of 'Swanky Sargent'. When The Great War broke out he signed up and spent time in India and Mesopotamia. He exhibited a mischievous streak even in uniform and used to get himself into trouble just so that when he was asked his name he could say, 'Sargent, Sergeant.'

It was also while in the army that he began to perform onstage, starting up a concert party to pass the time and entertain his comrades. It gave him a taste of the footlights. Back on Civvy Street he joined a concert party in Brighton, where he met his wife, Kathleen, who was a singer. It was Kathleen who suggested that if he was serious about showbusiness Max Miller was snappier than his real name, and he took her advice. They formed a double act for a while but it was clear that Miller was the one with the real talent and would stand more chance of making it alone. It was a shrewd decision. By the mid-1920s his career was taking off. He was booked by Fred Karno, who had discovered Chaplin and Stan Laurel, and by the end of the decade had appeared at the London Palladium. He was known not just for his risqué routines, but also for his appearance. Co-respondent shoes – named as such because they were supposedly the easily remembered flashy type worn by adulterers cited in divorce cases – plus fours, more usually seen on the golf course, kipper ties, trim silk jackets and tight-fitting trilbies.

Oh, and it is hard to tell by the few scraps of black and white footage that still exist, but the suits were dazzlingly gaudy, often a riot of red and blue, unheard of in those grey days.

By the early 1930s Miller was topping bills, appearing on the radio and releasing best-selling records. The Max Miller remembered today had finally broken through. Unlike his near contemporary George Formby though, Miller failed to make it as a film star. He shot fourteen movies, sometimes doing short spots which were no great stretch. He played a fast-talking publisher in *The Good Companions* with John Gielgud in 1933 and in *Hoots Mon!* a comedian called Harry Hawkins, whose routines were basically Miller's own, full to the brim with innuendo but slightly cleaned up for cinema audiences. Saucy material and saucy outfits were the name of the game for Miller, although under the jacket there lurked a secret. As he became more successful and put on weight he started to wear a corset to hold his belly in.

From the moment he strutted onstage he was in full flow: 'Thank you very much, I expected more but I'm satisfied . . .' He would get plenty of material out of his outfits, running his hands over his hips and thighs: 'I've got new ones on tonight, all rubber. Do you wear them, lady? You do look funny when you take them off, you look like a golf ball.' Gradually he would build to a bawdy climax while discussing his recent hunt for seaside lodgings. 'I went to Blackpool and I went round looking for rooms . . . An old lady came to the door . . . I said could you accommodate me; she says I'm awfully sorry I'm full up. I said surely you could squeeze me in the little back room, couldn't you? She said I could but I haven't got time now.'

And now here is a funny thing. This 'saloon bar priapus', as he was described by playwright John Osborne, was known as the filthiest comedian of his era but never swore. Everything was left to his audience's imagination. He'd sing a song then change direction or put on the verbal brakes just as everyone thought they knew what was heading their way: 'When roses are red, they're ready for plucking, when a girl is sixteen, she's ready for . . . . 'Ere!' As Bob Monkhouse later put it, 'paying the audience the compliment of letting them put the last word in'.

This linguistic sleight of mouth also meant that if he had a problem with the censors he could point to his routine and argue that he had said nothing wrong. There was something deliciously conspiratorial about his act. In his most famous rapid-fire riff he would pull out two joke books, a blue book and a white book, and ask the audience which one they wanted, the clean white one or the dirty blue one. They invariably went for the blue book, knowing full well that that was where the rudest innuendos were. 'I don't care what I say, do I?'

Miller had a tough streak and was not prepared to compromise. One night he was doing a hometown gig at the Brighton Hippodrome when someone backstage took offence and dropped the fire curtain on him, ending the performance and telling Miller he was banned for life. Miller didn't worry; he just chuckled and started gigging round the corner at the Grand Theatre instead. The Finsbury Park Empire once fined him for a quip about 'the girl of eighteen who swallowed a pin, but didn't feel the prick until she was twenty-one'[10]. He wore a lot of make-up onstage, and while quite clearly heterosexual was happy to play up to his camp side at a time when homosexuality was still illegal, joking, 'So what if I am?'

---

10 John M. East, *Max Miller: The Cheeky Chappie*, WH Allen, 1997, p.105.

Miller was a huge influence on rising young comedians. Walter William Bygraves was dubbed 'Max' because he did a neat impersonation. Tommy Trinder was said to have based his wide-boy patter on Miller. There was something of a rivalry between Trinder and Miller. One night after a show reporters asked for autographs so Miller provocatively signed them Tommy Trinder. At one point Trinder was accused of nicking Miller's material as well as his style. Later Trinder was accused of slandering Miller, saying that his career was on the slide and court proceedings looked possible. Trinder demanded all sorts of details about where Miller thought this remark had been made – on what date and at which performance – and, legend has it, asked all the questions separately so that Miller had to pay a lawyer each time he answered them. Trinder's intuition was right. Miller dropped the case in the end because at five shillings a time the letters were costing him too much. Every great comedian has a flaw, the bit of grit that makes the pearl, and for Miller it was money. There were rumours of affairs – and when he died it was revealed that he had had a relationship with his secretary Ann Graham – but it was the intimate relationship with his wallet that shaped Miller's life.

As a teenager and budding comedian, Bob Monkhouse once tried to sell Miller a joke outside the Lewisham Hippodrome. Many years later he was doing a charity gig at the London Coliseum and Miller sat in the wings and watched him. Afterwards Miller took him into his Rolls-Royce – number plate Max 1 – and deconstructed Monkhouse's act, telling him where to pause, where to be more audacious, but not dirty. He taught him the subtle trick of stepping back and clapping, and if it all went right the audience would clap too, almost without thinking.

Monkhouse was one of the lucky ones, getting free advice. Most comedians who encountered Miller are quicker to recall his legendary meanness with money. Variety comedian Maurice Sellars also met Miller after a show and was given some tips, but Miller wanted a tip in return, in the form of a drink. 'Then you can say you bought the great Max Miller a drink,' he added with a grin. Contemporaries joked that he was so mean that late in his career he was said to still have the first shilling he had ever earned.

Veteran entertainer Roy Hudd recalled being with a couple of friends at the Finsbury Park Empire and being invited up to the circle bar with Miller during the interval. They sat down, and as Miller was host Hudd expected him to order the drinks. They chatted but no order was forthcoming. In the end some fans appeared and, spotting Miller, shouted, 'What are you having?' Miller immediately responded with his own drinks order, adding, 'Can you get my young friends a drink as well'? After one theatre run at the Holborn Empire, despite it being traditional for the headline act to tip the orchestra, Miller finished by coming offstage, walking through the auditorium, jumping in a cab to Victoria and straight on the Brighton train. He was also said to have dug up one of the lawns of his grand house in Brighton to grow vegetables so that he didn't have to pay for them.

Miller was a past master at avoiding paying up when he lost a wager. He once had a gag that was near the knuckle for the day about a bus breaking down and the driver having a look at the engine to try to fix it. The female conductor shouted across, 'Do you want a screwdriver?' to which he replied, 'No, we're ten minutes late already.' He had a bet with bandleader Ray Ellington that he would tell the gag on the radio.

When he failed to tell it he claimed that the red light had come on and he had run out of time, but was going to tell it so refused to pay up.

Yet he could also be generous. He gave money to charities for helping the blind because he had been temporarily blinded in World War I, and he also helped out the homeless in Brighton, where he was said to own a huge amount of property. He loved Brighton and in London theatres would sometimes choose to go on second from last just to be sure of catching his train home. But it was his short-arms-long-pockets habit with his peers that landed him with a bad reputation. Having started out ducking and diving, it was a way of life for him. It got so bad some liked to have a laugh at his expense. One night on the London to Brighton train he was with some fellow performers, legendary madcap troupe the Crazy Gang, who ordered a large round of drinks but didn't tell Miller that they had made a special arrangement with the driver to make an extra stop just outside Brighton at Preston Park. When the train pulled into Preston Park they jumped off, leaving Miller to foot the bill. There was no doubt that he could afford it. During World War II Miller was the highest paid variety performer in the country. In February 1943 he was paid £1,025 for one week of shows at the Coventry Hippodrome.

Being near the knuckle meant that producers had to ask Miller to be on his best behaviour when they invited him to appear at the Royal Variety Performance at the London Palladium. Miller did tone down his act, and it worked because he ended up appearing twice, in 1937 and then again in 1950. But on the second occasion, against the producer's wishes, having planned to do a different routine, he did his old 'Blue book or white book?' intro and was said to have looked to the Royal

Box for an answer. The box was alleged to have replied, 'Blue.' That night Miller showed that he could be truculent as well as playful. He discovered that he had only been given a six-minute spot while visiting stand-up Jack Benny – another comedian who kept a padlock on his purse – had twenty minutes. Miller refused to get off when his time was up, prompting Val Parnell, the Managing Director of Moss Empires who ran the Palladium, to say that Miller would never work in his theatres again. Miller shrugged it off, saying 'You're £60,000 too late.' He knew that if the people wanted him the theatres would book him and, sure enough, he was eventually back at the Moss Empires once again.

But BBC Radio was stricter. Long before Sachsgate, Miller received a five-year ban from the BBC for making a single risqué remark in 1944. Telling a joke about a man encountering an attractive woman on a mountain pass, Miller was said to have remarked, 'He didn't know whether to block her passage or toss himself off.' This story, however, is disputed by a number of experts, including Roy Hudd, who thinks this gag is too rude, even for Miller. Through a series of Chinese whispers the rumour changed, and rubber-legged contemporary Max Wall was also said to be the culprit. Wall had been doing a show on the BBC and by accident had been faded out just before the climax of his routine. It was thought that maybe Wall had been censored by Auntie. Wall, however, says, in his autobiography *Fool on the Hill*, that it definitely was Miller, but that the gag was cracked offstage, not in front of the public. Maybe it was actually the 'Do you want a screwdriver?' gag that he had bet Ray Ellington he would tell on air, but ran out of time. Whatever the line that was broadcast and whatever the punishment, Miller's reputation as a naughty boy of stand-up comedy was cemented by it. And while he might have pussyfooted around the boundaries of bawdiness, everyone knew what was on his mind.

It may have been due to Miller's way of dancing around decency that in 1949 the BBC introduced its very own Green Book to rival Miller's blue and white ones. The *BBC Variety Programmes Policy Guide For Writers and Producers* introduced a code of acceptability for comedy, listing all the things a performer could not mention, from honeymoons, couples, fig leaves, ladies' underwear (for example 'winter draws on'), vulgar uses of 'basket' and being frightened by a donkey. References to commercial travellers also had to be avoided, and while one could not say 'nigger', one could say 'nigger minstrel'. Miller certainly had to tweak his material for broadcast after that. It seems like a ludicrous list now, but at the time it had to be followed or one's broadcasting career would be nipped in the bud. So seriously was it taken that writers worked hard to get around the rules, and in some ways the Green Book encouraged the growing band of radio and television comedy writers to be more creative.

But as television grew in popularity Miller's days at the top were numbered. There was something about his act, his persona and old-school delivery that did not translate to the new medium. The camera did not embrace him the way audiences did, or the way it would embrace Morecambe and Wise a decade later. It is hard to say exactly why Miller did not cross over onto the small screen. It was nothing to do with his act having to be tamed for television, as some have suggested. Like Jimmy Carr or Frank Skinner today, Miller could be just as quick-witted with his blue book tucked tightly into his pocket. Maybe he was slightly too old. By the time television came along as a major force he was already in his fifties. The tyranny of youth is no new thing, and it made life hard for Miller, whose suits, so distinctive onstage, made him look like a throwback onscreen. Music hall was dying and he had nowhere else to go. He was keenly aware that he was the last of a certain breed: 'When I'm dead and gone, the game's finished,' he once said. And as far as music hall went, he was right.

He still topped bills in the theatres that survived though and recorded *Max at the Met* in 1957, a terrific example of a live comedy album, full of fast-paced gags, stories told at breakneck speed and very little waffle. Today it would be billed as 'all killer, no filler'. Not the same as being there, but not far off. But in 1958 he suffered a heart attack, and though he continued to perform, took life more easily before dying on 7 May 1963.

Max Miller was not the only master of innuendo. George Formby was a contemporary of Miller who was not just a huge theatrical name but also one of Britain's first bona fide film stars. Formby's story is intriguing because, while it overlaps with Miller's in many respects, his career went down a different path, one that was more lucrative. Offscreen, offstage and sometimes on stage, Formby could push the envelope of acceptable behaviour just as much as Miller.

The Lancastrian laugh machine was not destined to be a performer, but if you were a betting man you might have had a punt on it. The oldest of seven children, George followed in the footsteps of his father George Formby Senior, 'The Wigan Nightingale', who was a big music hall star of his day, complete with a catchphrase, 'I'm coughing better tonight.' It was an odd catchphrase with a fatal punchline. It was based on the fact that George Senior had a genuine rattling cough caused by pulmonary tuberculosis, which would eventually kill him aged only forty-five when his son was sixteen.

His father had been the uneducated, illegitimate son of a prostitute, but Formby Junior, born George Hoy Booth on 26 May 1904, had an easier ride after his father had made his fortune. Unlike many of his comedy peers, he had a comfortable, solid upbringing, but he was not interested in a private education and trained to be a jockey. Yet the lure of performance was too much and despite his father's hopes that George would not go into showbusiness his appetite was whetted when he appeared in a couple of short films made during the Great War. Legend has it that on a trip to London young George saw another comedian using his father's material and claiming to be the 'New George Formby', and he vowed to keep the family name in lights.

With the following wind of his father's reputation, his career quickly took off, even faster when he started to play the banjo-ukelele. George had charm and appeal, not just with audiences but with the women he worked with. One-night stands and flings with chorus girls followed until in 1923 he met his wife Beryl, a clog-dancer on the same bill at a Castleford Theatre. She was not impressed by him and was as stubborn as George was easy-going. Yet George was attracted to her strong character and wooed her by befriending her father, who was a publican. Eventually he ground her down and they married in September 1924. As writer David Bret's definitive biography of Formby, *A Troubled Genius*, asserts, it would be the most important event in his life and one that would shape his career and help to turn him into a box office sensation.

Straight away Beryl announced that she would not have children because looking after them would mean that she could not look after George. She swiftly restyled him, getting him to ditch the flat cap and wear smart suits so that southerners would be able to relate to him better. She taught him performance technique – how to play to the galleries where the real hard-core fans were. She taught him to use his hands well when not playing the ukelele. Although, it would eventually transpire, George knew perfectly well how to keep his hands occupied. Beryl also kept a tight rein on the purse strings as soon as George started to earn money. When he was given a fifty-pound advance for recording some songs in 1926 she gave him a pound and put the rest in the bank. She was so cautious that many years later when the famous songwriter Jack Cottrell died, she refused to send flowers to the funeral on the grounds that as he was dead he wouldn't be able to see them.

George owed Cottrell much more than flowers. He had written 'With My Little Ukelele in My Hand' for Formby as well as umpteen other hits. It was this innuendo-laden song that first got Formby into trouble with the broadcasters. The BBC received so many complaints that a different song, 'Sunbathing in the Park', was played so that family audiences didn't hear the offending lyrics, which quite clearly implied what the ukelele represented – 'She said "Your love just turns me dizzy, come on big boy get busy" but I kept my ukelele in my hand.' Formby, however, never felt he went too far, or was vulgar. 'If you can't make people laugh without being vulgar then it's about time you packed it in,' he said during an interview towards the end of his career.

While Max Miller had shied away from a film career, George quickly discovered and embraced his screen potential, but this presented Beryl with more problems. His first big hit, *No Limit*, in 1935 found him winning the Isle of Man TT Races and the girl, both against the odds. In many of his films George played the put-upon everyman who ultimately won the day, bridging the gap between Charlie Chaplin's Little Tramp and Norman Wisdom's loveable underdog films a few decades later. Formby's gormless smile and buck teeth were a surprise hit, putting a grin on Britain as the country clawed its way out of a depression only to find another war looming. Beryl was fiercely protective and possessive, jealous of any woman that George talked to. During the shoot of his earlier film *Boots Boots*, in a tiny studio just off Regent Street, Beryl, who was also in the movie, was furious when she saw George chatting to Betty Driver – who would go on to become Betty Turpin in Coronation Street – even though Driver was only twelve at the time. The script was hastily reworked and most of Betty's footage ended up on the cutting-room floor.

By the late 1930s George was a huge star and making good money, partly because of Beryl's financial dealings – shrewd some would say, ruthless others would argue. She made sure George got a share of the writing royalties for one of his biggest hits, 'When I'm Cleaning Windows', by telling the writers Fred E. Cliffe and Harry Clifford that if he didn't he would not perform the song or any more of their songs and then no one would make any money out of it. She tried the same trick in 1937 when George was going to record Noel Gay's 'I'm Leaning on a Lamppost', which was to become his trademark song, more romantic than smutty – 'There's no other girl I'd wait for, this one I'd break any date for' – but Gay was successful enough to be able to refuse Beryl's demands, and she conceded defeat. A performance would barely go by over the next quarter of a century without Formby performing 'Lamppost' to rapturous audiences.

It was 'When I'm Cleaning Windows' that caused the most controversy though, with its Miller-like pulling back before the saucy pay-off – 'She pulls her hair down all behind, then pulls down her – never mind.' The dirty little ditty sold over 150,000 copies in its first month of release, despite, or maybe because of the fact that at the BBC the record was filed under NTBB – 'not to be broadcast'. The ban only prompted more interest and an even smuttier sequel. 'Window Cleaner 2', was released six months later: 'Now lots of girls I've had to jilt, for they admire the way I'm built, it's a good job I don't wear a kilt, when I'm cleaning windows.'

Success didn't make his relationship with Beryl any easier. She continued to object to any leading lady who was remotely attractive, sometimes with good reason. Formby was said to have had a fling with his co-star of *Keep Fit*, Kay Walsh, while Beryl was in hospital having a hysterectomy to make sure she never had children and could focus on George's career. She constantly tried to get Walsh removed from productions, infuriating directors and producers. When Formby and Walsh co-starred in *I See Ice* the director made two cuts of the final scene, one that Beryl saw in which Formby and Walsh were merely sitting together, another – for public consumption – in which Formby and Walsh actually kissed. Beryl's interference knew no bounds. On *Come on George* she made his co-star Pat Kirkwood cut her hair so that she would appear less feminine and be less appealing to George.

Beryl's preference was for leading ladies who were already married and she had a habit of interviewing prospective candidates herself.

Perhaps she had good reason to – George was heard to remark, 'When you have chicken every day you get tired of it by Friday.' There were arguments on set whenever Beryl saw George with a woman. During one break he was merely walking to the canteen with future sitcom regular Irene Handl when a major storm blew up. Beryl's suspicious nature was the only thing that was aroused.

By the late 1930s George was receiving £35,000 per film, a fortune in itself, plus royalties for monthly releases, with fees for live appearances and adverts for Feenamint laxative. He might have looked modest but he knew how to spend his earnings. In 1937 he took delivery of his first custom-built Rolls-Royce. He would accumulate 130 cars in the next two decades – all in Beryl's name of course. When it came to buying drinks, though, he was reputed to be as Scrooge-like as Max Miller. It was said that Formby only bought two rounds of drinks in his life, though he had a better excuse than Miller, with his dominating wife holding the purse strings.

Formby seems to have been two people, one off duty, another when the camera rolled. Pat Kirkwood called him 'cretinous', while another co-star, Phyllis Calvert, later described him as 'a very dull man'. He made a pass at Calvert even though they hardly hit it off, but when Beryl was not around this unlikely womaniser felt duty bound to make a pass at most of his leading ladies and also the extras, having an affair with Coral Browne during *Let George Do It*. As a devout Catholic he could never divorce Beryl, but fidelity was a different matter. He would use his dressing room, or whisk the lucky lady off to a hotel if time. *Let George Do It* was a huge success, thanks in part to its wartime propaganda message, with George as its anti-Nazi hero, punching Hitler on the nose and calling him a windbag. But even George's biggest supporters could not have predicted that the film would be a box office smash in Moscow for ten months running.

George's charity work during the war, appearing in a marbles competition for Finnish refugees as well as entertaining the troops in Europe, did his film career no harm at all – he was more successful than Errol Flynn and Bette Davies – and in 1941 he signed a six-picture deal with Columbia Films worth an astonishing £500,000. He certainly did his bit for the war effort, even though a locust flew right into his mouth during a show in Aleppo, ironically while he was singing 'It Serves You Right'. He had fans in high places too, being invited to perform for the royal family at Windsor Castle. George planned to do a cleaned-up version of his act but was told that they were more than happy to hear the unexpurgated version of 'When I'm Cleaning Windows'. In fact the royal audience worked out in George's favour. After the King heard the song, the BBC decided the nation could hear it too and lifted the ban.

His popularity extended in all directions. George built up an unexpected gay following during the war. *Bell-Bottom George* was a particular cult film, as the cast of the naval romp featured a large gay contingent, including future Carry On star Charles Hawtrey, among its extras. In one scene a character called Shapley, played by Peter Murray Hill, fondles George's chest and announces, 'I'm feeling a bit queer myself.' The censors had no problem with this, but Formby could still get into trouble with the authorities, even though he was a massive star. In one film, *Get Cracking*, he used 'pillock', which he claimed was normal in the north of England, but was still considered offensive on celluloid.

After the war George's film career slumped. His records still sold but the Columbia film contract had come to an end and he seemed to have fallen out of fashion. It happens to most comedians at some point in their career. Some have the mental strength to pull through, others fall by the wayside. The curse of the melancholic clown had struck again. Formby had never exhibited a dark side before, but he became severely depressed. In fact Beryl had him admitted to a psychiatric hospital in York under the pseudonym of Ingham. It was a complete nervous breakdown, and Beryl even said that if he could not be cured he should be sent to an institution. Her attitude changed, however, when he got a deal to tour Scandinavia – she decided that she knew better than the experts and against their wishes had George discharged. While his film career might have petered out, Formby was still a big star when it came to performing live, and not just in England.

Following Scandinavia, George went to South Africa. This was just before apartheid was officially introduced, but black and white people were already segregated. Beryl was insistent, however, that George met black audiences, and at one concert caused outrage by kissing a three-year-old black child who had brought chocolates for George. Their visit caused embarrassment to the leader of the National Party, Daniel François Malan. He personally called them to criticise their behaviour but Beryl put the phone down on him, saying, 'Why don't you piss off, you horrible little man.' They were asked to leave the country and went without any complaints.

Tours of Canada, Australia and New Zealand followed. At one point Formby was offered a tour of America, including $5,000 for one night at New York's prestigious Carnegie Hall, but he turned the offer down, suggesting that Americans would not understand him. But the endless travel was starting to take its toll. The marriage had become a sexless one, yet Beryl was more possessive than ever, scowling at female interviewers. George had recently been given morphine after collapsing while appearing in *Cinderella* at the Grand Theatre, Leeds. He was addicted to the painkiller for a while, and was only weaned off it when in 1951 he had a heart attack on his way home from a show and was treated by the royal physician Sir Horace Evans. He also contracted dysentery and had to have an emergency appendectomy. His depression returned, and for a while he went back to the York psychiatric hospital. It was a stark contrast to his sunny, happy-go-lucky 'turned out nice again' film persona. He was due to make another cheery film in Sweden, but Beryl put her foot down – not because of concerns about George's health, but because the leading lady, Anita Björk, had taken a shine to George. In fact his health was so bad and his depression so heavy, he announced his retirement. George had prematurely aged. He was not even fifty but had put on weight and looked ashen and worn out. Those late nights, long tours and cigarettes – forty Capstan Full Strength a day since the age of twelve – were taking their toll.

Retirement was short-lived. Less than two years later he toured Rhodesia (now Zimbabwe) and was back in the West End of London headlining a new revue entitled *Fun and the Fair*, supported by gap-toothed gagsmith Terry-Thomas. Despite getting rave reviews, Formby started to suffer from stage fright, but he was a driven man. Overcoming constant illness, he undertook a return trip to South Africa for charity, a major tour of Canada and seemingly endless dates around Britain, which seemed to put him right back at the top. There was life in the old dog yet. In the summer of 1960 he opened in *The Time of Your Life* at the Queen's Theatre Blackpool opposite a well-endowed exotic singer named Yana – a former Romford hairdresser's assistant whose real name was Pamela Guard. Yana was a star in her own right. She had released numerous records, appeared regularly on television and had offered first man in space Yuri Gagarin the loan of her open-top sports car – registration YG1 – for his visit to London. George was besotted with her, but the suspicion was that she was after his money and also that she was gay. Meanwhile Beryl had developed cancer.

In case it has escaped your notice, showbiz marriages during this era were never straightforward. Wives behind the scenes often seemed to play the role of bad cop to the comedians' good cop public face. Often the wives were ex-performers themselves. In some cases they concluded that the best way of keeping their husbands in check was to be with them even when they were onstage. Arthur Lucan was a music hall star who became a household name in the 1930s and 1940s after a series of hit films starring his cross-dressing alter ego, the benevolent if slightly befuddled washerwoman Old Mother Riley. His wife Kitty McShane kept an eye on him by playing his daughter on stage and screen. They were a public success, producing sixteen lucrative films on a shoestring budget, including 1952's *Old Mother Riley Meets the Vampire* with Bela Lugosi, but had a turbulent marriage. McShane, who was much younger, had numerous affairs, and although they remained co-stars onscreen in later films they filmed their parts on separate days. After Lucan's death in 1954 McShane wanted to keep the franchise going. She found another actor to impersonate Old Mother Riley and continued with the act. It was not a success though. Kitty McShane became more reliant on alcohol and was found dead at home in 1964 aged sixty. Maybe, on reflection, working together onstage is not such a sound idea.

Eventually Formby and Yana's fling came to an end, and soon after Beryl died in December 1960 Formby announced that he planned to marry schoolteacher Pat Howson, a family friend that he had known for some time. But on 6 March 1961, two days before their wedding, he had another heart attack and was dead within minutes. His interment in Liverpool on 10 March was the biggest showbusiness funeral in British history, with 150,000 people lining the route and his Lakeland terrier Willie Waterbucket whimpering as they lowered Formby into the ground. But Formby's troubles were not quite over. He wanted to give his fortune to Pat, but a family squabble over the will ensued, with his eighty-two-year-old mother – who didn't die until 1981 when she was over a hundred – arguing about her entitlement. In the end a settlement was reached. There was no happy ending for anyone though. Pat Howson died in 1971 aged only forty-six. 'Turned out nice again?' Not for George.

Max Miller and George Formby were the acceptable faces of bad behaviour in the period when music hall started to give way to home entertainment and comedians found that they could push the taste envelope with a mischievous grin and some charm. There was another comedian who was anything but family friendly, who put the 'offensive' in 'charm offensive'. We look on comedians today and think they are edgy, that they are nonconformists. Few were ever as edgy or as nonconformist as Frank Randle, music hall's ultimate Lord of Misrule, both onstage and, more particularly offstage. Formby and Miller both appeared in front of royalty; Randle was more likely to appear in front of the local magistrate.

Even Randle's name is a slippery, troublesome conundrum. He was an illegitimate child, born Arthur Hughes in a place that sounds rude in itself, Aspull, Lancashire, on 30 January 1901, but as well as Randle he was also known as Arthur McCoy, taking his stepfather's surname. He left school at thirteen and worked as an acrobat and then as a solo stand-up under the name of Arthur Twist before becoming Frank Randle. He eventually became a big star, fronting his own touring company called Randle's Scandals, towards the end featuring the future host of *Record Breakers*, Roy Castle. As a film star during World War II his movies were huge money-spinners, constantly breaking box office records.

So far, so conventionally unconventional for a clown. Randle's semi-educated, streetwise background of dubious parentage can be matched by all sorts of music hall stars. But there was something in Randle's DNA that just made him want to push things further and do things differently. He was not a typical gagsmith like Max Miller or a musical comedian like Formby; he specialised in satirical characters that bordered on the grotesque. Offstage as a young man, Randle was quite smart, distinguished even, but he had all of his teeth removed, which meant he could pop in different sets of dentures for each character he created, from a pipe-smoking old boatman to his most famous creation, the drunk old hitchhiker, complete with winning catchphrase 'I've supped some stuff tonight.'

Randle's hitchhiker was instantly recognisable, wearing shorts, carrying a rucksack, a bugle and some beer, hair on end, big boots on the wrong feet. His most famous routine involved him recalling the time he was chased by a randy bull, showing off his little legs: 'I tossed a sparrer for these an' lost.' Booze, sex and death were his favourite topics: 'Ah were at a funeral t'other day. Ah were comin' away from graveside. An' this chap comes up to me an' 'e says, '"Ow old are you?" An' 'ah sed, "Eighty-two." An' 'e sed, "There's not much point in you goin' 'ome then is there".'

Like Peter Kay today, he was a resolutely northern-and-proud-of-it comedian who reflected his audiences' own experiences back at them. He liked to prick the seriousness of theatre at any opportunity. He was an unlikely choice to do panto, but once he was playing Buttons at the Kingston Empire and could not resist faking a loud fart. The audience loved it, but the management fined him five guineas, which only made audiences love him more.

Writer, social historian and former comic musician with madcap 1970s combo Albertos y los Trios Paranoias C. P. Lee[11] says that there is no modern equivalent to Randle. Steve Coogan's Paul Calf comes close, he suggests, but Calf is nowhere near as dark. Randle's onstage boozy, belching threat 'Ah'll tek anybody on' might echo Calf's threats to 'bloody students', but Randle could be just as threatening in reality. There was something grotesque about his performances. There is a hint of Randle in some of the early work of the League of Gentlemen. The village of Royston Vasey seems bursting with Randle-like creatures, from the shopkeepers Edward and Tubbs to the monstrous children's

---

11 C. P. Lee, 'The Lancashire Shaman', Chapter 2, *Because I Tell a Joke or Two*, edited by Stephen Wagg, Routledge, 1998.

entertainer Papa Lazarou, but Randle was no mere character comedian. There was something sinister bubbling up from deep within his soul that drove him on.

Making his name in the 1930s he soon became even more ribald than his rivals Formby and Miller, liking to come onstage wearing a kilt and saying, 'By 'eck, I don't know where this draught is coming from – but I know where it's going.' Once, during a long-winded sketch based on *Cinderella* he thrust his hand up the fairy-tale princess's skirt, saying, 'Let's get to the point.' And he was no respecter of deadlines either. Like Ken Dodd he would go on and on – his anarchic shows would often finish well after midnight.

Randle was one of a number of comedians whose main following was in the north of England. He did have fans in London, but the crowds were maybe less sympathetic and he had to work harder to win them over. When he played in the West End, where he felt theatregoers were stuck up, he put on his best suit and put his false teeth on a velvet cushion, but the audience was not impressed. One night at the Finsbury Park Empire or the Wood Green Empire, depending on which version of events one accepts, Randle went down so badly the crowd started to throw coins at him – with malice rather than as a financial incentive to get off. The stage manager tried to protect Randle by bringing down the fire curtain in front of him, but Randle simply ducked under it, and through a hail of pennies shouted, 'Bastards.' They must have caught him in a good mood. He was also known to hurl his false teeth at hecklers.

A formidable woman called Cissie Williams ran the Moss Empires chain at the time. When a young Tony Hancock was about to play one of her theatres she caught sight of his shoes and deemed them unacceptable. Either the shoes went or he did. Williams got wind of Randle's antics and summoned him to her office to explain himself, saying that bad language was unacceptable. Randle was as cool as a cucumber and said that didn't she understand Italian – he was actually shouting, *'Basta, basta,'* meaning, 'Enough, enough.'

But it was offstage that Randle set the benchmark for dysfunctional behaviour. He was far more monstrous than he ever was onstage, an absolutely unpredictable Jekyll and Hyde figure. Russell Brand at his most devilish may have been shocked by some of the stunts that Randle pulled. He once drove his car straight up a tram track and refused to budge, playing chicken with the tram and shouting 'Get out of the way' until the very last second. His private life reflected his complex personality. He was a jealous, possessive tyrannical husband. In 1924 he married London-born May Anne Victoria Douglas, known as 'Queenie', at home. Marriage didn't change his behaviour, and while he had no children with Queenie, he was said to have fathered an illegitimate child by a fellow performer.

As a star, Randle did not suffer fools gladly and made little effort to get on with people. As much as his public loved him, the people he worked with were less generous with their plaudits. He once locked a four-foot, one-inch singer/dancer and pantomime cat Sadie Corre in her dressing room without any clothes, and another time chased her with a loaded Luger pistol. He clearly had a penchant for guns – he also fired at an extra during the making of one of his hit movies. He would smash up his dressing room with an axe if he was in a bad mood or throw empty beer bottles at mirrors, and he set fire to a hotel when he was unhappy with room service. Randle could cancel a show at a moment's notice if something annoyed him. He once arrived at the Garrick Theatre in Southport to discover that conditions backstage were not what he had been led to expect. 'No star dressing room, no star,'[12] he said and stomped off. Which was fine when he was a big star, but towards the end of his career managements became wary of booking him. If he was on song he was great, but he could be a liability too.

The rivalry with George Formby drove him to extremes. In the early 1930s Randle and Formby were equal top dogs on the northern circuit, but when Formby made his first film *Boots Boots* featuring his hit song 'Why Don't Women Like Me?' for Mancunian Films, his success rankled with Randle. When the comedians were both booked to play the Blackpool Opera House on the same night soon afterwards, Randle came on and declared, 'Ladies and gentlemen, it's perfectly clear that George Formby is the only star of importance in this show, so George Formby can entertain you now.' No doubt George Formby would have been quite willing to come on except for the fact that Randle had trapped him in a lift backstage. Randle then repaired to the pub next door until the furore died down. He was banned from the Blackpool Opera House for a year.

Formby was naughty but nice, Randle was mad, bad and dangerous to know. Class played a part in their rivalry. Though near contemporaries and geographical neighbours, George had had a comfortable upbringing while Randle's was tough. Randle was illegitimate; Formby came from a relatively stable background. Formby was suggestive; Randle came a

---

12 Very much a precursor of the rock and roll backstage motto: 'No Moët, no show-ay, no Chandon, no band on.'

lot closer to spelling out what he was thinking. Comedy thrives on these contrasts. Today Michael McIntyre is comedy's ultimate middle-class southern softie, while Peter Kay peddles a classy brand of northern working-class humour. Jack Dee is the Home Counties miserablist to John Bishop's cheery Liverpudlian. For every comedy Yin there is a comedy Yang.

Randle's most famous stunt involved hiring an aeroplane and bombarding Blackpool with toilet rolls after he had been convicted of obscenity. There is some dispute over this incident, however. It definitely happened, but Randle claims that he actually bombarded Accrington . . .

George Formby might have taken off sooner – and we aren't talking aeroplanes here – but Randle had successes of his own with Mancunian Films. During World War II he made a series of films – *Somewhere in Camp*, *Somewhere on Leave*, *Somewhere in England* – which were big hits in the north and, argue some, precursors of the Carry On franchise. After the war Randle continued to be successful. In 1950 he was one of the highest-paid stars in the country. He had a yacht moored off Blackpool, a fancy Lagonda sports car and a mansion on the Lytham Road. Three of Randle's shoestring budget films made a combined gross of £250,000. They were not sophisticated productions, merely vehicles for Randle to do what he did best. The script would simply say, 'Frank – Bus.' This was nothing to do with public transport; it meant, 'Frank'll come and do his business.' In 1949's *School for Randle*, very loosely based on the Restoration comedy *School for Scandal*, the star played a school caretaker, Flatfoot Mason, who turned out to be the father of a pupil. It was a cheap affair which nearly ended in tragedy when the final scene was being shot at Sale lido and the lighting rig toppled into the swimming pool, almost electrocuting a number of people.

One of blonde bombshell Diana Dors' first film appearances was opposite Randle in *It's a Grand Life* in 1953. Randle played an accident-prone soldier, a role that Norman Wisdom could have easily taken on. Dors was signed to Rank Films at the time, but had done something to upset them so was subcontracted to Mancunian Films and had to travel north. She did not like the idea, comparing it to travelling to Siberia. And she took an instant dislike to Randle, describing him as a 'disgusting, dirty old drunk'. *It's a Grand Life* showed that Randle could be as mischievous as ever. In one scene he blacked up in an attempt to upstage black pianist Winifred Atwell. The director decided this was a joke too far and pretended to shoot the scene, not telling Randle that there was no film in the camera.

Randle had his biggest problems onstage, particularly in Blackpool, where he met his match in the chief constable, Harry Barnes, a moral crusader who wanted to clean up the city. In 1943 Barnes complained to the management and had *This Is the Show That Jack Built* on the South Pier cancelled because it dealt with 'unsavoury matters', prompting a heated confrontation between Randle and Barnes, which you might call a frank exchange of views. It only made matters worse. In 1946, again on the South Pier, Randle's show *Tinker Taylor* was brought to a close by the police and local magistrates. They claimed that the show's agreed script had been 'embellished with gestures that were disgusting, grossly vulgar, suggestive and obscene'[13]. Barnes said that Randle had contravened the 1843 Theatre Act, performing material before it had been

13 Jeff Nuttall, *King Twist: A Portrait of Frank Randle*, Routledge, Kegan & Paul, 1978, p.83.

formally vetted. In 1952 he had problems with Barnes again when he was performing the following routine as part of his *Summer Scandals* at the Central Pier.

A silent Chinaman shuffled across the stage. Randle (Buttons) asked the audience: 'Is that King Farouk?' Cinderella to Buttons: 'I'd like to do you a favour.' Buttons: 'Ah'd rather have a boiled egg.' Cinderella: 'I'd like to talk to you.' Buttons: 'It's nowt to do with me. It'll be me father again.' And finally: 'There's a flea loose in the harem and the favourite will have to be scratched.'

It sounds pretty coy today, and even back then a comedian who was not a marked man would have probably got away with the vanilla sexual innuendo of a line like, 'I'd like to do you a favour,' but Barnes was out to get Randle, and the show resulted in four charges of obscenity and a ten-pound fine for each charge. It didn't put him off though. Randle continued to be outrageous, resulting in further charges. The battle with Barnes became an obsession in the way that a decade later Lenny Bruce would become fixated on his battles with the Establishment. The way Randle addressed his audience on the nature of his alleged crimes and the pressures on him eerily foreshadowed Bruce:

Ladies and gentlemen, you have seen that the little show we have presented for you this season has been under a great deal of criticism. You have seen that certain citizens, some of them quite eminent, have seen fit to call our performance, 'filthy', 'obscene', 'offensive', and that may well be their opinion, but I come to you ladies and gentlemen and ask you to be my final judges. I am, like you, a simple man, born of simple folk, a man of the industrial north of England. My pleasures are simple – my packet of Woodbines, my glass of Guinness. The simple joys of the seasons. Simple people of our kind understand the facts of life in a way that many of our critics don't. You will know that my little bits of fun are founded upon the facts of life and because you understand life and the realities of life – I ask you to be my judges.[14]

Barnes ground Randle down, and like Lenny Bruce he became so obsessed with being persecuted that he overlooked the fact that people wanted to see him being funny, not talking about his battles with the law. Randle's legal wrangles started to damage his shows, but then television came along and helped to finish the job. Like Max Miller, there was something about the way Randle bonded with a live audience that meant that he did not work so well squeezed into a box. Randle was truly larger than life, which meant he worked on the cinema screen, but somehow the small screen diminished him.

Randle made a few appearances in people's living rooms, but they did not work out. One was in a short-lived show called *Televariety*, a bizarre hybrid of *What's My Line?*[15] and variety acts. Tuberculosis and drinking beer by the crate-load did the real damage. Randle had always enjoyed a glass, and after each show would be up until the early hours drinking. When not performing he would disappear on three-day benders. If it was in the middle of a film shoot the rest of the cast would have to twiddle their thumbs until his return. Not surprisingly he had to deal

---

14 Nuttall, p.84.
15 In this game show panellists had to work out the occupation of guests by asking them yes or no questions.

with assorted drunk-driving charges during his life.

No amount of police bother could stop him from performing in Blackpool, and he kept on appearing there, treating each summons with contempt. But life was getting harder for Randle by the mid-1950s. He was being chased for unpaid tax and in 1955 was declared bankrupt. Only death could stop his rants, and in the summer of 1957 it did. On 7 July he died of gastro-enteritis. Within six years George Formby and Max Miller would also be dead. The golden age of music hall, as personified by these three entertainers, all bad boys in their own way, was also gone. One era of fighting the establishment would be over but there would be plenty more to come.

4

Naked Without a Fan

The Windmill Legacy – From Tommy Cooper to Rex Jameson via the Goons and Hancock

The Windmill Theatre on the edge of Soho just around the corner from Piccadilly Circus is like a living comedy character in its own right. The theatre got its name because it was located at 17–19 Great Windmill Street. There had actually been a windmill there in the time of King Charles II, but it disappeared during Queen Victoria's reign and in 1909 a cinema, the Palais de Lux, was built in its place. As bigger cinemas opened, this one lost out and closed, but in 1930 it was bought by Laura Henderson, turned into a small theatre and renamed the Windmill. The names that would grace its stage would go on to dominate post-World War II comedy. From Benny Hill to Bruce Forsyth to Tommy Cooper, if you didn't play the Windmill you really must have been funny in the head.

In the 1930s, however, business was still shaky. In 1932 the new theatre manager Vivian Van Damm had the idea for Revudeville, an all-day, non-stop variety show, but even this failed to perk up the box office takings until Van Damm – known as VD – had the idea of featuring nude women.

The only problem was that they had to stay still to avoid the wrath of the theatre censor, the Lord Chamberlain. Nude statues were not considered obscene, so living statues would be deemed acceptable too, prompting the catchphrase 'If it moves, it's rude.' Van Damm was very clever at steering a course around the rules. According to veteran straight man Nicholas Parsons, the Lord Chamberlain would be invited to opening nights, when, just to be on the safe side, the women would be less scantily clad than on subsequent nights. Van Damm didn't take too many risks though. When a living statue had a coughing fit, the curtain came down as soon as she started to jiggle about too much. Any nudity had to be strictly on the stage. If a performer spotted a man exposing himself she pointed him out to the stage manager and he was ejected, or at least told to put it away.

The shows attracted a curious crowd, invariably a lot of single men in large overcoats who would read their newspapers during the comedy turns, so it was a real challenge to grab their attention. Comics had to be very good very fast. The punters would arrive and sit at the back, but during the intervals would clamber over the seats to get to the front to get a better view from the footlights, a race that became known as the 'Windmill Steeplechase'. Handlebar-moustachioed war hero Jimmy Edwards dubbed it the Grand National, though any further horsey connections were strictly frowned upon. One enthusiast of the art of the *tableau vivant* was turfed out for producing a pair of racing binoculars when the nudes appeared. Another smuggled in a home-made pair of goggles, which unfortunately impeded his close-up vision, and he fell down the stairs and broke his leg.

The Windmill Girls were a huge success, and Van Damm even got away with them moving a little every now and again, as long as their bared essentials were hidden by large ostrich-feather fans. It was during the war that the theatre cemented its reputation, with continuous performances right through the Blitz, prompting the slogan 'We never closed,' promptly vulgarised into 'We never clothed.' It helped that the theatre appeared to have someone on their side in the Lord Chamberlain's office. When the inspector, Mr Titman – stop sniggering at the back – was due to visit, they got a tip-off and made sure they were on their best behaviour.

There were regular variety acts during the war years, but it was after peace broke out, when servicemen who had entertained the troops returned to Civvy Street, that the Windmill hosted the sort of line-ups that twenty years later money could not buy. Some performers were just out of uniform, others were barely out of school. The theatre was an education for them in more ways than they could ever have imagined. Tony Hancock was just leaving one day when he was stopped by a gentleman who asked for a favour: 'My dear chap, I did enjoy your act . . . could you possibly arrange an introduction to the third girl from the left?'[16]

It was the perfect place to learn one's craft. It you cracked the Windmill you could make it anywhere. The audition was both exacting and cursory, taking place in Vivian Van Damm's office. The thumbs up or down came very quickly, but luckily the theatre constantly needed new blood. Some still blew it. Spike Milligan torpedoed his first interview with Van Damm by apologising for turning up fully clothed,[17] while fellow future Goon Michael Bentine secured a booking as a double act with Tony Sherwood, calling themselves Sherwood and Forrest. Another Goon to be, Harry Secombe, who appeared at the Windmill in 1946, used to sing comic songs, blow raspberries and shave his face onstage in various different

16 *Daily Telegraph*, 21 November 2005.
17 Graham McCann, *Spike & Co.*, Hodder & Stoughton, 2006, p.63.

comic styles, although it is hard to believe he did the latter six times a day and still had skin. The nudes weren't too keen on his act either. They would sometimes slip if a splash of lather was left behind, giving them a bump and the audience an unsolicited thrill. It was at the Windmill that Secombe and Milligan, friends from the war days, first met Michael Bentine. Peter Sellers appeared at the Windmill for six weeks in 1948, sometimes in sketches, sometimes spoofing officers, though it was not Sellers' first stint there. Aged five, he had performed in a show with his overbearing mother Peg, who was a burlesque dancer.

Milligan, Sellers, Secombe and Bentine went on to create the Goons, who spawned Peer Cook who spawned Monty Python which spawned Reeves and Mortimer who spawned the League of Gentlemen and Little Britain. This surreal strand of comedy is arguably the only good thing to have come out of World War II. All of the Goons – as well as many others who played the Windmill – had been in combat. They had seen the best of humanity, but also the worst. Michael Bentine had been at Belsen concentration camp at the end of the war, and the horror of what he saw there had caused him to pursue a career in comedy. 'My decision to try and make a living as a comedian was prompted by my disgust at the wholesale slaughter of the war and the misuse of Science to achieve it.'[18] Bentine noted that three of the four future Goons had been in some kind of therapy. An unsettled psyche plus disgust for authority, which came from seeing what leaders put people through, cemented the anarchic philosophy of the *Goon Show*, a world where grown men retreated into an almost childlike state, complete with sound

---

18 Michael Bentine, *The Long Banana Skin*, New English Library, 1976, p.147.

effects, bizarre narratives and characters called Eccles, Major Bloodnok (Sellers again spoofing officers he had met in the army) and Neddie Seagoon. If a plot seemed to be going nowhere Secombe would simply blow his trademark raspberry, which always got a laugh. Milligan did most of the writing, which took its toll. He had the first of numerous nervous breakdowns during the third series and suffered from intermittent depression for the rest of his life. Comic genius and mental disturbance walked hand in hand with Milligan.

Secombe and Bentine seemed relatively sane by comparison with Milligan, though perhaps Bentine could see trouble looming, choosing to go solo after one series. Sellers, meanwhile, was a driven man but riddled with insecurities, conceited, abusive and prone to childlike tantrums. In some ways he never grew up. He was able to access a child-like innocence – even towards the end in his award-winning movie masterpiece of understatement *Being There* – like few others. He was a captivating presence onstage and more particularly onscreen, but off duty he felt he had no identity. For Sellers comedy was a mask which he was compelled to don. Like Milligan he would go on to great things away from stand-up comedy, but be haunted all of his life. Money, women and international success seemed to do little to ease the pain.

The other great name and troubled soul to emerge from the carnage of war and the Windmill was Tony Hancock, who was booked by Van Damm in the summer of 1948.[19] Another latter-day Grimaldi, Hancock's gift for laughter in front of an audience barely concealed the depression that could swallow him up offstage and offscreen. Born John Hancock

19 The debut album of Grimaldi fan Peter Doherty's first band the Libertines was called *Up the Bracket*, inspired by a line by Hancock, 'Are you looking for a punch up the bracket?'

on 12 May 1924 in Birmingham, his father had been an all-round performer, but had died when John was young. Hancock entertained the troops during the war as part of Ralph Reader's *Gang Show* before pitching up at the Windmill. Hancock's success led him away from pure stand-up on to radio, first playing the teacher to Peter Brough's ventriloquist's dummy in *Educating Archie*, before in 1954 landing his own wireless vehicle, *Hancock's Half Hour*. With his homburg hat and hangdog expression he was soon a major hit. In 1956 the TV version, written by Ray Galton and Alan Simpson, rewrote the rules of television comedy. This was arguably the first truly modern sitcom, with Hancock playing Anthony Aloysius St John Hancock, the bumptious, deluded anti-hero and ancestor of David Brent, Alan Partridge and Captain Mainwaring. Each week he was thrown into different situations. Sometimes he was a failed actor, sometimes a barrister. In the most famous episode he was simply giving blood: 'A pint? Why, that's very nearly an armful!' But Hancock was an anxious performer. The more successful the show became the more he worried that the supporting cast was stealing his limelight. Ego and insecurity make a combustible cocktail. First Kenneth Williams had to go, then Sid James, when he seemed to be as popular as the titular star. Then in 1961 the writers went too.

Hancock was highly strung. 'The lad himself' had always been anxious but one event made him worse. In 1960, when he was interviewed by John Freeman on *Face to Face*, he became introspective and more self-analytical. What did it mean to be funny? Why was he funny? How did he do it? The programme made him more insecure than ever. He had sleepless nights fretting over gags that had not quite worked. He would never be the same again.

While Galton and Simpson had a new hit on their hands with *Steptoe and Son* in 1963, Hancock did not hit it off with his new writers or his new network, ATV. Gradually his depressions became deeper and darker, his drinking heavier. It was a vicious circle. His alcoholism affected his work which in turn provoked more drinking. He was violent towards his mistress, Freddie, whom he married in 1965. One time when she tried to get him to stop drinking he broke her nose and damaged her eardrum. She attempted suicide herself. It was his second marriage but he was also unfaithful to Freddie. He didn't seem to be able to pull himself out of a professional and emotional tailspin. A live show at the Royal Festival Hall in September 1966 harked back to his illustrious past, revisiting old sketches complete with a wonderfully mock-pompous interpretation of *King Lear* and a send-up of bad ventriloquists similar to Peter Brough all those years ago. But there was a sweaty desperation to the show and it failed to recapture former glories. In 1968 he was contracted to make a television series in Australia – often a sign that one's star at home is waning. He only recorded three episodes. On 24 June he was found dead in his flat in Sydney, with an empty bottle of vodka and amphetamines by his side. A note said, 'Things just seemed to go too wrong too many times.' One man who knew what it was like to suffer from the black dog of depression was not surprised. Talking to *Q* magazine in 1989, Spike Milligan said Hancock was a 'very difficult man to get on with. He used to drink excessively. You felt sorry for him. He ended up on his own. I thought, he's got rid of everybody else, he's going to get rid of himself and he did.'

For Hancock and the Goons the Windmill had been the making of them, but not everyone emerged blinking into the light of Piccadilly

Circus as a star. Morecambe and Wise landed a spot but flopped and had to leave after a week. Ernie Wise cannily paid for an advertisement saying that they were leaving 'due to prior commitments', and they departed with their reputations intact. Performing all day and trying to grab the attention of punters who had only really come for the women, it was the comedy equivalent of the Beatles in Hamburg, though at the time Soho was not the seedy place it later became. It might be pushing it to say that backstage the Windmill was a bastion of respectability, but it was hardly a den of iniquity either. It resembled 'a nunnery gone potty', remembered one of the men who worked there in 2005.[20]

There were plenty more stars though. This is the story of two other names, one almost as famous as Milligan and Sellers, one almost completely forgotten. Yet they had much in common. In particular both battled with the bottle for most of their lives, and in both cases the bottle ended up winning. Rex Jameson blazed briefly but brilliantly. If you are under sixty, the name of Rex Jameson will probably mean absolutely nothing to you. Even his alter ego, Mrs Shufflewick, is unlike to stir any memories. Yet there was a time when Jameson's cross-dressing character topped bills, won awards and was a household name. Such is the harsh and fickle nature of comedy fame, particularly when one's ego is not strong enough to cope with the slings and arrows that fame flings at you.

Mrs Shufflewick was a terrific, almost timeless throwback, who would have fitted in perfectly in the music hall era and would have probably fared well today, yet somehow this utterly convincing monster made it big in the early TV – television, not transvestite – era. Jameson's Mrs

---

20 *Guardian*, 18 November, 2005.

Shufflewick is one of comedy's hidden missing links, a bridge between the lewd rudery of Marie Lloyd and the waspish innuendo of Julian Clary and Alan Carr.

Shufflewick, sporting feathered hat, gossipy manner, red nose, knock-kneed stagger and fondness for a tipple, was an instantly recognisable archetype of working-class London, a woman who drank at her local, the Cock and Comfort in the Balls Pond Road, and on cold nights wore a fur scarf that would have been the envy of Mrs Slocombe on *Are You Being Served?* – made of 'genuine untouched pussy'. Like Mollie Sugden's Mrs Slocombe, Shufflewick was a strange mix of snobbery, pseudo-gentility and past-the-knuckle Chaucerian bawdiness. At one point Mrs Shufflewick was a huge star, working onstage and on radio alongside some of the biggest names in comedy. Today Shufflewick is almost forgotten. As is the story of her creator Rex Jameson.

Part of Jameson's downfall, as with George Leybourne and so many others, was his fondness for alcohol. There is a story that Jameson was once booked to do a show and the stage manager was so concerned about him getting drunk that he locked him in his dressing room, planning to let him out only when he was due onstage. One should never underestimate the ingenuity of the desperate drunk, however. Jameson is reputed to have got a stagehand to buy a bottle of whiskey for him, slipping him the money under the door. When the stagehand got back he held the bottle to the door and Jameson put a straw through the keyhole. Sometimes it was hard to see where the bibulous Mrs Shufflewick ended and the boozy Rex Jameson began.

Jameson's origins were unknown, even to him. Rex never knew who he was. He was left on the steps of Trinity College Hospital in Greenwich in the summer of 1924 when he was only two weeks old and brought up by his foster parents George and Mabel in Southend. Life in the Essex seaside resort had a big influence on him. Music hall performers did summer seasons on the pier and the young Rex saw the hordes of east Londoners coming down for their holidays, the hen-pecked men accompanied by noisy, chatty, bossy Mrs Shufflewick prototypes. In the late 1930s his family moved to Finsbury Park, north London, just in time to be bombed by the Germans when World War II started. By 1942 Rex was in Egypt. He had joined the RAF and was appearing in Ralph Reader's *Gang Show*, where being thin and barely five foot tall, he was quite often cast as the token woman. He was in good company – Tony Hancock was Rex's flight sergeant. When they were stationed in Cairo and the other performers went off to the brothels, Hancock and Rex headed for the bars and drank themselves stupid. By the time the war was over he had decided on his career and a new surname – changing from Coster to Jameson, after the whiskey.

By the late 1940s Jameson was making a name for himself. As well as 'Shuff' he had a grumpy comedy vicar character: 'Good evening to you, my flock, and now you can flock off.' Eventually he got his turn at the Windmill, with an eight-week stint. It was certainly great training, he later recalled. 'Six shows a day . . . For the first three shows you had men in raincoats playing with their tortoises.'[21] When not performing he would drink in the Bear and Staff round the corner on the Charing Cross Road, a well-known but discreet haunt for gay performers at a time when homosexual acts were still illegal and carried a prison sentence.

Homosexuality was a difficult issue for Jameson's generation. Jimmy

---

21 Patrick Newley, *The Amazing Mrs Shufflewick: The Life of Rex Jameson*, Third Age Press, 2007, p.33.

Edwards, another Windmill veteran, was outed as a homosexual late in life, against his wishes. He was also a major drinker, and in his Sussex village the police got used to him and took a benevolent stance to his antics. One night they escorted Edwards home having found him singing *La Traviata* in the street. To avoid embarrassment they covered the dress he was wearing with a coat.

Jameson's sex life, certainly until the decriminalisation of homosexuality in private between consenting adults in 1967 and probably after it too, was illicit but hectic. While working in the West End of London he went cottaging – cruising for gay sexual encounters – in the toilets in nearby Dansey Place. This was a well-known gay hangout until just after the war in a small street just off Shaftesbury Avenue on the edge of Chinatown, known as 'Clarkson's Cottage' as it was close to a famous theatrical costumiers run by Willie Clarkson. The Cottage was so well-known that after the war a rich gay American charmed by the graffiti on the walls bought it to have it shipped home and installed in his New York garden – he was frustrated and horrified to discover that Westminster Council had thoughtfully cleaned off the suggestive graffiti before shipping it.

BBC Radio soon got wind of Jameson's work onstage, but when he auditioned for Auntie he was politely informed that his vicar's jokes about religion were not permitted, so he developed the cockney charlady he had been trying out. The embryonic Gladys Shufflewick was born, complete with unnamed hubby and friend Lily, who she liked to accompany on pub crawls. It was a character that Jameson inhabited so thoroughly that broadcasts never billed him under his own name, and critics, who only heard the voice and saw pictures, often assumed Mrs Shufflewick was genuine. And so, it seemed, did Jameson. The

Joseph Grimaldi: The godfather of modern comedy used laughter as a way of coping with intense personal angst. Grimaldi's wife died in childbirth and his only way forward was to hurl himself further into his work, bringing pleasure to the masses but dying in pain.

'The saddest eyes in the whole world.' Dan Leno, one of the numerous comedy heroes whose love of making people laugh took a toll on their own psyche. Before he died Leno would have a stint in a lunatic asylum.

Only four feet tall, Harry Relph, alias Little Tich, was one of music hall's biggest stars. Hit songs of the day could always be relied upon for a splash of innuendo. 'I could do, could do, could do, could do, could do with a bit' dates from 1891.

Marie Lloyd: She may have sung 'I'm one of the ruins that Cromwell knocked about a bit', but abusive husband Bernard Dillon may have knocked Lloyd about a bit.

Charlie Chaplin and Roscoe 'Fatty' Arbuckle in 1914: the calm before the storm. One Hollywood great would be brought down quickly by scandal; the other would have his reputation savaged but would continue to be box-office dynamite for many years.

'... Evoked my libidinous curiosity.' Charlie Chaplin was drawn to the volatile Joan Barry. Despite being victorious in a paternity case, the scandal coincided with a decline in his cinematic prowess.

Hollywood made the first twentieth-century comedy superstars but it also broke them. Behaviour in prohibition-era California could have given Caligula's Rome a run for its money in the debauchery stakes. To some, Roscoe Arbuckle was the sacrificial lamb; to others he was a symbol of everything that was immoral about the movie business.

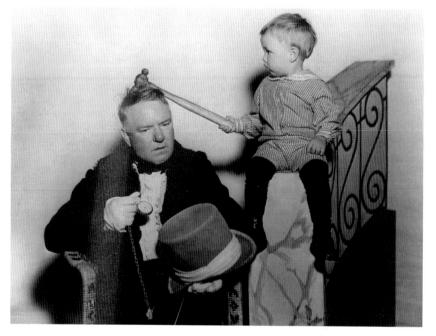

'Who put pineapple juice in my pineapple juice?'
W. C. Fields was brilliant at acting drunk, but after many years of drinking maybe it came easily. He is getting hammered again here in *Old Fashioned Way* (1934).

Max Miller: Generous with his time, Miller entertained the troops in World War II. But despite being one of comedy's richest men, he was less generous with his money. Quick with a saucy gag, less quick when it came to buying a round of drinks.

Withering looks: George Formby's wife Beryl was intolerant of his female co-stars. Googie Withers appeared with Formby in *Trouble Brewing* (1939), but Beryl would not let Withers talk to her husband off-set.

Polished performer: Northern legend Frank Randle was comedy's ultimate rebel.
If you were lucky, he threw his teeth at you; if you were unlucky, he pulled out a pistol.

'We never clothed.' If you could make it as a comedian when the audience only wanted to see the motionless naked women, you could make it anywhere. Tony Hancock, Bruce Forsyth, Tommy Cooper and Harry Secombe were among the future greats who graced the stage while the dirty raincoat brigade did the 'Wimbledon Steeplechase'.

Mrs Shufflewick: 'Just a little something to shove down your guts.'
The permissive society was a long way away but Rex Jameson's creation Mrs Shufflewick
found a way of getting filth on the airwaves in the 1950s before slipping into obscurity.

identity crisis was soon full blown. He soon began to do Shuff in full drag, even though radio listeners could only hear his voice, arriving at the Paris Theatre in Lower Regent Street by taxi, stepping out in costume and paying the cabbie, who was none the wiser. But it seemed to do the trick. Along with the young Frankie Howerd he was one of the stars of the BBC's *Variety Bandbox* – 'Here we all are then, full of port and ready to sport.' Jameson capitalised on his rise with live shows, set up by his manager Joe Collins, the father of Joan Collins. He was also cast in some straight plays but didn't enjoy them. Jameson was comedy through and through, and that was all he wanted to do, towards the end of his career not looking back on his dramatic digressions with much fondness: 'I was drunk for most of the run', he told his biographer Patrick Newley.

Shufflewick was not the first drag act to make it in broadcasting. That honour went to Douglas Byng, who used to sing 'Nobody Loves a Fairy When She's Forty'. Byng was a complete contrast to Jameson, something of a grande dame of drag, always elegant, whether in or out of a dress and exquisitely well spoken. Barry Cryer recalls that in 1996 he was at a BBC party at Alexandra Palace, and after one of his old shows had been screened Byng got up to use the toilet, opting for the sink rather than the urinal. When challenged he had a short answer that silenced everyone in the men's room: 'I am an actor.'

Jameson's act sailed about as close to the wind as one could get in the early 1950s. The rules in the Green Book still held sway, but clever performers such as Max Miller and now Jameson would navigate a course around them with a nod and a wink to those listeners who got the gags. The innuendo was perfectly clear to anyone who wanted to hear it, but at the same time Jameson made sure that he didn't infringe the rules on decency: 'This sailor walked in. I think he must have been in the Navy himself because he kissed me on both cheeks. And I was doing me shoelaces up at the time. He turned to me and said, "Would you care for a little something between your lips?" I said, "What did you have in mind?" He said, "Oh just a little something to shove down your guts."' Even by today's post-watershed standards it is crude. One can imagine Julian Clary breaking into this straight after his controversial 'I've just been fisting Norman Lamont . . . Talk about a red box,' remark at the British Comedy Awards in 1993.

The development of Mrs Shufflewick may have been partly inspired by Jameson's friendship with Hylda Baker, a legendary comedy figure in the early 1950s who later found mainstream fame in the ITV sitcom *Nearest and Dearest*, in which she played pickles heiress Nellie Pledge. Baker was famously difficult to work with. When *Nearest and Dearest* was being filmed she would often forget her lines and did not get on with her co-star, former stand-up Jimmy Jewel. When there was a stage version of the show and Hylda Baker dried up, Jimmy Jewel looked at the audience and said, 'I'm not helping her.' At her house in Blackpool, where she flew a flag when she was in, she used to keep monkeys and was known to take them into work. Onstage she employed a silent tomb-faced stooge, rather like Edna Everage did with Madge a generation later, getting through over eleven, including Matthew Kelly, in her career.

Yet Baker and Jameson seemed to hit it off. Jameson used to spend a lot of time with Baker – and her monkeys – at her London flat close to the British Museum. Looking at pictures of Baker, in fur scarf and hat, she and Shuff could have borrowed each other's wardrobes. The only thing they didn't share was accents – Baker was defiantly northern,

Shufflewick a committed cockney, but they both sported a glazed look and a wobbly stance after imbibing one too many tinctures.

By the mid-1950s Jameson had moved on from radio. He was topping the bill in the country's biggest theatres and was a huge TV star, voted television personality of the year by *TV Mirror*. He toured with another great female impersonator, Norman Evans, and the Goons. Morecambe and Wise could often be spotted further down the bill along with the likes of the Dagenham Girl Pipers. Onstage he relished the chance to be rude: 'I went to see my doctor the other night. He said have you had a check-up lately? I said no, a couple of Hungarians.'

But variety was dying and television was taking over, although Rex looked like he was successfully making the transition. He appeared on the box with Terry Scott and Jon Pertwee. He didn't get on with the latter, in later years recalling, 'To put it mildly he was a cunt.' Rex barely had any time off. When he did he would spend it cruising, drinking, going to the cinema or putting bets on, fag in hand. But tastes were evolving fast. By the end of the 1950s radio had turned to music rather than comedy, TV was also evolving and Mrs Shufflewick's face did not fit any more. Jameson had made plenty of money but had gambled and drunk most of it away. In 1960 he was declared bankrupt. Even though he still worked regularly in the 1960s the money went on the tax that he owed. That plus booze and betting.

As the decade wore on Shuff became a caricature of her early self, and she had always been larger than life. She became more sozzled onstage as Jameson became more boozy offstage. His behaviour got worse, and stories about Jameson did the dressing-room rounds. When he did a season in Jersey there was a stream not far from the theatre, and rumour had it you could tell when Rex had had a little too much to drink, as he had a habit of falling in the stream and could be spotted walking along as if nothing was wrong in full Shufflewick drag with added pondweed on his head.

Stage managers knew all too well that he had a drink problem so tried to get round it by putting him on earlier in the evening before he had had too much. Even though he was the headline act he would sometimes go on first. This meant that as Mrs Shufflewick Jameson had to fake drunkenness onstage, but then ironically afterwards he would get drunk for real. Once, after his own performance, he fell from the circle bar into the stalls. The alcohol seemed to work as a muscle relaxant and painkiller, and there was nothing major injured except for his dignity.

Jameson could regularly be spotted on the streets of London the worse for wear, a tiny figure in a green cap, oversized coat and hangdog expression. Cabbies would refuse to pick him up until he slipped into character and announced with a grand slur, 'Tis I, your mother, take me home.' Drinking was affecting his performances, and although he still had a following, theatres were wary of booking him as stories of nightmare performances started to circulate. At the Civic Theatre in Barnsley Jameson acquitted himself well in the first half, but after a few snifters in the interval had difficulty getting back onstage. When he finally managed it he simply did exactly the same act again and could not understand why nobody was laughing. Shufflewick started out sober but then got ruder and drunker as the evening wore on, and lurched further and further off-script. One Brighton show was so filthy it closed after two nights.

By the early 1970s life had reached rock bottom. Jameson was living in a damp, rented two-bedroom flat in Kentish Town. The wallpaper was peeling off the walls and the furniture looked like it had been salvaged from a skip. The smell of stale smoke, stale beer and stale urine was terrible. Jameson once told Patrick Newley who managed him for a while that he had not had a bath in twenty-three years, and it looked as if he didn't intend to start now. But the state of the flat didn't really matter as Jameson was rarely there. If he wasn't gigging or staying in digs, he was installed in a pub somewhere in London, hoping an old fan would recognise him and buy him a drink, or going through the racing pages and putting his last few pence on a horse.

It was a long way from his golden era, but while his public profile had taken a dive there were advantages. Homosexuality was now legal and Jameson could live a more open gay life. And when he performed, increasingly in the proliferating gay clubs around the capital, such as Camden Town's Black Cap 'The Palladium of Drag', he could let rip in a way he never could on BBC Radio.[22] His renewed popularity came with its own problems though. When appearing at cult venues such as the Vauxhall Tavern, well-meaning fans would send bottles of beer to the dressing room topped up with vodka or gin, resulting in chaotic car-crash performances. Jameson and alcohol were rarely parted. He would always carry a small bottle of whiskey in his pocket, and if he did have a tea or a coffee there would be a substantial nip in it. Some of the clubs he played were extremely rough. He once did a gig at the Elephant and Castle pub, which was filthy, smelly and full of drunks. Jameson should have felt at home there, but after giving it his best shot to no avail he announced, 'I have

---

22 The Black Cap, just round the corner from Julian Clary's Camden Town house, renamed its upstairs bar the Shufflewick Bar in honour of Rex Jameson, who recorded a live album there in the 1970s.

played some of the finest variety theatres in the country and I can truthfully say that this is the worst fucking dump I have come across.' He ducked just in time to avoid being hit in the face by a beer bottle arcing through the air with considerable force.

Gradually though, with the help and encouragement of Patrick Newley, he started to make a comeback. As a favour his old chum, melodramatic songstress Dorothy Squires, invited him to support her at the London Palladium on condition that he stayed sober. Somehow he managed it, and in front of an audience that included another old mate from the Windmill days Danny La Rue and writer Barbara Cartland, he got great reviews and was able to ramp up his asking price. But there were still regular lapses. He was invited back to the Palladium by Squires in 1976. Newley recalls Jameson turning up with two full carrier bags, one containing his costume, the other containing his drinks. He pulled out a bottle of whiskey and said, 'Don't worry. I'm only having the one.' He once went to a friend's flat and offered to cook while they were out. When his friend returned the flat was on fire and Jameson had passed out drunk on the living-room floor. One night he was so drunk he lost his toupee, and the next day there was a frantic dash around town trying to find a replacement.

Gradually, however, the drink and the lifestyle took its toll. By the time Jameson was in his mid-fifties he looked two decades older whether in or out of his dress. Mrs Shufflewick had not aged very gracefully either. Her nose was redder than ever and her clothes were becoming increasingly threadbare. The tragi-comic character was still loved but had become more tragic than comic. No amount of greasepaint could hide the ruddy complexion and broken veins, but he kept on working right to the end, which came without warning on 5 March 1983.

Jameson was living in Camden Town by then and fittingly he had just popped out to buy some cigarettes and Guinness when he had a heart attack and collapsed. He was rushed to the Royal Free Hospital in Belsize Park but was dead by the time he got there. He was only fifty-eight years old. At his funeral at Golders Green Crematorium loyal fans and celebrities from the contemporary drag circuit and the old musical hall era gathered. Danny La Rue and Ernie Wise were among the big names. Light entertainment legend Dickie Henderson said, 'If they dropped a bomb on this lot there wouldn't be a poof left in England.' Despite Jameson's death his legend lives on. The likes of Julian Clary, Graham Norton and Alan Carr might not wear dresses, but their penchant for smutty asides keeps Mrs Shufflewick alive.

The Windmill Theatre gave showbiz breaks to all sorts. World War II had shaken everything up. The absurdity and horrors of war left a generation of performers with a sense of infinite possibilities. Anything could happen now. Comedy had a new irreverent streak and a lack of respect for authority. This made for great ground-breaking comedy, but at the same time it produced more comedians than ever who had a dark side. It is worth noting that Morecambe and Wise, an act without any discernible shadow, were just that little bit too young to see active service in the war. This may be the reason for their Bring me sunshine-y disposition. It might also be the reason why they did not fit in with the spirit of the Windmill and didn't complete their booking there.

Some graduates of the theatre of war, such as Rex Jameson, would fall victim to the psychological fallout. Some would come through it. And some would look as if they had overcome the trauma only for it to enter in the final act with a vengeance. Tommy Cooper, that beloved gentle giant of family entertainment, falls into this final category. It is perhaps no coincidence that his most famous onstage routine involved producing endless bottles of spirits as if from nowhere. By the end of his career Cooper was producing endless bottles of spirits offstage as well.

Thomas Frederick Cooper, born on 19 March 1921 in Caerphilly, Wales, where the cheese comes from, was not born big. In fact the midwife said he was a weakling, and his mother had to give him nips of brandy to keep him going. It certainly did the trick – he was eventually well over six feet tall. And maybe those drops of alcohol gave him an early taste that would blossom into that bottle-a-day regime.

Eventually the family moved to Exeter, where his father had an ice-cream van. Like many entertainers, Cooper was shy offstage and had something of a reputation for being an outsider. If he was known among his school chums at all, it was for his interest in magic. Before he was ten he had his first magic set. He would practise the tricks in private, and when he had perfected them set up shows for his friends. It would take time, however, for Cooper to realise that his skill was not so much in sleight of hand but the natural gift for clowning, which had always been there but took time to break through. His sheer physicality was funny, giving him a head start – lantern jaw, broad shoulders, six foot three and a half inches of lumbering lunacy.

During the war Cooper was in the army, joining the Household Cavalry, rising to the rank of Corporal of Horse and developing the onstage style that would serve him so well. It was while entertaining the troops in Egypt as part of the Combined Services Entertainment Unit that he reputedly grabbed a fez from a passing waiter and donned it. His act might not have been complete but his look was. Soon after the war, while he was still in the Middle East, he met Gwen. After a two-week courtship they were married, and Tommy and 'Dove' would remain together until he died. For a while they were also a professional double act, but it was clear that it was going nowhere and Tommy had to branch out alone doing what he called 'cod magic and comedy'.[23]

The late 1940s were a tough time. There was still rationing and austerity was the order of the day. It was hard to make an honest living, and Tommy came up with some ingenious ways to supplement his income. With a friend he pretended they had hot tips for races, selling them for two shillings a time. They collected the money from workers on their way home with bulging pay packets and fled before the results came in. It all went well until Cooper was recognised due to an early TV appearance, and he had to steer clear of some areas for a while. But stage work was picking up. He had an agent, Miff Ferrie, and soon he could concentrate on comedy not conning. Ferrie was not a great judge of comedy, but he was good at doing a deal, whether for Tommy or for himself. Cooper would often moan about the tight contract that Ferrie held him to, but Cooper's assiduous biographer John Fisher, suggests that this might just have been a way for him to cover up his own parsimony, pleading poverty when rounds of drinks were being bought. In fairness cash was tight everywhere

---

23 John Fisher, *Tommy Cooper*, Harper, p.64.

in those years. People quickly got into the habit of not spending money unless absolutely necessary. Cooper used to do the old Groucho Marx gag: 'I've got a clause in my contract that says I have to be cremated. That way my agent can get 15 per cent of my ashes.'[24] In cafes he would say, 'You get the teas, boys, and I'll get the chairs.'[25] The most famous apocryphal story is of him catching a taxi and putting something in the driver's pocket as he got out saying 'have a drink on me'. When the driver looked there was no tip, just a tea bag. When writers told Cooper he owed them money for doing their material on television he often tried to argue that as the piece had been used on TV the broadcaster had to cough up.

Cooper might have had a cuddly exterior, but there was a tougher streak that did not just manifest itself where money was concerned. If an audience gave him a hard time he could give them one back. At that legendary bear pit the Glasgow Empire, where Des O'Connor later faked illness to escape the stage, Cooper felt so unappreciated he walked to the front of the stage, told the audience to 'fuck off', packed his bags and caught the next train out of the city. London club gigs could be difficult. Places such as the Blue Lagoon in Carnaby Street and the Bag o' Nails in Kingly Street were notorious hangouts for villains back then. Guns had to be handed in at the door with coats. But gradually Cooper was learning his trade, and eventually he got the chance of a stint at the Windmill after his fifth audition for Vivian Van Damm, doing six shows a day for six weeks for thirty pounds a week in late 1949. Whether it was the importance of the venue and the fact that having it on his CV

24 Ibid., p.84.
25 Ibid., p.100.

would help him get better bookings or the naked women constantly milling about backstage, Cooper was particularly nervous here. Just before one performance he went to grab his fez and grabbed a pudding basin instead, putting that on his head by mistake.

But hard work and simple stunts such as pushing a knot up and down a piece of string did, as it were, the trick, and got Cooper noticed. The old guard of comedy was noticing him too. In the late 1950s Max Miller encountered Cooper, maybe spotted a kindred spirit, was suitably impressed and gave him one of his trademark white snap-brim trilbies. As far as we know he didn't send him a bill either. Cooper and Miller were certainly spiritual soulmates when it came to spending money. There was no single event that made Cooper an overnight sensation. He just grafted and grafted until he rose through the ranks, building up a huge fan base. He played clubs up and down England; he played Las Vegas; he did a TV special with Bruce Forsyth and Frankie Howerd. But the work was hard. There was a lot of travelling involved, and a lot of late nights in smoke-filled rooms. It is hard today to believe how much audiences smoked in the 1960s, but look at any archive footage of Baileys in Watford or the Night Out in Birmingham and you can barely see the audience for the fug.

Cooper was not averse to a bit of sleight of hand to get noticed, 'borrowing' tricks he had seen on trips abroad. One of his famous routines, playing the tune 'Autumn Leaves' on the piano until he and the piano were covered entirely in leaves, was not original; he had seen it done in Las Vegas. Today, when anything and everything is just a computer click away, he would not have been able to get away with it, but back then it was unlikely anyone in his audience in the

UK had seen it done before. Gag theft is often frowned upon, but at least when Cooper did it he added his own unique personality to a riff.

His routine with a variety of hats, acting out a story and playing all the parts – fireman, policeman, soldier, etc. – by pulling the relevant hats from an increasingly muddled crate, also seemed original to anyone in the UK unfamiliar with the ancient art of chapeaugraphy, the manipulation of headgear, which had gone on in shows on the Continent for centuries. 'I've got to get a bigger box,' he would say as the routine got increasingly chaotic. Sometimes, of course, a routine is just in the comedy ether and performers do it without knowing it has been done before. Cooper used to do a routine where he played tunes on car horns hanging from his overcoat. Both Bill Bailey and Harry Hill have done routines playing more recent pop classics on car horns, but I doubt whether they were thinking of Cooper – or for that matter, each other – when they came up with what I'm sure they thought was a brilliantly original idea.

Even Cooper's most famous exchange – with the Queen after the Royal Variety Performance, may have been more second hand than it seemed. Cooper was said to have asked the Queen if she liked football, and when she replied, 'Not particularly,' he asked if he could have her FA Cup Final tickets. John Fisher suggests that this line might first have been used by Bud Flanagan to the Queen Mother and that Flanagan may have repeated it to Cooper, not knowing he would magic it away for his own use.

As Cooper started to make good money he was often at loggerheads with Miff Ferrie, who he felt had too tight a stranglehold on his affairs.

Cooper would write to him calling him 'Little Caesar' and Miff was understandably miffed. There was also the small matter of Cooper embarking in the late 1960s on an affair with Mary Kay which meant that Miff had to be discreet when settling hotel bills. From 1967 Kay had started travelling with Cooper as his assistant, but very soon this blossomed into an affair that would last until Cooper's death. He was not a womaniser taking advantage of groupies on tour, but it was just that he was devoted to two women.

And at the same time there was a noticeable increase in Cooper's alcohol intake. When he appeared in a small part on the *Mike and Bernie Winters Show*, Miff was put out because Cooper arranged the fee himself – a cask of whiskey. Miff thought it was demeaning for a star to be paid in booze but presumably he was also disgruntled because he didn't receive 15 per cent as his commission either. At first a quick drink helped to settle Cooper's nerves. It is not easy making an audience laugh without saying anything. People thought it was effortless, but of course just walking on took a lot of effort, and he thought that alcohol might help. And until it got out of hand maybe it did.

Cooper and drink seemed to go hand in hand. He was not known publicly as a drunk, and it was not part of his stage persona as it was with Rex Jameson. Yet looking back it is remarkable to see how often he used to refer to drink both in his act and in interviews. It was almost a cry for help, as he told interviewers, 'I never drink before a show. If I did my tricks might start to go right.' He did a very neat trick of making a small whiskey glass disappear into thin air by slamming one hand down on the other. And then there was another classic Cooper line: 'Sometimes I drink my whiskey neat. Sometimes I take my tie off and leave my shirt hanging out.' You do not make that many jokes about a subject unless it is on your mind.

Then there was the gag about being stopped by the police. 'I was driving home the other week and a policeman stopped me. He said, "Is this car licensed?" I said, "Yes constable. Would you like a gin and tonic?"' This may have been partly inspired by a real event. In the late 1950s Cooper was stopped by the police and was set to face charges until he agreed to do a gig for a police charity instead.

By the mid-1970s, however, Cooper's star had risen and was falling again. It was not his talent that was at fault but his health. Those years of smoky late nights had taken their toll – his own habit of smoking up to forty cigars a day didn't help – but more importantly he was drinking heavily. There were recordings when he had to have cup after cup of black coffee before dress rehearsals and recordings so that he could be coherent. According to John Fisher, in 1978's *Cooper – Just Like That* TV show he missed cues, turned his back on the audience, argued with a fan and at the end of one edition could be heard muttering 'rubbish' as the credits rolled. It was assumed to be a joke but maybe he was aware of how shambolic he was getting. It was a shame that his own joke was not coming true – having a drink before a show didn't make the tricks go right, it made the comedy go wrong.

His punctuality was getting worse too. He arrived onstage late, sometimes didn't have the right props with him and was not firing on all cylinders. And like Mrs Shufflewick one could hear the clink of bottles in his bags as he arrived. Like a magic trick anything might emerge from Cooper's plastic bags as long as it had an alcoholic element to it – green Chartreuse, yellow advocaat, vodka, gin, brandy or whiskey. He once asked for gin at breakfast in a hotel and poured it on his cornflakes, saying it was healthier than fatty milk. When he did drink milk it was to line his stomach before another binge.

The drinking took a toll on his domestic life. Gwen was also fond of a drink, and rows between them could become heated and even violent. By the end of the 1960s Gwen had been in touch with Miff Ferrie, saying they were going to get a divorce. The marriage rumbled on however. When Cooper had a heart attack in Rome in 1977 which might have killed lesser men, the doctors had an easy, brutal explanation: chronic alcoholism was cited as a cause. It was a scare but it didn't stop him. He was clearly in denial, constantly trying to make light of his drinking. He once told producer Dennis Kirkland he was only allowed one glass of Dubonnet. When it was pointed out to him after a liquid lunch that three bottles had been consumed, he argued, 'I've only used one glass.' Legend has it that his meanness and his alcoholism collided backstage – he would lock his booze away so that no one else could get at it. He would even lock the phone away so no one could make phone calls which would appear on his bill. During fights at home crockery was smashed and furniture thrown. Dove tried to find the funny side when she talked to the press, explaining that was why they did not have any matching chairs. It was not easy living with Cooper: 'He was the nicest, kindest and most awkward man in the world' she said.[26]

This could not last for ever. By the 1980s Cooper's star had declined and he had some odd bookings. He even supported The Police – the

---

26 Ibid., p.367.

band, not officers who wanted to nick him – but he was still a big enough name to be a guest on ITV's prime-time variety show *Live From Her Majesty's*. As he proceeded to do his act, pretending to pull increasingly odd items from under his cloak (in reality Jimmy Tarbuck was passing them through the curtain), he suffered a heart attack, crumpled and fell. It seemed like another trick, but soon it was clear there was something wrong, and for the sixteen million viewers at home the programme cut to a commercial break. When it returned the old maxim 'The show must go on' really did kick in. Despite Cooper's large feet still protruding from under the curtain, Jimmy Tarbuck introduced the rest of the show. If Cooper could have chosen a way to die, it might have been something like this.

Cooper's death was a huge shock to the public. He was only sixty-three but his health had been failing for years. There were leg problems, bronchial problems and heart problems. He knew he had to give up drinking and smoking but struggled. One time in front of Bob Monkhouse he cracked open a can of lager and lit up a panatella. Monkhouse said he thought he had given up. Cooper gestured to the weak alcohol and thin cigar and replied, 'You can't call this smoking and you can't call this drinking, can you?'

Eventually the Windmill wound down in the mid-1960s when Soho became filled with more explicit strip clubs, but it had a revival as a breeding ground for a new generation of comedians at the start of the 1990s. I remember being invited down there for the filming of *Paramount City* – the new name of the venue – the BBC's answers to Channel 4's cult shows *Friday Night Live* and *Saturday Live*. I was given a very generous glass of white wine as I walked in, but that was about as good as it got. The programme did not really capture the thrills, spills and devil-may-care kinetics of a live comedy show. *Saturday Night Live* had the Thatcher-bashing young gun Ben Elton as host; *Paramount City* had Arthur Smith. Or maybe it was the lack of naked fan dancers.

Arthur would go on to be one of the best comperes on the circuit, but at not much more than thirty, his face didn't fit. With his crinkly Sid James skin and hangdog expression he already looked middle-aged. Viewers may have thought he had been knocking around Great Windmill Street since Peter Sellers and Tony Hancock were treading the boards. The producer of the show, Janet Street-Porter who had made her name with 'yoof TV', didn't think he fitted the bill either, describing him as 'a thoroughly irritating man, neither young, attractive or witty'. *Paramount City* marked the end of the comedy road for the venue. Some of the acts that appeared there – Steve Coogan, Jack Dee, Frank Skinner, Caroline Aherne, Jo Brand, Mark Thomas – went on to brilliant things. A number of them became stars as big as the first generation of Windmill comedians. And some would do battle with their demons in public and private. The Windmill might be gone today, but without it comedy would not be the same.[27]

---

27 I popped down there today to check. It is actually called the Windmill again, but the emphasis these days is firmly on tits and not titters. No sign of Mr Titman checking up on business.

5

The TV Times

Mr Comeback, Mr Slick and the overgrown schoolboy

Benny Hill never made it past Vivian Van Damm's auditions at the Windmill. The aspiring comedian did frequent the theatre though. He may even have been one of those men in overcoats who took part in the daily Windmill Steeplechase. He was certainly smitten by some of the performers he saw there, and we aren't talking comedians. He used to send regular fan letters to Ann Hamilton, one of the (clothed) dancers, who went on to appear regularly with Morecambe and Wise.

While the Windmill spawned one batch of troubled comic geniuses, there were plenty more tormented souls with a scurrilous streak cutting their teeth elsewhere. And as England returned to a semblance of normality after World War II they managed to find new outlets for their expansive, needy egos. Benny Hill may have been thwarted but he did not give up. This strange man, both sex-obsessed and peculiarly sexless, continued to graft away and eventually became massive all over the world.

Alfred Hawthorne Hill was born in Southampton on 21 January 1924. Comedy was everything to him. When he died, wifeless and childless, in a modest flat in west London, his estate went to relatives he barely knew, if at all. This was a man who truly lived for laughter and did not show much interest in quotidian preoccupations such as having a family of his own, although he was devoted to his mother. When she died in 1976 he kept the Southampton house he had grown up in exactly as it was as a shrine to her.

It is not widely known, but performance was in Hill's genes, while the minutiae of sexual activity was also part of the family business. His father and grandfather had both been circus clowns, but his father also sold condoms by mail order from his backstreet shop in Southampton. Hill's first job was as a milkman. He was not the fastest milkman in the west, and he was not the happiest milkman on the south coast either. He gave it up and followed in his family's showbiz footsteps, heading to London and working in variety. Unfortunately the war got in the way and he was conscripted – initially missing his call-up papers due to being on tour and being briefly thrown into prison. In uniform he avoided front-line combat and entertained the troops as part of the 'Stars in Battledress' corps.

After the war Hill worked in clubs and theatres, for a while as a straight man to future *On the Buses* star Reg Varney. History could have been so different – Peter Sellers had tried and failed to get that gig. Hill was one of the first performers to see the potential of television and he bombarded the BBC with script ideas. His persistence paid off. By 1955 *The Benny Hill Show* was one of the biggest draws on the box, and Hill became one of the first major British TV comedy stars. He was not just the corny 'dirty old man' we think of today; he was an innovative, constantly inventive clown. At a time when television technology was so primitive and cumbersome it was virtually steam-driven, he used split-screen techniques to play all the characters – male and female – in panel-game spoofs.

Hill's genius was closer to that of early movie stars such as Chaplin, who was a fan, and Buster Keaton than modern comedians. And his love of a visual gag that could have come straight out of a silent movie paid off – without the need for subtitles Hill was able to sell his programmes around the world. In 1990 his show was running in ninety-seven countries, and he was one of the few British TV comedians to make it big in America, where even Frank Sinatra tuned in to watch the ex-milkman from Southampton slap a small bald man on the head. Prisoners in San Jose Penitentiary rioted when lights-out meant they could not see *The Benny Hill Show*. Michael Caine, who worked with Hill in *The Italian Job* in 1969, was another admirer, but his tribute seemed to sense that there was something not quite right about Hill. 'He has a face like an evil cherub – a cherub sent by the devil.'

But Hill wasn't as original as some might have thought. He once invited a girlfriend on a trip to Paris. She was expecting oysters, romance and flowers; instead they ended up spending all their time in the hotel room – watching French television, with Hill hoping to pick up some ideas (there are also stories of him taking notes at other comedy shows in France and when American performers visited the UK). Like Tommy Cooper he cannily took advantage of the fact that Britons did not travel abroad very often back in the 1950s and early 1960s, and there was little chance they would have seen the original versions.

Despite his success, Hill was a classic case of comic insecurity. But while others took a swift slug of Dutch courage from a bottle and stepped up to the plate onstage, as soon as Hill was successful he bid the theatre a relieved farewell and stuck to the television. He didn't like performing live and turned down chat shows and anything that didn't involve following a script.

The romantic life of Benny Hill remains a mystery. The aforementioned trip to Paris which turned out to be all about research and development sounds typical. He had few relationships, and it was rumoured that he was either gay or a frequenter of prostitutes. Like Frankie Howerd, Hill never married. Also like Howerd, he talked of relationships with the opposite sex – he claimed he had proposed to three different women but had been turned down each time. He was also anxious about his weight but had a fondness for the catering truck on location. 'I have plenty of will power, but not a lot of won't power,' he once joked. In the 1970s he started taking amphetamines to suppress his appetite. The drug, better known as speed, may also have contributed to his idea for speeded-up comedy footage, being chased by scantily clad women across parks and through streets. Maybe he was taking the diet pill benzedrine – better known as bennys.

It was once said that all political careers end in tragedy. The same could be said for a lot of comedy careers. Despite his huge success – and making huge amounts of money for Thames Television in international sales – Hill fell out of favour in the 1980s with alternative comedy promoting non-sexist humour. New Ben on the block Ben Elton was a notable critic, suggesting that although he was a talented comedian Hill's portrayal of women was old hat. Certainly they tended to be bimbos or hags in Hill's world, but in his defence feminists should note that during those Keystone Kops-style fast-paced skits Hill was usually being chased, not doing the chasing.

Eventually Thames responded to the criticisms, and in 1989 his contract was not renewed. Some say that this contributed to the decline in Hill's health. Without television he suddenly had little purpose. He was not a social animal, and back then there was no reality TV or shows set in the Australian jungle where out-of-favour celebrities could go to rehabilitate themselves. It was an odd death, alone at home at some point between 18 and 20 April, 1992. Yet in some respects, as with Cooper, Hill died as he lived. Cooper died onstage, Hill in front of the television. His flat was just a short stroll from Teddington TV studios, where he had had so much success.

Hill lived on after his death in the most macabre of fashions. Over the same weekend that he died, Frankie Howerd also died. When the tributes came flooding in for Howerd, Hill's body had not yet been discovered. But the press did try to contact him and went via his old producer Dennis Kirkland, who kindly provided a quote that Benny was 'upset' on his behalf. It was only afterwards that Kirkland decided to visit his chum and had to get into Hill's flat by climbing a ladder. There he found Hill dead in his pants with his shirt unbuttoned and his shoes and socks off, in front of the television. The post-mortem concluded that he had died before Frankie. It was not a good weekend for comedy. A big chunk of comic history died that weekend in April 1992.

Frankie Howerd had first met Hill way back in the late 1940s. Hill had seen Howerd auditioning for an ex-servicemen's show and complimented him, saying that he seemed much more experienced than he actually was. They then went their separate ways, only to be reunited nearly half a century later in death. Like Hill, Frankie Howerd was a contemporary of the Windmill gang but carved out his own path. His life is a case study in bouncebackability – making it to the top again just when you've hit rock bottom. His life is also a case study in the dysfunctional nature of comedians. It was quite clear to anyone who ever saw Howerd in performance that it was just that. A performance. There was a darker, more difficult, suppressed side that was due in part but not entirely to his homosexuality at a time when being gay was still illegal. Howerd is a prime example of a comedy misfit, who would have found it almost impossible functioning successfully in mainstream society, playing by normal rules. It was comedy or bust for him.

Howerd was born Francis Alick Howard in York on 6 March 1917, and brought up in Eltham, south-east London. In his less-than-candid autobiography, *On the Way I Lost It*, penned when he was not openly gay, he indulged in a touch of light self-analysis. He thought that his unusual personality was due to a bump on the head as a baby. In later life he distinctly recalled falling down the stairs: 'Five tumbles as my head hit various stairs then – bang – an almighty bang at the bottom.[28] If you are reading any innuendo into that sentence that's your filthy mind. There didn't seem to be any major neurological damage, but Howerd grew up a shy child. His father was in the military and he spent a lot of time with his mother. When his father was invalided out, the young Frankie felt that his dad had intruded on his party with his mother. He was pretty self-contained but a regular church-goer, and at the age of thirteen he became an unlikely Sunday school teacher.

Speaking to an audience was an odd move. Like W. C. Fields, Frankie

---

28 Frankie Howerd, *On the Way I Lost It*, Star, 1977, p.14.

had a stammer, but also like Fields, he learned to turn it to professional advantage. In later life it would be covered up in public by the comical repetition of words, ums and aaahs, as if he was hesitating, rather than having difficulty speaking. He was determined to be a performer despite this impediment. He auditioned for RADA but failed to get in so decided he would pursue a career in comedy, where he could have more control over his destiny. He put on his own shows in Scout halls and old people's homes and for a while called himself Ronnie Ordex, which he thought had more star quality, before joining the army in 1940 and being posted to exotic Southend.

It was here that he developed his act, playing with gags and stories and stretching his monologues, stopping just short of snapping point. He was still very naive though, sometimes failing to spot a joke even as he was telling it. One night at the Palace Theatre in Westcliff he introduced his next song, the old Marie Lloyd classic, not realising the double meaning of its title 'I Sits Among the Cabbages and Peas'. The curtain promptly came down; he was hauled off and told to get out of the theatre by the manager. He was clearly still honing his style. For one song he performed as part of a trio in ATS uniforms, Miss Twillow, Miss True and Miss Twit. He was Miss Twit.

Somehow this awkward figure rose to the rank of sergeant and was posted to France, where for a while he was an interpreter, despite barely speaking the language. One day his major asked him to find out how many women were pregnant in the local village. Howerd garbled his Gallic and went round asking if any women wanted to have a baby. He was nearly run out of town by *hommes* brandishing pitchforks.

After being demobbed, Howerd's career quickly took off following a spot of chicanery in which he faked his way on to an army show by putting his old uniform back on. Howerd's self-image can be seen by the words he used to describe himself on variety posters in those early days, known in the trade as bill matter: Borderline Case. Soon radio discovered this borderline case, and he was a hit on *Variety Bandbox*, where his catchphrases – 'Please yourselves'; 'Poor soul – she's past it' – soon made him a star. Sometimes though he went too far and fell foul of the broadcasting guidelines. In banter with band leader Bill Ternent, Ternent would say something like, 'I've been orchestrated,' and Howerd would suggestively reply, 'Dirty old devil' prompting letters of complaint. Howerd cannily negotiated a way round the rule book – like Rex Jameson, bending the regulations rather than breaking them.

His success meant that his tours were getting bigger, and he was moving up the running order, but Howerd still didn't play the star, always opting for the same three-guineas-a-week digs. In *On the Way I Lost It* he is decidedly shy about his sex life, suggesting – not very convincingly, considering what other people tend to say about life on the road and backstage – that nothing much went on because chorus girls were very moral. It is worth noting, however, that while he still technically lived at the family home in Eltham he kept a flat in London, where maybe he was more sexually active. 'I was now a big boy: romance with the ladies involved something more than lemonade and gallant hand-kissing outside the church hall.'[29]

Being gay was still extremely difficult in the early post-war years. A performer's sexual orientation was often well known in showbusiness

---

29 Ibid., p.79.

circles, but due to the law discretion was essential. Stories of assignations which might have jeopardised his career if they had come out did the rounds of the backstage gossip-mongers. Luckily there were well-established ways to keep the press quiet. His tour manager suppressed a story on the eve of a Palladium show in 1950 by getting the reporter drunk on good claret at the Savoy. One of the guests on *Variety Bandbox* was Gilbert Harding, the celebrated panellist on the radio game show *What's My Line?* Harding was gay as well as being a hopeless alcoholic. When he went to meet Howerd at his flat Harding was rude and insulting and drank Howerd dry before wetting himself on his way to the toilet. They did, however, become friends, with Howerd describing Harding as 'lonely and confused'.[30] Maybe he saw something of himself in him.

Howerd's success was partly down to the excellent writers he employed, such as *Goon Show* collaborator Eric Sykes, *Steptoe and Son* creator Johnny Speight and Ray Galton and Alan Simpson, who went on to work with Tony Hancock. There was a reason he picked his writers carefully. Without a script Howerd, like Hill, floundered, although his distinctive style meant that he could even make floundering sound funny. Though not always. On one memorable occasion he replaced Gilbert Harding on *What's My Line?* and was so stricken with nerves he could not think of anything to say. When he did speak his stammer returned with a vengeance. Even onstage, where he felt most comfortable, Howerd suffered from nerves. He was not the first comedian and would not be the last to vomit violently into his dressing-room sink just before a performance. But the world of live comedy was changing. Howerd's

---

30 Ibid., p.90.

break on to radio and then television came at just the right time, as the live variety circuit started to wither. Audiences were shifting from going out for their laughs to staying in. At one point there were over 400 theatres around the country, but after the war first radio and then television killed them off.

The best thing to happen to Howerd around this time was that he took on what he called a personal manager. Dennis Heymer, previously a waiter at Simpson's-in-the-Strand, would be his lover until his death. By 1956 they were living together discreetly in Holland Villas Road, west London. Given the illegality of homosexuality, it was understandable, yet even in his 1977 autobiography he was still concealing the truth, saying that Heymer had 'a keen eye for the birds'.[31] According to biographer Graham McCann Howerd had previously had an 'intimate friendship' with a fellow performer, but Heymer had a clear appeal. He was smart where Howerd was scruffy, calm where Howerd was fiery, easy in his skin where Howerd was uncomfortable, tolerant where Howerd was needy. In effect he was all the things Howerd – and so many neurosis-riddled comedians before and since, who have a sense of 'otherness' – would have liked to have been.

Everything was going swimmingly with his career until Howerd thought he could fulfil his original ambition and become an actor. He ditched what he did best in return for plays which had mixed results. The transition was awkward. Once a comedian always a comedian though – when he was offered the part of Bottom opposite Titania in *A Midsummer Night's Dream* at the Old Vic in 1957 he called it the Tit and

---

31 Ibid., p.145.

Bum Show. 'Here's to a warm hand on your opening,' said one telegram from a well-wisher, a line that Julian Clary would unconsciously rework many years later. Howerd certainly wasn't in it for the money – thirty pounds a week compared to the hundreds he had been earning in variety. The reviews were good for now – *The Times* called him poetic – but worse was to come. A new play, *Mr Venus*, received scathing reviews and closed after seventeen days. If it was an early case of stunt casting – bringing in a celebrity from another discipline to pep up the press notices – it had failed, damaging the production and Howerd's marketability.

In April 1957 he spent time in a private nursing home in Harrow. His condition was described as nervous exhaustion, but it may well have been the first signs of a nervous breakdown, his depression triggered by the major crisis in his career. Howerd's decision to be an actor had backfired badly. If this was today he might have ended up in the Priory. There is nothing new about a comedian having a crisis or a breakdown. Joseph Grimaldi overcame the seismic grief of the death of his wife and baby by hurling himself into his work and came back stronger than ever. Some, such as Dan Leno, could not come back at all. It looked for a while as if the same fate might befall Frankie Howerd, who did not have that much work to hurl himself into.

When he tried to return to comedy it seemed as if his funny bones had fled the scene of the crime. He took any jobs he could find, but even summer season in Scarborough was a disaster. It was 1959 and it looked as if Howerd's career was over. He slipped back down bills and was turned down for numerous parts. He seemed to be cursed. Things looked promising when he started rehearsals playing Fagin in a major production of *Oliver!*, but he was axed before the show opened. It was as if he was showbiz's number-one persona non grata. He stopped going out and stayed at home, watching television and drinking too much.

A nervous breakdown in the early 1960s marked Howerd's absolute nadir. He felt so defeated he even considered quitting comedy, selling up and opening a pub. After his mother died in 1962, Howerd's psychological isues deepened. He tried therapy and psychoanalysis and even a new treatment, taking LSD, following in the footsteps of Cary Grant and Aldous Huxley, in an attempt to expand his mind and come to terms with himself. Dropped off at a private clinic by Dennis, he was left alone after taking the drug to write down his thoughts and memories, spending a weekend there before returning home. It did not seem to do him much good. He would dip in and out of analysis for many years after that, but still seemed as gloomy and despondent as ever. What helped more were the offers of work that were slowly but surely starting to come in again.

This was largely thanks to his new agent, Beryl Vertue, who had faith in him. At the *Evening Standard* Awards in 1961 he made an impromptu speech which went down very well. Afterwards Peter Cook – who had just won an award with Dudley Moore, Jonathan Miller and Alan Bennett for *Beyond the Fringe* and was the toast of the town – suggested he play the club Cook was planning to open, The Establishment. Howerd took this with a pinch of salt and even when the offer came in was keen to turn it down, suggesting that he could not do cabaret and had never done it before. Beryl reassured him – cabaret was what he had actually done at the *Evening Standard* Awards. He needed to develop this intimate underplayed side of his storytelling and The Establishment was the perfect venue.

Howerd was a revelation. He did a longer set than planned, nattering to the crowd in his inimitable 'Titter ye not' style. Though of course Galton and Simpson had chipped in too. He was soon in full flow: 'I'm no Lenny Bruce. If you've come expecting a lot of crudeness and a lot of vulgarity I'm sorry, you won't get it from me, so you might just as well piss off now.'[32] Afterwards the work started to come in again, from films to television. An appearance on satire show *That Was the Week That Was* cemented his return. Howerd was asked to talk about the government's latest budget, and despite not being a political animal got all the best jokes from his writers and delivered a brilliant thirteen-minute routine, famously describing reporter Robin Day as having 'cruel glasses'. It should have only been eight minutes but the studio laughter made it overrun. Howerd was cast in the lead of *A Funny Thing Happened on the Way to the Forum* (when it was revived *Paramount City*'s Arthur Smith was offered the role of Howerd's understudy but declined) and appeared regularly on television and in Carry On movies. Against all the odds, Howerd had bounced back.

By the end of the 1960s he was a mainstream star all over again as put-upon slave Lurcio in the ribald BBC hit *Up Pompeii*. 'Imagine Italy is the shape of a woman's leg. Well, Pompeii is situated not quite high enough to be interesting.' If only his private life had run as smoothly. Despite his relationship with Heymer, who was so supportive that at times Howerd described him as his 'male nurse', he was prone to making advances towards any young man whose path he crossed. Success seemed to have an adverse effect on his private life. It did not calm him down at all. He seemed compelled to live dangerously. He would sometimes

32 Graham McCann, *Frankie Howerd: Stand-up Comic*, Harper Perennial, Fourth Estate, 2005, p193.

ask his TV producer to say he was working if Dennis called, when he was actually out cruising for anonymous sexual encounters. Though how Howerd, with his unmistakable hangdog face and wonky toupee flapping in the breeze could ever remain anonymous is a mystery.

Howerd was of course not the only star taking a big risk in a less tolerant age. In 1953 actor John Gielgud had been prosecuted for 'persistently importuning for immoral purposes' – 'cottaging' – and in November 1962 Wilfrid Brambell, best known today as the co-star of *Steptoe and Son*, was arrested for a similar offence outside a toilet on Shepherd's Bush Green. Brambell's defence was that he had been to a party at the nearby BBC Television Centre and while in search of a taxi was caught short – it had all been a misunderstanding. He was given a conditional discharge and fined twenty-five guineas including costs. His career survived, but it was touch and go for a gay comedian in the pre-legal days.

Funnily I've been to the same toilets myself. In recent years the venue was turned into a stand-up comedy club called Ginglik, and I recall a very young Michael McIntyre there. He was stricken with nerves and after his performance was ridiculously overcritical about his short set. He was clearly talented but no one would have predicted that half a decade later he would be comedy's biggest star. Or that along with Russell Brand he would conspire to make comedy in the UK so popular.

Howerd was on safer ground when his advances were less random. In 1961 comedian Bob Monkhouse had been doing summer season in Great Yarmouth and had rented a big house so that his wife and children could stay with him. As the season came to its end and school resumed, his family returned to London. One day Monkhouse was alone watching a movie with the curtains drawn when there was a call from Frankie Howerd, who was appearing nearby. The camel-faced clown wanted Bob's advice and asked if he could pop over – he promised to bring a nice slice of Battenberg with him. Soon afterwards there was a knock at the side entrance and Howerd appeared. He came into the lounge and quickly revealed his problem. He was thinking of getting married, he explained as he sat on the sofa next to Bob, and wondered if there was something wrong with his sexual equipment. At which point he whipped down his trousers and pants to demonstrate, pulling the younger comedian's hand on to his chest. Monkhouse could barely get away, particularly when Howerd grabbed his hair. Eventually he managed to extricate himself from the situation and fled to the kitchen where he had a good wash before Howerd appeared and offered him a soiled napkin: 'Souvenir?'[33]

Monkhouse knew that Howerd had a reputation for this kind of behaviour, but it still came as a shock to him to be the subject of Howerd's advances. In later years Howerd continued his pursuit of anything in trousers with a pulse. In the mid-1970s he was working on *The Frankie Howerd Variety Show* for BBC Radio. Howerd had long had a reputation among BBC producers for being 'difficult', which may have contributed to his earlier fall from grace. The original producer for the show had left, to be replaced by a young man called Griff Rhys Jones. The writing team included three enthusiastic but fairly raw Oxbridge graduates, Clive Anderson, Jimmy Mulville and Rory McGrath. They turned up at Howerd's flat in Edwardes Square, Kensington, and as soon as the door was shut he started plying them with drink. Howerd was drinking heavily

33 Bob Monkhouse, *Crying with Laughter*, Arrow, 1994, p.188.

himself by this time, and before they conducted post-show inquests he would put bottles of whiskey, gin and vodka down in front of his youthful team so that they could join him. They liked a drink, but they were not used to this much being available.

One time, after a few drinks had been downed, he tried a similar trick on McGrath to the one that he had used on Bob Monkhouse fifteen years earlier. His technique tended to be to drop his trousers or grab his chosen subject's groin. Paul Ross was also on the receiving end of Howerd's amorous advances, but politely declined. In 2004 on a television documentary about Howerd Ross suggested, 'Ninety per cent of people who worked with Howerd were propositioned by him.' Paul's younger brother Jonathan joked that he was rather put out that he had never been the subject of Howerd's amorous attentions.

Howerd had a crafty habit of engineering situations. Sometimes writers would come round and he would say he was having a shower but they should continue the meeting. Other times he would ask a writer to test the temperature of the bath water for him – even though he was already in the bath. He would complain about a bad back and ask them to rub some cream on him. Polite refusals were met with a curt 'You don't know what you are missing.' Behind the farcical side of the story, however, there was something more sad. Howerd was drinking way too much – triple gins before dinner – and taking amphetamines to keep himself going. He was not happy. He felt overlooked when rival Larry Grayson was given the job of presenting *The Generation Game* – Grayson hasn't just nicked my act, he thought, he's nicked my job. He had always suffered from low self-esteem, and he felt cheated once again. As the 1970s came to an end it looked as if he was about to fade away fairly gracefully.

Yet we have to remember that Howerd defied the idea that there are no second acts in comedy. In fact he had three or four acts, having more ups and downs than an overactive elevator. Just as he seemed washed up for good he would be discovered by a new generation. As Frank Skinner once noted, they were worshipping Jesus on Sunday and by the following Friday calling for his crucifixion. Better men than Frankie Howerd had fallen out of favour and – if Jesus' publicists are to be believed – returned.

In the 1980s Howerd came back yet again when was picked up by the post-alternative-comedy student fraternity. He spoke at the Oxford Union, and merchandising stalls at his gigs did a roaring trade in T-shirts spoofing Frankie Goes To Hollywood's famous big-lettered Katharine Hamnett designs. Except that his version featured the slogan 'Frankie Says Titter Ye Not'. If he was around today he would be making yet another come-back and some enterprising soul would be printing out 'Twitter Ye Not' T-shirts by the truckload. But the strain was showing. The always-prominent lines on his face were getting more deeply etched. His suits looked scruffier. The old wig that never matched his real hair looked odder. His ailing constitution was not helped by the drinking. Frankie Howerd died of a heart attack on the way to hospital on 19 April 1992 just after Benny Hill, although, as we have just seen, Hill was quoted as being 'upset' about Howerd's death, which must be the first time a dead comedian has paid tribute to a fellow dead comedian.

If Howerd and Hill were the twin pillars of scandalous early TV comedy, Bob Monkhouse is the unlikely third man. Monkhouse is an intriguing figure, a man who, unlike Frankie Howerd, did not go out of fashion because he was never really in fashion. He was just an ever-present shiny-faced figure on the screen. Yet behind the smile and the much-maligned smarm there was somebody every bit as psychologically complex, every bit as neurotically confused and every bit as badly behaved as his peers.

Monkhouse may not have been chased by demons, but he certainly had issues. How else could he have come up with the brilliant observation that comedy is the ultimate coping mechanism, that anything nasty has to be 'rolled up in a joke to reduce it in size'? Laughter may have been his Freudian default buffer, a way of keeping emotional suffering at bay. Monkhouse, the high priest of one-liners, worked hard at analysing his comedy and understanding how it related to his life story: 'Some of us, myself included, can write our pain, encapsulating and sealing it away in a one-liner like a devil trapped in a bottle, defenceless against our mockery.'[34]

Although from a materially comfortable background himself, Monkhouse read up on Freud and used the father of psychoanalysis to explain why so many comedians have come from harsher origins, observing that Freud said, 'Humour is used as a weapon by the have-nots against the haves.'[35] Materially Monkhouse might have been comfortable, but that does not mean he was not deprived emotionally. This would certainly go some way to explaining a bleak streak of self-loathing in his gags: 'I was not wanted. Two weeks after I was born my mother tried to have an abortion.' By one of those journalistically satisfying quirks of comedy fate, there was a further Freud–Monkhouse connection. Monkhouse briefly ran a club in

34 Ibid., p.324.
35 Ibid., p.49.

Newcastle called Change Is. One of the acts that played there was future Liberal MP Sigmund's grandson Clement.[36]

Bob Monkhouse's grandfather had made the family fortune from custard powder by the time Robert Monkhouse was born in Beckenham on 1 June 1928. Bob's father Wilfred was an accountant, who became quite distant when Bob was in his teens, while his mother Dorothy was strong-willed and self-controlled. He says he can only remember one occasion when she hugged him – during the war when flying bombs were dropping on south London and they took shelter in a stairwell.

His brother John was five and half years older, so Bob was something of a loner with friends but no one close. John was his father's favourite and during the war he joined up, leaving Bob lonelier than ever. He was chubby when he was young and inevitably cracked jokes to avoid taunts, but then when he lost weight and did not need jokes to deflect jibes found that he liked to do it anyway. At twelve and getting a good education at Dulwich College, he was already sending jokes to comedians and verses to Christmas card manufacturers: 'No holly in my garden bed, no holly do I miss, just mistletoe above my head so I can send a kiss,' for which he was paid a shilling by R & L Locker in Stoke-on-Trent.

By seventeen he was performing in amateur shows and concert party nights, and big names were buying his gags. As we read earlier Max Miller was appearing in a touring show at Lewisham Hippodrome, not far from Bob's home. It was the dog days of music hall and the show was as much about the naked women as the comedians, as the initials of its title, *This Is the Show*, subversively implied. After hassling for a

---

36 Ibid., p.324.

week Monkhouse got his gags to Miller, and his dresser came to the stage door and paid Bob five shillings.

Monkhouse soon hooked up with Denis Goodwin. Denis was a year behind Bob at Dulwich College and they were never really friends there, but Goodwin was ambitious and after they had left school tracked Monkhouse down. Goodwin was clearly even more troubled than the average stand-up. His father had died in the war; he hated his stepfather and according to Monkhouse had already attempted to kill himself by drinking Charlie Chaplin's favourite penis paint, iodine. Monkhouse and Goodwin formed a double act, but performances did not always go to plan. One night at the Ridgeway Working Men's Club in Hammersmith they sang 'The Alphabet Song', a hit for Perry Como and later made famous in a TV routine by Morecambe and Wise and special guest Angela Rippon. Monkhouse kicked off the routine as usual, 'A – I'm adorable, B – I'm so beautiful,' but before he could get the next line out someone intervened with, 'C – you're a cunt.'

His personal life was not going quite to plan either. Bob's cold relationship with his mother came to a head when he wanted to marry his girlfriend Elizabeth. His mother took her aside and said that if she married Bob she would cut him off without a penny. But she didn't disapprove of Elizabeth and recommended that she transfer her affections to Robert's older brother, who, like his father, had become an accountant. The wedding went ahead on 5 November 1949 regardless. For a while it seemed as if Bob's mother wouldn't turn up, but in the end she did. Dressed all in black. Later, when Monkhouse helped his wife write a reconciliation letter the reply was a torn-up picture of a farmyard Bob's mother had helped him paint when he was a little boy. It is not surprising that he bottled up his emotions.

Behind the dimpled toothpaste-advert smile his comedy often had a darker edge to it than it might have seemed to the casual observer. He used to joke, 'They laughed when I said I wanted to be a comedian. They're not laughing now.' This might have been one of his most famous jokes – and knowing his family background it carried a brutal private pay-off too – but it was not entirely original. Its roots can be seen in a joke told by one of Monkhouse's comedy heroes, Max Miller: 'Comedy is the only job you can do really badly and people won't laugh at you.'

Monkhouse, however, seemed to be getting on OK, particularly with women. In fact, he may have been comedy's most unlikely Lothario, notching up various affairs during his first marriage. He had always been interested in women ever since, aged fifteen, a housewife had taken him in hand during a summer party and led him into a bathroom upstairs and Monkhouse was so excited he tried to control himself by thinking of his German grammar. There was a less enjoyable sexual awakening a short while after at the King's Hall cinema in Penge, when Monkhouse dozed off while watching Tyrone Power in *Son of Fury*. He awoke to find an old man with his hand inside his trousers. When he realised what was going on, Monkhouse rushed out of the cinema and caught a bus home. It would be a few years before he caught up with Tyrone Power again.

By the end of the 1940s Monkhouse and Goodwin's career was taking off, and they were hired by BBC Radio. But while writing the all-star show *Calling All Forces* Monkhouse's life got messy. The guest on the second show was Diana Dors, then a pneumatically endowed rising star soon to be dubbed Britain's answer to Marilyn Monroe. Monkhouse was convinced that Dors was looking at him flirtatiously between delivering her lines, and the recording seemed to take on a ruder hue than intended.

When Dors for instance asked co-star Max Wall, 'How long is it since you kissed a woman?' the audience of servicemen saw a phallic gag in there that even Monkhouse – always brilliant with wordplay – had not noticed. This kind of double entendre peppered the rest of the show. At one point Wall chucked his script in the air in despair. Audiences at home were outraged. Why was everyone in the studio laughing so raucously? Was Dors topless? And on a Sunday too.

In a foretaste of the Sachsgate scandal over fifty years later, Monkhouse and Goodwin were summoned to see Pat Hilliard, the head of variety, like two naughty schoolboys. In front of six other senior members of the BBC the duo were put on probation and told that Dors would no longer be a guest. And from now on they had to submit their scripts on the Wednesday before transmission to give those in charge plenty of time for censorship. Luckily the outcome was different to that for Jonathan Ross and Russell Brand. When the ratings came in, it turned out that listening figures had been going through the roof, and the audience appreciation index was equally spectacular. The weekly blue pencil censorship session was dropped and Dors invited back. The BBC knew a hit when it had one on its hands, and in 1951 the show even went on a tour of army bases in Germany, bringing Monkhouse and Dors closer together. The follow-up, *The Forces Show*, however, was less successful. A young Tony Hancock hated Monkhouse's writing, remarking one day at a read-through, 'This is shit! And it's written on shit paper, so I'll take it away and have a shit and wipe my arse with it!'[37] Writers Ray Galton and Alan Simpson were brought in. They

---

37 Ibid., p.97.

formed a more successful relationship with Hancock and helped to make him a star.

Perhaps Bob had other things on his mind. In 1952, while Monkhouse's wife was away, he was invited to a party at Diana Dors' house. Her husband Dennis Hamilton, who had a reputation for violence though never convicted, was there, and the mood was not what you would expect of the austere 1950s. Blue movies were being screened in one room; alcohol flowed and women of easy virtue paraded around. Monkhouse got chatting to a woman called Anita, and after a while Hamilton invited them up to a special room, decked out like a harem with a mirror on the ceiling. He shut them in and said they had fifteen minutes. But as Monkhouse was removing his clothes he could hear giggling. The penny dropped. The mirror was one-way, and the other guests were on the other side watching. He didn't want to be involved even if his genitals did, and as Anita grabbed them he grabbed his trousers and made for the door. 'What a waste,' said Dors when she appeared on the other side.[38]

The flirtatious friendship with Dors was to turn more serious, when Dors told Monkhouse that Dennis Hamilton was away on business in New York. Monkhouse was determined not to let the opportunity go to waste and rented a flat for the weekend for fifteen guineas in Stratford Court off Oxford Street – in Denis Goodwin's name. After a Sunday-morning rehearsal the writers and cast were free. Denis asked Bob what he was up to and, keeping his plans secret, he said he was going to the cinema to see Jacques Tati in *Monsieur Hulot's Holiday*. But instead he

---

38 Ibid., p.100.

offered Dors a lift home. She said it was OK, she had a car and offered Bob a lift instead. They finally made their way to the flat in a chauffeured white Rolls-Royce that Dors had borrowed from a film-star friend. Not quite as discreet as Monkhouse had planned, but he wasn't complaining. Monsieur Hulot would have to wait.

On their way back to the theatre Bob asked when they could meet again, but Dors said they couldn't because if her husband found out he would kill both of them. Oh and, by the way, he wasn't in New York; she had made that story up to give Bob the psychological all-clear. In fact Hamilton was at home with flu and was destined to find out about their tryst. One night in 1956, at a party held by harmonica player Larry Adler, Monkhouse was walking in with his wife when Hamilton grabbed him by the lapels and took him into the garden. According to Monkhouse's autobiography, Hamilton pulled out a cut-throat razor and said, 'I'm going to slit your eyeballs.'[39] Monkhouse's reflexes kicked in and he kneed Hamilton in the testicles, then ran in and grabbed his wife and fled. But he was not in the clear by a long way. A boxing promoter told Monkhouse that one of his fighters had been offered money to beat him up and had also heard talk of a contract out to kill him. Monkhouse didn't know what to do. For the next few years he lived nervously, wondering what was around the corner, whether anyone would be waiting for him or might have tampered with his car. Then in January 1959 he had a stroke of luck. Hamilton died. The papers called it heart failure, the truth was that it was tertiary syphilis. Monkhouse could relax and concentrate on his work. And other women.

---

39 Ibid., p.112.

By his mid-twenties, despite being married Monkhouse was 'dallying with every pretty actress and singer in our shows'.[40] At times he could have dallied for England. Success clearly opened plenty of doors in the unlikeliest of places. There was a 'night of passion with an exotic strip-tease dancer at the Sunset Strip Casino nightclub in Norfolk'.[41] Mona Maravillosa said she had been a dancer in a show Bob had done at the Alhambra in Glasgow a few years earlier, but try as he might he could not remember her. Eventually in bed the penny dropped. Mona had been a man in the previous show.

In Southsea in 1959 the star of one show, Yana – George Formby's future crush – threw a tub of cold cream at him because she was upset she was the only member of the cast he had not made a pass at. He made up for it with her in Glasgow in 1963. During Bob's promiscuous days, his affairs felt like shows, another form of entertaining the punters – 'a one woman audience to be persuaded and entertained and thanked before moving on'.[42] Sentiments Russell Brand might have echoed in his libidinous youth.

By the late 1950s Monkhouse's career was thriving. so much so that he and Denis Goodwin were too busy to write their TV series, *Fast and Loose*. In fact they were so worried about the amount of work they pulled a stunt that bought them more time. At the end of the first edition of their show Monkhouse pretended to faint on air. Everyone was shocked – even the continuity announcer – and the show was suspended, giving the duo time to get the rest of *Fast and Loose* written.

---

40 Ibid., p.167.
41 Ibid., p.176.
42 Ibid., p.182.

The public at the time never knew they had been duped. This wasn't the only incident of cheating on television in those monochrome days. For a while Bob Monkhouse appeared on *What's My Line?* One panellist, Lady Isobel Barnett, always got the right answer. Then after six weeks the seating arrangements were changed and Monkhouse found out why. When he sat in her chair he could see the reflection of the card with the answer held up to the audience at the start of each round in the glass window on the technical control booth. Monkhouse used his inside knowledge for laughs. When a nude model appeared he asked, 'Does your job require any kind of suit?' When a chamber-pot maker was on he asked, 'Is there an end product?'

Monkhouse was the consummate professional. Nothing could put him off once the cameras were rolling. On 17 February 1956 he fronted ITV's first variety show on its first night of transmission, greeting his audience with a feisty 'Hello, traitors!' Little did the audience know that during rehearsals he had had an unexpected Frankie Howerd-style encounter with one of the stars, Tyrone Power. The Hollywood icon, who Monkhouse had idolised all those years ago in *Son of Fury*, was booked to do some skits on the show, and Monkhouse went to meet him in his hotel to go through the lines. Power was in the bath and invited Monkhouse in too. Not just into the bathroom, but into the bath itself. Monkhouse explained that he was married, to which Power pointed out that he was too. Monkhouse might have played away with Diana Dors, but this was a step too far.

But while Monkhouse's career was going from strength to strength the behaviour of his partner Denis Goodwin was giving him cause for concern. It was clear that while Goodwin was a gifted writer, Monkhouse was a much better performer. He just got slicker and more relaxed, where Goodwin was awkward. When they made a sitcom *My Pal Bob*, the solution was to feature Goodwin in bubbles onscreen rather than in person. But this was a short-term solution and Monkhouse could see that Goodwin's behaviour was becoming increasingly strange. One time Monkhouse had an illicit weekend in Brighton with a woman called Billie, who worked for them. As their train pulled out of Victoria Station they spotted Goodwin on the platform. Then when they were in their hotel Billie spotted Goodwin standing impassively in the street. Later roses arrived in their room. Goodwin had delivered them while they were out.

Goodwin also intervened when Monkhouse had a liaison with a woman in the cast of *Cinderella* when he was appearing at the Manchester Palace. Bob's wife Elizabeth heard about the affair when an Italian-sounding man phoned her and tipped her off. She came rushing up to Manchester and Bob had to do a quick cover-up. Luckily the woman in question managed to convince Elizabeth that she had a crush on another member of the cast. What was more disturbing, however, was that according to Monkhouse later Goodwin claimed it was him who had assumed the fake accent and tipped off Elizabeth. One night he turned up at Benny Hill's Maida Vale flat drunk and got even drunker on Hill's only bottle of alcohol, British sherry. Monkhouse had to come and take him home and while they were talking Goodwin confessed that he had made the call.[43]

Goodwin always seemed to be the one who had the bad luck. Even onstage, where he was more comfortable than in front of the camera, he had mishaps. One night during a performance in Bournemouth Monkhouse's

43 Ibid., p.138.

pet dog slipped its lead in the wings, ran onstage and bit Goodwin on the ankle. Monkhouse wanted to break up the partnership, but it was problematic. He knew Goodwin was emotionally unstable and worried what the consequences might be. Then, in the early 1960s, a convenient opportunity occurred. Through a fortunate series of events and coincidences Goodwin was offered the chance to move to America and write for Bob Hope. The ultimate Hollywood comedian had wanted both of them, but they were too expensive so this was the chance for a natural break, Goodwin going and Bob staying in England and chipping in when Hope visited the UK. It did not work out well for Goodwin though. The job was not as rewarding as expected; tax was high; and after a while he returned to the UK to work without Monkhouse. But the strain was too much and his marriage broke up. He set up home with a younger woman but his drinking and dark moods got heavier. In 1975 Denis Goodwin took an overdose of sleeping tablets, washed them down with vodka and died, aged forty-five.

As Goodwin's life had spiralled out of control, Monkhouse was settling down. He was one of television's biggest stars thanks to his skilful hosting of Sunday teatime crossbow gameshow *The Golden Shot* and his latest catchphrase, 'Bernie the bolt.' In October 1973, having divorced his first wife, he married Jacqueline Harding. This put an end to his womanising. It was true love, although maybe the date of the wedding showed a more practical side to Monkhouse – his accountant had advised him that October was the most tax-efficient month for a marriage.

But scandal of another kind was just around the corner. Monkhouse had been a huge success as the presenter of *The Golden Shot*, but ratings seemed to mean nothing when the producer was tipped off that Monkhouse was taking bribes in return for plugging products on the show. It was said that he had been seen receiving a big brown envelope in a restaurant from a representative of Gillette and then that Sunday a new type of Gillette razor blade had been given away on the programme. The brown envelope had actually been a book, not a big wad of used fivers, but it was agreed that Bob would leave the show and the press statement would say he was resigning to pursue other avenues. There would be no mention of kick-backs, but there would be a comeback. Monkhouse's successor Norman Vaughan was a great comedian but no host, and the public knew it. When they saw him in the street they would say, 'You want to get off that show.' Eventually he did and was replaced by black ex-footballing stand-up comedian Charlie Williams, who some felt was even worse. Vaughan went on holiday, and three weeks later, arriving back at Heathrow Airport, a baggage handler saw him and shouted, 'You want to get back on that show.' But instead ATV looked to Monkhouse again and he hoisted it back up the ratings until it finished in 1975.

There was, however, still time for one further scandal, when in 1977 Monkhouse was charged with conspiring to defraud film distributors of hiring fees. In those pre-video days Monkhouse was an obsessive collector of old movies, buying prints from all sorts of sources around the world. This was never for financial gain, more for fun and because Monkhouse was a devotee of cinema. However, the film companies claimed that he had deprived them of income and a letter from Terry Wogan's ten-year-old son Andrew thanking Bob for lending him a film to screen at his birthday party was used as evidence. Terry Wogan sprang to Monkhouse's defence and asked in court that if Bob had lent him a book would he have been depriving Maidenhead library of income? Monkhouse was eventually acquitted at the Old Bailey in 1979.

The case cost him time and money but revealed a side of Bob that the public did not know about. He had also collected tinned food alongside over 50,000 tapes of TV programmes crammed into an outbuilding, prompting a whole different meaning to the phrase Bob's full house. He owned one of the first video recorders in the UK and actually did comedy a service – he had tapes of episodes of Peter Cook and Dudley Moore's shows which the BBC itself had wiped. But his meticulous cataloguing was weird. He even corrected running times in old editions of the *Radio Times* and amended published line-ups. Remember the suggestion at the start of this book that comedians are not normal? Forget the sex, drugs and drink, that was really not normal. Yet this example of obsessive–compulsive disorder helped him to clear his name – he could explain where he had acquired every film and how he had never done it for profit, only for love and his passion for the movies.

This thoroughness inevitably extended to his gag-writing too. He kept books of every joke written (two ring binders full of Monkhouse-isms were once stolen, and while he appealed for their safe return a nation of Monkhouse-haters hoped they had been pulped – bad news for them; he got them back) and a Rolodex of one-liners arranged by subject. Sometimes the more comedy changes the more it stays the same – more recently, when Jimmy Carr was starting out he would keep his gags about everything from cats to politicians on a PalmPilot. Name a subject; Carr could call up a quip for every occasion.

Monkhouse's career was back on track. He had never quite fallen from grace in the way that Frankie Howerd and Benny Hill did, but he had plenty of critics who knocked everything from his oily sincerity, which they said was false, to his tandoori tan. (Monkhouse explained that he suffered from vitiligo and wore make-up and used a sunbed to hide the blotchy skin that was a sign of the condition.) Even though he had never really been part of the Frankie Howerd/Benny Hill/Tommy Cooper gang, when alternative comedy broke through in 1979 and comedy opted for a year-zero mentality somewhere between Pol Pot and punk rock, Monkhouse was very much perceived as part of the frilly-shirted elite – not a quality stand-up comedian but the presenter of cheesy, intellectually undemanding light-entertainment game shows such as *Celebrity Squares* and *Family Fortunes*. Yet he kept plugging away on television and onstage, and, as a true comedy fan, gave a number of new comedians such as Emo Phillips early breaks on *The Bob Monkhouse Show*. This allowed Bob to gain a foothold in the comedy new wave. He was admired by the likes of Alan Davies, and like Bruce Forsyth was invited on to newer shows such as *Have I Got News For You*.

Monkhouse eventually died of prostate cancer on 29 December 2003, aged seventy-five, outliving two of his three children. Gary had been born with cerebral palsy and had died aged forty, Simon died of a heroin overdose. Monkhouse proved that if you stick around long enough, you can shake off any scandal, any scurrilous gossip, and become a comedy legend. And Bob kept up the gags until the very end. 'You'll be glad to hear I can still enjoy sex at seventy-four. Which is great because I live at seventy-six.' In fact he was still joking after his death. In 2007, thanks to computer trickery, he fronted an advert promoting prostate cancer awareness. The visuals were false but the jokes were true Monkhouse: 'What killed me kills one man per hour in Britain. That's even more than my wife's cooking.' A joker to the end. And beyond.

*　*　*

Hill, Howerd and Monkhouse thrived by sticking mostly to the stage and the booming medium of the small screen, but one cannot write about the dark side of British comedy without touching on the less-than-golden age of British cinema. The lives and careers of comedians who dabbled in the big screen were often mixed affairs, and when it comes to talking about affairs, the *Carry On* team took the collective biscuit. Take a deep breath now. Matronly Hattie Jacques left stalwart *Dad's Army* star John Le Mesurier for a younger man, cockney car dealer John Schofield, after sixteen years of marriage. Schofield moved into the main bedroom with Hattie while the ever-reasonable John moved into the attic. When not spending his meagre Carry On wages on gambling, Sid James is alleged to have pursued Barbara Windsor with a determination that would have won him a gold medal if persistence was an Olympic sport. Meanwhile Tony Hancock was involved with John Le Mesurier's third wife Joan, who left Le Mesurier for a year before returning to him when Hancock's erratic behaviour became too much. It was said that Le Mesurier was so easy-going and so fond of Hancock that he tolerated this indiscretion. When Le Mesurier died his self-penned obituary notice in *The Times* said that he had 'conked out'. It sounds like the rest of the British film comedy scene should have conked out through sexual exhaustion.

Kenneth Williams, on the other hand, claimed to be celibate, but there may have been another side to him. It has been widely assumed that Williams was gay. His generally camp demeanour and his appearance as half of the (gay slang) Polari-speaking duo Julian and Sandy in *Round the Horne* did little to dispel this theory. He was a friend of playwright Joe Orton and his partner Kenneth Halliwell and used to accompany them on holidays to Tangiers, where Orton certainly indulged in plenty of readily available sex. It is hard to believe Williams did not get involved, but he did have a particularly complex emotional make-up. Williams' father died of accidental poisoning in 1962, and it has been suggested that Williams may have been a suspect when it was thought that his death was suspicious. He was exceptionally close to his mother, towards the end literally very close – she moved into the flat next to his near Regent's Park. Williams died on 15 April 1988 having taken a mixture of painkillers and sleeping pills. It was assumed to have been a tragic accident rather than suicide, but what is certain is that like so many comedians he suffered terribly from depression, despair and the inevitable insecurity. His last diary entry simply read, 'Oh what's the point?'

Fellow eccentric Charles Hawtrey's life was equally bleak towards the end. Before making it in the Carry Ons as a perennial pipsqueak he had appeared with George Formby and Will Hay. Hawtrey was definitely gay at a time when one could go to prison for one's sexuality. Hawtrey had few friends, but in his diary Williams recalled visiting him in his house in Deal on the Kent coast. It turned out he was a collector of brass bedsteads. The house was crammed with them, and he was convinced they were the key to his fortune, not the poorly paid Carry On films. Hawtrey smoked and drank heavily and was promiscuous whenever possible. It was said that he pursued footballer George Best but failed to score. In 1984 he made the headlines when his house caught fire. Hawtrey had been in bed with a young man and a stray cigarette had caused the blaze. His life was saved when a fireman carried the half-naked and wig-less star down his ladder. He seemed to rather enjoy the attention. At least he retained a degree of humour about himself. Before he died on 27 October 1988 the doctor said he might have to have his legs amputated. Hawtrey turned down the offer, saying he preferred to die with his boots on.

By the late 1960s the British film industry was on its uppers and the comedy fraternity was scrabbling around for whatever work it could find. One of the few outlets was soft porn, which was thriving, with cinemas in Soho and dubious fleapits around the country airing corny, cheap films that took the low comedy tradition of the Carry Ons and dragged it even lower. Dubbed sexploitation movies, these films had very few redeeming features. The young struggling performers trying to get a foot on the acting ladder were probably embarrassed by them, while the older comedy legends who topped up their pensions should have been ashamed of themselves. *The Confessions of a . . .* films with Robin Askwith and the *Adventures . . .* franchise were some of the tawdriest offenders. Barry Evans (plus Diana Dors, Benny Hill's old sidekick Henry McGee and Stephen 'Blakey from *On the Buses*' Lewis) all starred in *Adventures of a Taxi Driver* in 1975 before Evans went relatively legit as the teacher in ITV sitcom *Mind Your Language* in 1977. Bespectacled film veteran Richard Wattis, who had made his name playing comic civil servants, starred alongside Joanna Lumley in *Games That Lovers Play* in 1970. Perhaps most surprisingly, Irene Handl, who had appeared with George Formby and Tony Hancock on the big screen, appeared with porn icon Mary Millington in 1977's *Come Play With Me*, a smutty romp set on a health resort. Handl might have lost some dignity, but she did retain her clothes. It was a blessing in disguise that home video killed off the porn film industry in Britain. It meant that comedians had to be funny again and not just go through the motions in tawdry skin flicks that were like Carry Ons with a little more taken off. At least at the Windmill they were perfecting their craft in front of the toughest of audiences. Here they were just the bread wrapped around the saucy seaside postcard filling.

But the oddest, darkest and most unlikely contribution to the British sexploitation film saga was Norman Wisdom. The knockabout funny man had been a superstar in the 1950s and early 1960s at home and in Europe – particularly communist Albania, where his films were the only ones from the decadent West that were released, because Wisdom portrayed the little man triumphing over the capitalist state. He had even been acclaimed as Britain's answer to Charlie Chaplin, who said that Wisdom was his 'favourite clown'. Wisdom's career had got bumpier as the 1960s progressed. He had been offered the chance to pursue a career in Hollywood but turned it down to be close to his young family following the break-up of his marriage. Instead in 1969 Wisdom took the plunge and starred in the light-weight sex comedy *What's Good for the Goose*. Wisdom wrote the script, sang and wrote the theme tune, and played straight bowler-hatted assistant bank manager Timothy Bartlett, who is bored with his routine life and is sucked into the world of free love and hippie fun in, erm, Southport, where in one memorable scene he ends up removing his wedding ring, letting it all hang out and dancing to real-life hairy rock band the Pretty Things. Wisdom's character soon swaps his tie for a paisley cravat and his suit for a suede jerkin. At least that was when he was wearing clothes, which was preferable to seeing him in his white pants, about to hop into bed with Sally Geeson. He was fifty-four at the time. The British audience was protected from some of the rudest excesses, but a longer less-censored version was released in the rest of Europe, though probably not in Albania. Wisdom died on 4 October 2010 aged ninety-five, but his career as a comedy film star probably died the day the cameras rolled on the set of *What's Good for the Goose*.

6

From Cocksucker to Cook

The trials of Lenny Bruce and the travails of Peter Cook

Do you remember television's unashamedly unreconstructed 1970s action romp *The Persuaders*, starring Roger Moore and Tony Curtis? Moore played the suave, dashing, Harrow-educated Brett Sinclair, while Curtis played the streetwise Danny Wilde, who had graduated from the University of Life via World War II service in the US Navy. If cigar-devouring TV impresario Lew Grade had decided to cast a couple of comedians in the lead roles, Peter Cook and Lenny Bruce would have been shoo-ins. Cook was the perfect well-mannered gentleman, Bruce a natural smart guy. The contrasts were already there. When the Anglican met the Jew. And as we shall see, in reality their colourful lives inter-twined and overlapped just like in a TV script. The only real drawback was that by the time *The Persuaders* was made, Lenny Bruce was dead due to a lifestyle that always threatened to catch up with him, and Peter Cook's glory days were floating away on a sea of pills, booze and half-hearted performances.

In 1960 theatre critic Kenneth Tynan called Lenny Bruce 'the sharpest denter of taboos at present active . . . a true iconoclast who breaks through the barrier of laughter to the horizon beyond where the truth has its sanctuary'. Tynan was correct, but Bruce was more complicated even than this eloquent paean implied. He didn't just dent taboos, he revelled in them. He was a drug addict who carried a suitcase of medication including all manner of uppers and downers with him wherever he went. His luggage resembled a pharmacist's Aladdin's cave. Tuinol was often prescribed to help people sleep, but Bruce was intravenously injecting methedrine when he took it. If he wanted to sleep, kicking the methedrine habit would have done the trick.

At one point Bruce also had a ready supply of Dilaudid on hand. This was a painkiller normally prescribed to patients suffering from terminal cancer or serious injuries. Bruce, who made his living out of his gift of the gab, would come out with a convincing sob story about his serious migraines and charm doctors into writing out prescriptions. Anyone less persuasive would have to make do with aspirins. He knew so much about drugs that if the comedy ever dried up he wouldn't need to train very long or very hard to be a pharmacist.

Bruce was the kind of person that we have met again and again in this book, a terrific comedian but a flawed human. Perhaps he was conclusive proof that the two skip merrily down the yellow brick road of showbiz hand in hand. It was the same tunnel-visioned self-destructiveness and stubbornness that made Bruce a star that also made him so difficult to live with. It was no surprise that after a performance which flew by in a blur of off-the-cuff comic riffs he could only find solace in a needle or a woman. How would you relax after a show? Settle down with a good book? Bruce, born Leonard

Alfred Schneider on 13 October 1925 in Mineola, New York, was clearly a driven man. But what drove him?

Bruce was already causing trouble long before he was making people laugh and making up his own rules. As a kid growing up on Long Island he used to steal other kids' lunches and once broke into a cupboard and stole the school Red Cross collection of thirteen dollars to pay for a pair of sneakers because his parents could not afford to buy them for him. It was the tail end of the Depression and money was tight. His mother Sally was a waitress who harboured showbusiness dreams of her own, while his father Myron, known as Mickey, worked hard but never made a lot of money. School in North Bellmore was unappealing and he used to sleep at his desk. Leonard was clearly no academic, but a keen self-educator, finding solace in books, which he read voraciously, and listening to his little radio under the sheets at bedtime.

Life at home was constantly fraught. His parents didn't get on and he was often farmed out to aunts and uncles. There are conflicting accounts of whether it was his mother who walked out on his father or vice versa. What is clear is that Lenny had a tough childhood and had to learn quickly how to fend for himself. His father had actually been born in Kent and for a while lived in Wardour Street in Soho, a stone's throw from where Bruce would make his UK debut in Greek Street six decades later. Lenny may have inherited his self-destructive streak from his erratic, unpredictable mother. He certainly shared her desire for fame, but there was also a suggestion of mental instability in her family, which may have been passed on.

As a young teenager he worked on a nearby farm and lived with the farmer's family. By 1942 America had entered World War II and Lenny joined the US Navy. War was fine – he liked the mix of confusion and routine, and saw action at Anzio and Salerno in Italy. He was easily bored and the conflict kept him interested. When the war was over he was less interested and decided to get his ticket out of the navy by claiming he was a transvestite. Four naval psychiatrists interviewed him: 'Do you enjoy wearing women's clothing?' 'Sometimes' 'When is that?' 'When they fit.' They may not have laughed at this early comic routine but he bagged his ticket home.

Bruce's entry into comedy was almost accidental. In 1947 he changed his name to Lenny Bruce and considered becoming an actor, but before you can say 'oedipus schmoedipus' fate stepped in. His mother had become a dancer and been booked to perform in a local club. When the compère failed to turn up she asked her son if he would introduce her. Bruce got a big build-up as he strolled onstage but then momentarily froze as a heckler shouted, 'Bring on the broads.' There was a pause. The heckler repeated his cry. Then almost without thinking Bruce replied, 'I'd like to, but then you wouldn't have any company at the bar.' Not the greatest comeback he would ever deliver, but he got a laugh. Later he compared the buzz he got from the audience to the buzz he got from his first hit of heroin. He was hooked.

Success came in the form of talent-show victories and radio appearances, but Bruce had not found the style that would make him stand out from the pack. He was what you'd call a hack comic, doing clean material, impressions of Hollywood gangster James Cagney and character actors such as Peter Lorre. But when he was complimented on the fact that his act did not rely on toilet humour he started thinking about what was so funny about toilet humour and about what it was acceptable to say onstage. He then became more lewd and more outrageous, in his material and in his behaviour, constantly pushing back boundaries.

As Bruce's career progressed, however, he could not stay out of trouble. On 23 April 1951 was arrested for impersonating a clergyman and trying to raise funds for an organisation supporting a leper colony in British Guiana. He was charged with vagrancy and panhandling, but his quick-thinking chutzpah got him off. The police were so confused by his story, about having two names and two careers, one in charity and one in comedy, that they seemed to overlook the fact that he was dressed as a priest. Bruce was found not guilty. He had made $8,000 in three weeks in Miami. He gave $2,500 to the lepers and kept $5,500 for himself. He could clearly talk his way out of a sticky situation offstage as well as on it.

That same year he married a burlesque dancer or, more accurately, a stripper, known as Harriet Lloyd but who worked under the name of Hot Honey Harlowe. It was a stormy relationship, but for a while it worked. Bruce was never the most faithful of husbands. Working the burlesque joints around New York City, temptation was never very far away, and he and Honey seemed to have an unwritten rule that if it wasn't thrust in her face she would put up with it. She was no saint either. Before she met Lenny she had been in prison for attempting to rob a candy machine, and this was her third marriage. In 1955 they had a daughter, Kitty, but separated later that year.

Bruce was always good at coming up with money-making scams. When trying to make a film in LA in the mid-1950s he advertised his services as a gardener. He would barely start the job when he claimed he had to go off and get some food. He was paid upfront of course and never came back. He would do ten of these stunts a day, and the money he raised went to finance a couple of z-movies, called *Dance Hall Racket* and *Dream Follies*. Both were sleazy exploitation films set in the burlesque world. No great stretch, then. Bruce co-wrote the screenplays and had bit parts in them. His wife appeared in the films, and, even weirder, his mother too, using the name Sally Marr. Eat your heart out, Sigmund . . .

Gigging in burlesque clubs toughened up Lenny's act the same way the Windmill turned amateur turns into professionals. Comedians had to compete for the attention of the audience, who were really only there to see the strippers. Comedians were like the posh articles in *Playboy*, the grouting which held together the main attraction. Bruce certainly had a sense of humour about his role. One night at the Cobblestone Club in Los Angeles he decided that if you can't beat 'em you might as well join 'em. When the stripper left the stage naked, Bruce came on wearing nothing but a pair of black socks and an insouciant expression that said, 'Haven't you seen anyone naked before?'

Drugs had not really played a major part in Bruce's life until his late twenties, though his problems with drugs may ultimately have dated back to his time in the navy. Following a bout of hepatitis he started to suffer from lethargy. He would doze off while talking or while dictating notes about his act (the latter suggests it wasn't that compelling at this early stage). He had even fallen asleep while driving and ended up in a ditch. While in Philadelphia he went to see a doctor, who prescribed amphetamines – uppers that would help to pep him up, though at the time they were more commonly prescribed to women as diet pills because they suppressed the appetite.

Bruce had dabbled with heroin but only really got hooked when he was twenty-eight. He had formed friendships with jazz musicians such as Joe Maini who regularly used drugs. He described the feeling as 'like a sunflower opening in my stomach'.[44] He started injecting on a regular basis and going down to rough neighbourhoods to score. At first he didn't like using needles but he did like the result. He was still very creative though. In the summer of 1955 he hustled enough money to shoot his own TV pilot. A hard-hitting stand-up show? A televised version of the burlesque clubs he knew so well? Neither. It was a children's show entitled *Fleetfoot*. But this was not your normal children's show when it came to casting. The extras were all played by junkie friends of Maini, and when not in shot they could often be seen shooting up.

It should be pointed out that much of the medication Bruce obtained was on prescription. He seemed able to charm doctors into dishing out drugs as easily as he could charm women into bed. And Bruce had now developed a particular penchant for injecting. Not just heroin, but aspirin and penicillin. It was almost as if he was seduced as much by the para-phernalia and the ritual of injection as by the pharmaceutical high itself. The matches, the cotton and the spoon, and the process of finding a suitable vein, filling the syringe with blood and injecting was as important to him as the actual narcotic consequences. When he was on the road he would check into his hotel room and immediately set about concealing his stash, taping gear behind drawers, taking out the light switch and cramming in a small bottle next to the fuses. The cops would never look there, he chuckled to himself.

Drugs soon came to dominate Bruce's life as much as performance.

---

44 Albert Goldman from the journalism of Lawrence Schiller, *Ladies and Gentlemen – Lenny Bruce!!*, Penguin, 1991, p.343.

He was as experimental with his narcotics as he was with his act. During one visit to a pharmacist to get something for a sexually transmitted disease he spotted a bottle labelled methamphetamine hydrochloride. He had recently heard that Bela Lugosi, famous for playing Dracula, had been addicted to this. If it was good enough for Dracula it was good enough for Bruce.

His narcotic excesses would shame a lot of hard-bitten hard-boiled jazz musicians. He knew all about drugs and would vary his intake. Sometimes he cut down on heroin and stuck mainly to uppers and downers. He also developed a penchant for peyote, a hallucinogenic drug derived from a cactus. One night he and his friends grabbed a group of strippers from the Pink Pussycat Club and drove out to the legendary Joshua Tree in the California desert. The strippers couldn't understand why none of the men wanted sex, but the boys were having such a good time on peyote they forgot about the strippers. Ironically he did not smoke pot because he believed it heightened sensations. As he wrote later in his autobiography *How To Talk Dirty and Influence People*, 'I've got enough shit flying through my head without smoking pot.' But as a libertarian he was a passionate advocate of its legalisation. It was only part of a plant, after all, and as for the argument that it was a gateway drug, he asked how many murderers of fellow crap game players ended up inside because they had started off gambling at bingo?

By 1956 Bruce was making a name for himself in LA and launched a residency at Duffy's Gaieties off Cahuenga Boulevard. It was everything Bruce wanted – jazz, girls, an edgy atmosphere. Once again he ended up onstage naked – well, naked apart from a mink stole and silk stockings. They were wild days. Honey had usually tolerated Lenny's antics when she was not present, but one time she shared a bed with Lenny and another woman and when she saw the look of delight on his face she decided enough was enough. No more orgies. At least not in their house.

After splitting and getting back together numerous times – echoing his own parents' turbulent behaviour – Bruce and Honey were finally divorced in 1957. This marked a new start for Lenny, whose humour turned darker and angrier than ever, while moving away from the lewd material that had made him a notoriously sick comic. He was at the forefront of a new kind of post-war comedy. Clued-in, alert and hip, boasting a stream-of-consciousness style aligned to Jack Kerouac's beat literature, Allen Ginsberg's poetry and the jazz of John Coltrane and Charlie Parker. Bruce was not the only comedian following this path at the time. He clearly owed a debt to Mort Sahl, who was America's top satirist, capable of dissecting the daily news and finding the funny angle to every political event. But Sahl was never cool. He was clean-cut; he did not drink, smoke or take drugs, and appealed largely to the middle-class liberal intelligentsia, who liked his jokes about the Korean War and his jibes at communist Russia.

By 1957 Bruce had built up a full act, a stand-up set as we would recognise it today, and he started getting reviews. Lenny Bruce was a true shock comic, who held a mirror up to the twisted society he was confronted by. As Kenneth Tynan suggested, he wanted his audience to be shocked, but by the right things. Bruce wanted to lay bare the hypocrisy of a society that allowed segregation depending on the colour of a person's skin but got upset about four-letter words. Bruce was breaking away from the comedy mainstream, not just in terms of material but also appearance. Others wore tuxedos and ties, Bruce wore a denim jacket and jeans or a chic Nehru jacket, coming across as the hip high priest of stand-up.

Bruce might have been a topical comedian like Mort Sahl, but apart from that he could not have been more different. It was no surprise that he felt most at home gigging in liberal laid-back San Francisco, where his residency at Anne's 440 started in January 1958 and where he developed his legendary Religions Inc. routine, riffing on the way that Christianity was little more than big business with the possibility that a little criminality was thrown in for good measure, complete with jive-talking preachers greeting the Pope, 'Hey Johnny, what's shaking baby?' Routines and riffs like this helped Bruce's career to take off. Great reviews were followed by album recordings in an age when comedy albums could top the charts. An appearance on Steve Allen's influential television talk show confirmed Bruce as a national star – not the sick commentator he had once been but a commentator on a sick society. By the time he headlined at the Cloister in Chicago in 1958, arranged by Playboy boss Hugh Hefner, he could get away with anything, even joking that celebrities in the audience included murderers Leopold and Loeb and 'the lovable Adolf Hitler'.

By the late 1950s Bruce was the ultimate jive-talking jester, whose act covered everything from politics and religion to sexual behaviour and American foreign policy. He was also a celebrity. One notable 1959 TV appearance was on a bizarre, compelling period-piece called *Playboy's Penthouse*, hosted by Hugh Hefner, who chatted to Bruce about everything from nose-blowing to tattoos. Somehow Bruce was able to hold these two lives together. Some of the time at least. His fans loved him;

they knew his records and wanted to hear the routines live. Sometimes Bruce gave it to them – Father Flotsky, the 1930s prison break spoof, for instance – but usually he liked to shake things up onstage, throwing in material about race, challenging liberal persuasions by getting a light for his cigarette from a black member of the audience and complaining that the fan had 'nigger-lipped' his cigarette. There was invariably an awkward silence before the fan laughed and everyone could relax.

His hit album *The Sick Humour of Lenny Bruce*, released at the end of the decade, caught him in full, ferocious flight, imagining Hitler carving out a career in showbusiness and the Catholic Church running itself as a criminal organisation. It was amazing that he was able to find the time and head space to generate so much material when at the same time he had a drug habit that was costing him $600 a week. In New York it was tougher to score and he would call in favours from the jazz fraternity, risking being busted all the time. Later he would use a gold-plated syringe, but he had little time for hygiene, using an old eye dropper and a far-from-box-fresh needle.

He was by now attracting the attention of the police not for his act but for his offstage activities. In August 1959 two cops stopped him in the car park on the way to his booking at the Crescendo Club in Los Angeles. They pulled up his sleeves and when they saw the needle marks immediately took him down to the station. After a night of making calls and begging and pleading, Bruce got off by giving the arresting officer some larger fish. Bruce called some dealers and arranged for them to deliver to his house. As they were handing over the goods, the police pounced. It was a deal that Bruce allegedly did regularly while in LA to get off the hook himself.

Bruce was becoming more vocal than ever in his attacks on mainstream America and more successful. In February 1961 he caused a sensation at Carnegie Hall in New York. This was a long way from the dives and flophouses he had been playing a decade earlier. His gigs in New York attracted the widest of audiences. Not only fellow performers, from Mel Brooks to Sammy Davis Junior, but also intellectuals, men in metal-rimmed spectacles who would scratch their chins and nod sagely at every swipe at society. He enjoyed attracting such a wide range of fans. He also got a kick out of those who didn't like him. That, he concluded with the arrogance of someone convinced they were right, was their loss.

In September 1961, he was back on the road and was busted by the narcotics squad. If the new decade was supposed to usher in a more permissive age, no one seems to have told the Philadelphia police. They burst into his hotel room and found thirty-six ampules of the heroin substitute methedrine along with needles and syringes. Bruce insisted that it had all been legitimately prescribed, but he was carted off to police headquarters on a stretcher. The scene was darkly comic. Bruce was perfectly capable of walking, but when the police reached the lifts he refused to get off the stretcher so they stood it on end – upside down with his head almost touching the elevator floor.

In court his defence was very persuasive, arguing that nothing had been found that matched what was on the search and seizure warrant. The warrant boasted a long list of drugs, just not the right ones – there was no opium, heroin, Demerol, cocaine or marijuana for instance. The prosecution case was consequently weak and the police could offer no reason why they had decided to go to Bruce's hotel room, denying that it was because he was a famous name that would look good on their charge sheet. In the end a Philadelphia grand jury sided with Bruce and the case was dropped.

Bruce had got off but his problems were only starting. He had become a marked man and had to tread carefully. He would always make sure he carried copies of all of his prescriptions so that he could prove that every drug on him was legitimately obtained, but the police attention was starting to get to him. He began to feel that he was being persecuted. His real problem was nothing to do with drugs and everything to do with what he said onstage. Lenny Bruce was arrested for obscenity for the first time on 4 October 1961, at the Jazz Workshop in San Francisco. He had appeared in the city many times before but started this gig by explaining bluntly why he was not appearing at Anne's 440 as usual. Anne's had had a change of policy, he explained with a smirk: 'I can't work at 440 because it is overrun with cocksuckers . . .' That last word was not a word usually heard onstage, even late at night in San Francisco.

This was an introduction to an incendiary set that dealt with politics, religion and sex, but most of all with language. Bruce wanted to get down to the nitty-gritty of semantics and explore why certain words cause offence. He suggested that anyone offended by toilet humour had had bad toilet training as a child. He then did his landmark routine about the verb 'to come', with the words eventually spewing out of his mouth at the speed of an express train. '"To" is a preposition, "come" is a verb.' The sexual context of 'come' is so common that it bears no weight, and if someone hearing it becomes upset, they 'probably can't come'. When asked what his influences were his answer was simple: 'I am influenced by every second of my waking hour.' A very Russell Brand-ish thing to say. It was a diverse act that took in all manner of historical and contemporary references, from speculating on Moses and Christ coming back, to discussing the lifestyles of prostitutes and asking how people can live normal lives in the modern world while the threat of nuclear war constantly hangs over them. The audience had never heard anything like it. And neither, it seemed, had the policeman who arrested Bruce.

In his defence his attorney Albert Bendich said that Bruce was working in the tradition of social satire as exemplified previously by the likes of Jonathan Swift, Rabelais and Aristophanes. The defence centred on Bruce's act being about social hypocrisy, people saying one thing and meaning another. He was setting out to show that words contained no essential harm within themselves but had a meaning imposed on them from the outside.

The case was hard-fought. To the very end Bruce did not know if he would be victorious. As the verdict was read out he sweated. He was found not guilty of violating Section 311.6 of the Penal Code of the State of California. However, from this point on his performances would be regularly monitored and he even took to recording them himself to prove what he had said onstage. For now though he could still see the funny side. Later that night he wrote a note to his accountant suggesting that the whole arrest was a planned publicity stunt, and as such any costs should be tax deductible.

Sometimes it was hard to spot where Bruce was coming from politically. He simply had no belief in the Establishment. It didn't matter who you voted for, he might have said, the government always wins. No one was safe when Bruce was in full flight. He was an equal-opportunities sacred-cow demolisher, putting the boot into the left as happily as he put the boot into the right, heaping particular opprobrium on the liberals who supported black causes but never had blacks over to dinner in his routine 'How To Relax Your Coloured Friends at Parties'. 'The world is sick and I'm the doctor,' said Bruce, whose humour might have busted taboos but only to stimulate debate. His critics might have called him immoral, but to his fans he was the most moral of social commentators.

It was only a matter of time before Bruce got an invitation to appear in England and it came in 1962. Peter Cook had opened The Establishment club at 18 Greek Street on 5 October 1961. It was the epicentre of intelligent, oppositional comedy, consolidating the satire boom that had been kicked off with the success of *Beyond the Fringe*, the box-office smash featuring Cook, Dudley Moore, Jonathan Miller and Alan Bennett. Dudley Moore played jazz piano with his band in the basement and regulars included future stars John Bird, John Fortune, Willie Rushton and Eleanor Bron, all overseen by the dashing, handsome Cook, as thin and elegant as a character in an Egon Schiele painting with a fondness for bespoke mohair suits. Cook had a particularly adventurous booking policy – he would later revive Frankie Howerd's career and promote Aussie surrealist Barry Humphries aka Edna Everage – but the first major name he signed up came from further afield.

In the spring of 1962 Cook had a cancellation and seized the opportunity to invite Bruce. The deal was sealed, but as soon as Bruce arrived there was clearly a clash of cultures. On meeting Jonathan Miller and seeing the *Beyond the Fringe* linchpin carrying a crash helmet, Bruce tried to bond by asking him what he rode. He expected the answer to be something like a Harley-Davidson or, failing that, a Triumph. Instead Miller explained that he had come on a motor scooter . . .

Cook was shocked that his booking was a shambling wreck. Even allowing for jet lag he was in a bad state. No sooner had Bruce arrived than he was booted out of his hotel when a mixture of prostitutes and syringes were found in his room. Bruce ended up staying in Cook's Battersea flat. His new English friend asked if there was anything he needed and the answer was very simple. Bruce wanted some drugs. At this point two very different worlds truly collided. Cook, for all his laid-back cool, was not au fait with the world of narcotics, dodgy prescriptions and sniffing lines of white powder off a mirror, and was at a loss. He then had an idea. Dudley Moore moved in jazz circles, he would be able to help. But Dudley could not get anything stronger than aspirin. Eventually Cook returned empty-handed, terrified that his American friend would fly into a rage. Instead he caught Bruce in one of his benign moods, and he asked for chocolate cake instead, which was much easier to score in SW11.

The irony was that in England at the time of his visit heroin was still legal. Bruce was intrigued by the British take on drugs, though less interested in the prospect of morphine suppositories. Why take heroin by sticking it up your rear? Surely injecting it into a vein was all part of the fun? Yet Bruce seemed happy during his London sojourn and was a popular figure. He briefly pursued Judy Huxtable, who was to become Cook's second wife, but for once had no luck.

Bruce did occasionally fail to turn up at the club – Cook had to fill in for him – but when he did perform he was a sensation, despite sections of the press denouncing him as obscene. This was not George Formby, Max Miller or the Windmill. This was not the world of Mrs Shufflewick innuendo. The English audience had never seen anything like it and there were some notable walkouts. Russian poet Yevtushenko left, as did play-wright John Osborne. Objects were thrown onstage, which shocked even Bruce. One night Bruce was riffing about Catholicism and the actress Siobhan McKenna, who was there with her boyfriend, heckled him. Bruce responded: 'Well, if you don't like it you must leave and take your son with you.' Cook spoke to them on their way out and a small brawl ensued in which his lip was split. When Cook complained McKenna reportedly said, 'These are Irish hands and they are clean.' To which Cook replied, 'Well, this is a British face and it's bleeding.'

London had never seen anything like Lenny, particularly when he left the stage for a fix during the show. Some thought this was a daring gimmick, an example of liberal-baiting *epater les bourgeois*, but it was no joke. Bruce was a hardened addict by now. His career had peaked at Carnegie Hall, and police harassment was getting to him. His righteous anger was spilling over into obsession, and soon the balance of his act would tip over and it would be less about comedy and social comment and more a litany of Bruce's own personal grievances.

But English audiences took to him, and Cook wanted him to return. The Establishment however was less keen on him returning to the Establishment. In April 1963 Bruce was booked to perform there again but a moral panic drummed up by Fleet Street newspapers resulted in him being arrested by immigration officers as soon as he stepped off his plane. He was deemed an undesirable alien and immediately deported. Home Secretary Henry Brooke condemned him for his 'sick jokes and lavatory humour' and said that because of this it was not in the public interest to have him in the country. Cook tried to find a way round this. One night, while having dinner with author of *Catch-22* Joseph Heller, he spent hours on the phone trying to work out if Bruce could sneak into England by flying to the Republic of Ireland and crossing to Wales via the ferry from Dun Laoghaire. It wasn't to be. Cook's club lost £2,000 in legal fees and cancelled bookings, and England was deprived of a return visit.

Bruce's brief British tour marked a turning point in his career. Cops were in the audience when Bruce opened at the Troubadour Club in West Hollywood in October 1962. There was even one policeman who was fluent in Yiddish just in case he decided to be obscene in that language. He seemed distinctly unhappy on a subsequent tour of Australia. At Aaron's Hotel in Sydney in September 1962 he didn't like the stage, the microphone or the set-up. He harangued the audience and the club owners. He eventually said, 'I'm going to do something that's never been done in a nightclub before. I'm going to piss on you.' The run was cancelled after one night.

Back in America he felt more hunted than ever. In December 1962 he was gigging at the Gate of Horn in Chicago in the basement of the Rice Hotel and was charged with obscenity again. Interestingly the show was recorded by *Playboy* so there was ample opportunity to see how police statements about his act were taken out of context in court. These were routines that Bruce had done many times already, about Germans, black people and Christ and Moses coming back to earth. At the Gate of Horn show another stand-up comedian, George Carlin, was arrested as an audience member for refusing to show identification. They were placed together in the back of a police van. Later Carlin himself became famous as a free-speech campaigner, arrested for obscenity after performing his 'Seven swear words you can't say on TV' routine, which owed a major debt to Lenny.

Bruce was particularly anxious when the Gate of Horn trial started as he knew that the judge, the prosecutor, his assistant and the entire jury were Catholic and might have a more reactionary moral attitude. In San Francisco, where he had been acquitted of the same charge, the arresting officers had said that his material did not arouse their prurient interest, but his attorney was not allowed to use the same defence here. The prosecutor was aggressive, accusing Bruce of using a word that 'started with a f and ended with a k and sounded like '"truck"'. The trial was adjourned and Bruce went to do a gig in Los Angeles, where he was arrested on a narcotics charge. He was suddenly caught in his own personal catch-22 situation – if he went to Chicago to defend himself he would be charged with jumping bail in California. If he stayed he would be found guilty in absentia. He chose to stay and was found guilty in absentia. Eventually, however, the case went to the Illinois Supreme Court, where it was argued that 'the obscene portions of the material must be balanced against its affrmative values to determine which predominates'. After deliberation the Supreme Court found in his favour, concluding that 'we must concede that some of the topics commented on by the defendant are of social importance'. Bruce was discharged.

But he was becoming more and more fixated on his troubles and talking about his court cases in his act, even going as far as to read out court transcripts onstage. He studied books to fight his own cases. It was no good. Drugs busts, arrests and general hassle were becoming the norm, and his morale was low. By 1964 things were spinning out of control to the point where Bruce could barely go about his business. He was putting on weight and was no longer the Nehru-jacketed epitome of cool. Every waking second seemed to be about being busted. In March

1964 he was arrested twice in the same week at the Cafe Au Go Go, a 350-seater French-style coffee house in Greenwich Village, where he performed wearing a plaster cast on his leg due to a sprained ankle.

At one point a newspaper reported that Bruce had *not* been busted for obscenity. In this world turned upside down that was more news-worthy than yet another obscenity charge. Bruce's notoriety was becoming legendary. On 1 June on the satirical television show *That Was the Week That Was* the cast spoofed a graduation ceremony by awarding Bruce, in absentia, the honour of doctor of letters 'to the man who won fame using them four at a time'. The four-letter words Bruce said that he objected to were 'kill', 'maim' and 'hurt'.

A week later he was due to open in San Francisco, where he was arrested for obscenity again. At times the hounding of Bruce took on an absurdist hue. But there was a serious side to the overzealous policing of his gigs. Apart from sex and drugs all Bruce wanted to do was perform, and it was getting increasingly difficult for him to do that. A booking at the Alamo in Detroit in 1964 was cancelled on the orders of the Detroit Board of Censors without the right of a judicial hearing, even though Bruce had appeared at the same venue without any major issues over the previous eight years.

But he did have support from the artistic and liberal community. Before his New York trial for alleged obscenity at the Cafe Au Go Go over eighty prominent public figures signed a petition supporting him and arguing that he should be able to perform free of harassment and censorship. Among those who offered Bruce support were Bob Dylan, Jonathan Miller, Woody Allen, Arthur Miller, Richard Burton and Paul Newman. Their argument was a familiar one, that Bruce was a performer 'working in the field of social satire in the tradition of Swift, Rabelais and Twain'. Bruce might make use of the vernacular in his nightclub performances but he was doing it in the context of 'his satirical intent and not to arouse the prurient interests of his listeners'. Above all, this was an issue which drew on the fundamental right to freedom of speech in the American Constitution's First Amendment, the petition argued. 'It is not a function of the Police Department of New York or any other city to decide what adult private citizens may or may not hear.'

The case was as important as the *Lady Chatterley's Lover* obscenity case in the UK in 1963. Maybe even more important. Bruce had cut his teeth in the ultra-repressive McCarthy era, when anyone with left-wing views was in danger of being condemned as a communist and hounded out of their job. His use of language was a statement of intent that Americans were now living in freer, more liberal times, ripping into the core and hypocrisy of modern-day values and beliefs. The question the court had to answer was whether Bruce's Cafe Au Go Go performances were obscene in substance, not just in language. After a lengthy trial that included a break in the summer for the judge to take his holiday, the verdict was reached and announced on 4 November 1964. Bruce was found guilty. An appeal later in the year didn't help either. It was hard for Bruce to claim he showed remorse when he had continued to do the same material elsewhere. He was duly sentenced to four months in a workhouse. It was a sentence, however, that he never served. In late March 1965, while free on appeal, Bruce fell out of a hotel window and smashed up his ankles and hips. Peter Cook reportedly smiled when he heard that Bruce had shouted 'I am Superjew' as he fell.

Bruce was now injecting the wrong drugs in the wrong places

– dissolving Percodan and injecting it into his biceps where there was a risk of an abscess forming, turning gangrenous and endangering his life. An abscess duly formed and two quarts of pus burst out of his arm. He was hallucinating. He was in a wheelchair but he needed to work to cover his medical bills. In the same month that he celebrated his fortieth birthday he was also declared bankrupt. He looked for venues with a ramp up to the stage. At home he was surrounded by books and legal documents. He certainly wasn't an ordinary comedian any more and planned to sue the governors of the states where he had been busted for their breach of his civil rights.

On 18 April 1966 he was due in LA for sentencing on a three-year-old drugs case. The result was a huge relief – a one-year suspended sentence and a $260 fine . . . plus probation for two years. It should have been a relief that he did not receive a custodial sentence, but somehow he did not feel victorious. Instead he became more depressed.

Bruce died on 3 August 1966 at home at 8825 West Hollywood Boulevard. It was not a dignified death. He was found in his bathroom on the floor with a needle in his arm, having fallen off a toilet seat. One of the tragedies about his death was that by this time Bruce was no longer a full-time junkie. This was a one-off fix that went horribly wrong. His major addiction at the time of his death was sweets. Like Elvis Presley a decade later, he had become a bloated version of himself, weighing over fourteen stone. The offficial cause of death was given as 'acute morphine poisoning caused by an accidental overdose'. Record producer Phil Spector bought the negatives of the corpse taken by the police to keep them out of the press and passed his own judgment on the cause of death: 'Lenny died of an overdose of police.' Conspiracy theories abounded. Had he been silenced for speaking out? We may never know the truth. On the plus side, on 23 December 2003 Bruce was granted a posthumous pardon for his obscenity conviction by New York Governor George Pataki.

So how did the paths of Bruce and Cook collide so beautifully and so briefly? To see how Peter Cook ended up in Greek Street we need to go back to St Chad's Nursing Home in the seaside town of Torquay in Devon, where on 17 November, 1937, Peter Edward Cook was born. It would be nearly twenty-five years before their paths crossed, but in that time they would go through some very similar and very different experiences. After Lenny Bruce's death, Peter Cook's subsequent life and career would eerily echo that of his American friend.

As with Bruce's antecedents, there was talk of mental illness in Cook's family. Peter's grandfather Edward, traffic manager for the Federated Malay States Railway, suffered from depression and shot himself with a revolver in May 1914. Both also had fractured relationships with their fathers. While Bruce left home when he was barely into his teens, Cook only met his father, Alec, for the first time when he was three months old. Alec Cook worked in the colonial service in Nigeria, and separation was to become a theme of Peter's childhood. When Alec returned to Nigeria the following summer Peter's mother Margaret accompanied him, leaving Peter in the hands of nannies and grannies. When war came leave was hard to come by, and home visits were rarer than ever as Peter was growing up. After the war the family was reunited, but there was an emotional gap between father and son that could never be bridged and may have had a lasting effect on Peter Cook's ability to form relationships. Any belated bonding was stymied when Peter was packed off to St Bede's School in Eastbourne when his father was posted to Gibraltar. There was one good thing that came out of the British public school system though – Peter Cook learned to be funny to avoid being bullied.

As Cook grew up, comedy became an obsession. After St Bede's he boarded at Radley in Oxfordshire, where, like Bruce, he had a solitary side and devoured books – P. G. Wodehouse, *1066 and All That*. Radio comedy was becoming important too. He had a habit of feeling ill on Fridays so that he would be sent for a rest in the sanatorium, which had a radio. By a strange coincidence his funny turns always seemed to occur when the *Goon Show* was being transmitted.

Cook's future seemed laid out before he was even in his second decade: he was expected to follow his father into service overseas. But at Radley he was unhappy. The day started with icy showers and institutionalised bullying. He was once beaten for drinking cider at the Henley regatta by Ted Dexter, an older pupil and future England cricket captain. Reports at the time describe him as either withdrawn or aloof. He was even more miserable when his father was posted back to Nigeria, but he perked up when his mother decided to return to England and he could spend the school holidays with her outside the seaside resort of Lyme Regis.

Cook eventually found his niche as the school mimic, in particular sending up one of the dining hall's butlers, Arthur Boylett, whose drone would later provide the inspiration for Cook's monotone megabore, E. L. Wisty. As his confidence grew he started to perform in school plays and revues. Cook later admitted he had 'wanted to be an entertainer since puberty'. Onstage he flowered; offstage he started to pursue pupils from the nearby girls' school. His hit rate was pretty good, and he regularly came second on his year's 'Top Ten Tarts' chart, one time having a brief sexual encounter in the school organ loft. He was number one when it came to the stage though. His satirical school show, a thinly veiled attack on the colonialism that helped to pay his fees, *The Black and White Blues*, was so successful there was a thriving black market in tickets. His future might not lie in the diplomatic corps after all. In the section he filled out himself on his final school report before heading to Pembroke College, Cambridge he wrote under 'Plans': 'BBC, Films, TV, sherry'.

According to his biographer Harry Thompson it was not sherry but a different form of alcohol that got him into trouble during his gap year. While in West Germany he got drunk, fell asleep on a train and woke up in East Germany. He was immediately thrown into a cell where he claimed, as a joke, political asylum, saying that he wanted to defect. This was the mid-1950s, a period when the Cold War was getting particularly frosty; in 1961 the Berlin Wall would be erected. Luckily a sympathetic guard took pity on him and rather than have him sent to the gulag Cook was dropped off at the border to slink home with a hangover and a good anecdote under his belt.

At Cambridge he was that strange mix of introvert and extrovert typical of stand-up comedians. When they are on they are on, when they are off they want the world to swallow them up. Cook quickly made his name among his own social group, yet it was six months before he approached the famous Footlights Society. When not studying or writing sketches for revues he would be sneaking women into his rooms. He was a success on every level. In fact before he graduated his work was already being performed in the West End by the likes of Kenneth Williams.

By the time Cook left Cambridge his life had already taken off. He invested in property while developing an interest in gambling that would last a lifetime. He had met his future wife, Wendy Snowden, and had already written one of his greatest sketches, 'One Leg Too Few', which would later be performed with Dudley Moore, about a one-legged man auditioning for the part of Tarzan. 'I've got nothing against your right leg. The trouble is neither have you.'

But the seeds were already being sewn for Cook's self-destruction and even his early death. On a family trip to Libya he contracted jaundice, which damaged his liver. He would never be able to drink to excess again without doing harm to his health. Career-wise he had been booked to appear at the 1960 Edinburgh Festival in an irreverent satirical little thing called *Beyond the Fringe*, with three other Oxbridge alumni, Dudley Moore, Alan Bennett and Jonathan Miller. *Beyond the Fringe* was an epochal ground-breaking smash hit, making stars of the quartet, transferring to the West End and Broadway and kick-starting the satire boom. The West End run at the Fortune Theatre – the night before opening on 10 May producer William Donaldson had taken Cook and Co. to see a porn film – made fortunes for its backers, though not so much for the stars, who started out on seventy pounds per week and a small percentage of the gross takings.

In October 1960 critic Kenneth Tynan had enthused about Lenny Bruce in the *Observer*. By May 1961 his allegiances seemed to be shifting closer to home. He called *Beyond the Fringe* 'a revolution in revue'. Everyone loved the show. Even Cook's father and, reportedly, the Queen, who giggled at Peter Cook's positively anarchic impression of Prime Minister Harold Macmillan as a doddery old fool in the 'TVPM' sketch. Macmillan was never named as the subject of the sketch but everyone knew who the skit was skewering. And, legend has it, just to compound the irreverence Cook added some extra lines to his character's ramblings on the night when Macmillan decided to see the show for himself: 'When I've a spare evening, there's nothing I like better than to wander over to a theatre and sit there listening to a group of sappy, urgent, vibrant young satirists, with a stupid great grin spread all over my silly old face.'

There were fringe benefits too. Cook's new friend Dudley Moore availed himself of women who had previously spurned him, but Cook had to miss out – he had proposed to Wendy Snowden during the Edinburgh run so felt that he was off the market. He had to make do with a regular slot in the *Observer* instead. One of his famous cartoon captions featured two bowler-hatted gents discussing latest trends onstage: 'You know, I go to the theatre to be entertained. I don't want to see plays about rape, sodomy and drug addiction. I can get all that at home.'

As the 1960s dawned, Cook was a figure of boundless energy, always on the lookout for the next opening. Having seen the booming nightclub scene in Germany during his gap year he could not believe there wasn't a similar club in London. He was determined to be the first person to open one. The Establishment Club was a former strip joint called the Club Tropicana. Cook made it the place to be and be seen in 1961, long before London really started swinging. Making it a club was a canny move. As it was for members only, it did not have to kowtow to the heavy censorship of the Lord Chamberlain, who still vetted any material that went into theatres and crossed out anything unacceptable with a blue pencil.

Lenny Bruce was a sensation at The Establishment; Frankie Howerd was reborn there; and Barry Humphries also had an intriguing spell but with mixed results. Bespectacled suburban Melbourne housewife Edna Everage did not go down quite so memorably. At this point in his career Humphries was better known for his roles in West End musicals such as *Oliver!*. For a while Humphries appeared in a Lionel Bart musical entitled *Maggie May*, but he was only onstage at the start and finish so he spent the time in between refreshing himself: 'One night I appeared at the end of the show without make-up and in modern dress, when in fact I was meant to be a one-man band with cymbals and a mouth organ,' he told the *Independent* newspaper.

Humphries described himself during his drinking days as 'a dissolute, guilt-ridden, self-obsessed boozer', so he was probably cut out for a career in comedy. The turning point, however, came in 1972 back in Australia, when he awoke in a drunken fug in a car park having been mugged. Having reached rock bottom he dried out, joined Alcoholics Anonymous and cleaned up his act. In fact Humphries was one of the people who would later recognise that Peter Cook was heading down a similar trajectory and tried to get him to sort his life out too.

While Bruce's career went into a nosedive from which he would never recover, Cook's career continued to thrive as he took on new challenges. In 1965 during the making of the British film *The Wrong Box*, Cook met Tony Hancock, another instinctively gifted comic talent trying to keep a lid on his demons. Peter Sellers was also one of the stars. Director Bryan Forbes said that both Sellers and Hancock 'were searching for an elusive bird of happiness which eventually destroyed them both'. The same could probably be said of Cook. Hit live shows and hit TV shows with Dudley Moore, hit clubs and even a hit magazine in *Private Eye* did not seem to be enough for this prodigious, unique individual. There always seemed to be a higher peak to scale.

Cook's film career, sometimes with, sometimes without Dudley Moore, was the first indicator that things would not always head in an upwards trajectory. *The Wrong Box* had mixed reviews and the Faust update *Bedazzled* was also decidedly flawed. Cook, however, was not short of confidence and began to see himself developing a career beyond the world of comedy, maybe as a modern-day romantic lead in the mould of Cary Grant. By the summer of 1967 and still only twenty-nine, he and his wife Wendy were considered a glamorous young couple on the A-list and always invited to the best parties. Home life with their two children in their large Hampstead house seemed to come straight out of the pages of a society magazine. Dinner-party guests included Peter O'Toole and John Lennon; the wine and conversation flowed.

But life was not that simple. Behind the veneer of cool, things were not running smoothly. He was already seeing Sid Gottlieb, a fellow Tottenham Hotspur supporter but also a doctor specialising in the treatment of drink and drug addictions. Even if Cook did not have a serious problem, he had enough self-awareness to realise that he was in danger of developing one. As Lenny Bruce had done many years earlier, he was developing an interest in amphetamines, which gave the user confidence and an almost superhuman burst of energy but also a bleak, depressing comedown. He had come a long way from shock at Lenny Bruce's drug habits only few years earlier.

By 1968 his marriage was not looking quite so secure. Wendy had moved to Majorca, and while the couple were still officially married, the boundaries were more blurred. There was an affair with a Swedish au pair and Cook embarked on a relationship with his old friend, actress Judy Huxtable. At one point in the affair, she became pregnant and had an abortion. Eventually the Cooks separated; Peter moved in with Judy in Notting Hill, and Wendy was given custody of their two daughters, Lucy and Daisy, which helped to drive Peter to drink and more drugs. In November 1970 he was found drunk at the wheel of his car and the following April given a one-year driving ban. Peter and Wendy were divorced in 1971, just as Peter and Dudley prepared for their tour of Australia and New Zealand. It was a difficult time for the comedian, who had had a decade of success. Like many comedians Cook had an addictive personality. Infidelities were a way of achieving intimacy, but fleeting dalliances did not fill the void. Not even the laughter of the nation could do that. For someone so confident there was a nagging insecurity bubbling away not very far from the surface. But how could a man so brilliant go so wrong?

By 1970 Cook's fortunes had changed. His marriage was over and so, it seemed, was his film career. *The Rise and Rise of Michael Rimmer*, a prescient project about focus groups taking over the media and dominating politics, was released in November and was a critical and commercial flop. And things got even worse when in 1971 he was invited to host a TV chat show, *Where Do I Sit?* All of a sudden Cook, the great talker, a raconteur on a par with Peter Ustinov, seemed lost for words. Drinking too much and taking too many prescription drugs before filming probably didn't help. When Kirk Douglas walked on, Cook meant to say,

'How are you?' but it came out as, 'Who are you?' He might have been unprepared but he wasn't that unprepared. The BBC was flooded with complaints. One viewer complained that Cook was a drug addict so Cook phoned him live on air. The result was an excruciating mixture of car-crash TV and Beckett-like absurdity as the man got out of the bath and said that he couldn't stay on the line because a) he was dripping wet and b) because he wanted to watch the show. In fact the bad publicity had done some good – ratings were rising – but that was not enough for the BBC, which cancelled the twelve-part series after the third week, opting for a new chat show instead fronted by journalist Michael Parkinson.

The only conclusion Cook could reach was that he was not interested enough in other people. Like many comedians, there was a level of self-obsession that was essential when it came to creativity, less essential when it came to empathy. Cook's career had surely hit rock bottom. Laughter was like oxygen to him. He constantly craved it and without it began to die a little. His confidence had taken a huge knock. He had always got bored easily, and comedy had been his way of dealing with it. He was now in danger of becoming a bore himself. Even worse, he had always had an air of nihilism about him; now he was turning that nihilism on those closest to him, Dudley Moore and his own second wife Judy Huxtable. Moore described the conundrum that was Cook as 'professional confidence combined with personal un-confidence'.[45]

Gradually his moods became more extreme, due to a combination of mood swings, drugs, drink and depression. Dudley Moore singled out

---

45 Harry Thompson, *Peter Cook: A Biography*, Hodder & Stoughton, 1997, p.303.

the point at which he believed Peter Cook became a fully fledged alcoholic. It was on 2 October 1971 when the duo were on a tour of Australia and he received a cable from Wendy saying that their daughter had suffered a severe asthma attack due to the decor in Peter and Judy's home, which she had moved into. Moore recalled Cook writing a reply, sealing the envelope, drinking himself insensible and walking fully clothed into the pool of the President Motor Inn in Melbourne. Judy also saw the problems first hand, as Cook drank from lunchtime, paused for the show then drank himself to sleep afterwards.

Various factors contributed to his dramatic decline during the Australian tour. He missed his family but maybe he also missed England and what it represented – success. Their Australian tour went well, but Cook was in too much of a drunken stupor most of the time to appreciate it. The drinking affected the shows and his relationship with Moore, which was becoming increasingly turbulent. The rivalry that had always simmered under the surface boiled over one night in New Zealand when Cook had collapsed into bed and Moore stayed up playing the piano. In the middle of the night Cook appeared, lurching out of the lift in nothing but his underpants, overcome by a wave of alcohol-fuelled paranoia that Moore might be attempting to seduce Judy. Perhaps the paranoia was understandable. Dudley did make a pass at Judy at one point, but was rebuffed.

The drinking continued on his return to England, at parties, in clubs and generally anywhere that there was a bottle around. On the opening night of *Behind the Fridge* on 21 November at the Cambridge Theatre he reached a new low. Cook was already drunk by the time the curtain was due to go up, possibly due to the fact that Dudley had been the surprise subject of *This Is Your Life* earlier on the same day, suggesting that he was the more successful half of the partnership. Cook passed out backstage and had to be dressed by director Joe McGrath. The start of the show was delayed and a chorus of 'Why are we waiting?' started. Meanwhile in the wings Dudley Moore improvised his own version: 'I'll tell you why we're waiting . . . the cunt is drunk, the cunt is drunk, he's out of his fucking mind.'[46] When Cook was finally about to go onstage nerves hit him like a bolt of lightning and at one point he froze in the wings. Yet once in front of the audience the magic was still there. He received better reviews than Moore, which could not have gone down well with his long-suffering partner.

He seemed to have a phenomenal amount of energy and still seemed able to be creative despite his lifestyle. He and Moore found time to make the eye-poppingly filthy first Derek and Clive album, recorded during downtime during the New York run of *Good Evening*, which was widely bootlegged. The idea started when Cook wanted to record a sketch about the worst jobs anyone had ever had. His worst job involved the buxom starlet Jayne Mansfield: 'I had the terrible job of retrieving lobsters from her bum.'

This was not actually the first time Cook and Moore had pushed at taboos on tape. While doing *Beyond the Fringe* in New York they had recorded *The Dead Sea Tapes*, an outrageous conversation purporting to involve various associates of Jesus that hadn't made it into the Bible and not a million miles away from some of the religion-baiting riffs of Lenny Bruce. *Derek and Clive* was followed by two official hit albums, *Come*

46 Ibid., p.316.

Again and *Ad Nauseam*, the latter complete with its own sick bag, to save anyone with sensitive stomachs having to rush to the loo while they were listening to routines about the Pope, Jesus and the Holocaust, which were also captured on film for *Derek and Clive Get the Horn*.

A decade earlier Lenny Bruce had asked Cook to get drugs for him in London. When *Good Evening* ran in New York it was Cook that had to ask his host for a fix. At dinner one night with Judy at the house of *Catch-22* author Joseph Heller he pestered his host to get him some drugs. He had brought uppers and downers from London but had no idea what their equivalents were in America. As the show travelled across the country, Cook's dependence on narcotics seemed to increase. Eventually in Los Angeles he hooked up with Who drummer Keith Moon and had the chance to fulfil one of his lifelong ambitions and make a hit record. Unfortunately the drugs flowed rather too thick and fast in the recording studio and barely a note was recorded.

Cook found plenty of time for womanising while Judy was back in England. Peter and Dudley were not just competitive onstage; they were fiercely competitive when it came to bedpost notches. As their show toured America the duo took advantage of their groupie-pulling rock-star status and slept with as many women as was humanly possible, fore-shadowing the behaviour of future stand-up superstar Frank Skinner a decade later. But things were getting worse for Cook. At the end of the tour Moore announced that he did not want to work with Cook again and chose to stay in America when Cook flew home.

This left a dangerous void in Cook's life. 'I'm rootless,' he joked on Michael Parkinson's BBC chat show, but maybe there was a deeper truth to this. When he was busy he was a functioning alcoholic, but with no major projects on the go he drank, ate and put on weight. He seemed simply bored with life. Luckily the original Derek and Clive album when eventually officially released proved to be a big hit, and with some reluctance Moore agreed to work with Cook again on the two, increasingly bleak, painful sequels that followed. But even when working hard Cook managed to find time to drink. When he was filming the flop Sherlock Holmes spoof *The Hound of the Baskervilles* in 1977 he would be picked up by car at 6.30 a.m. every morning, but still found time to down a bottle of wine before arriving at the studio. When he guested on the Lol Creme and Kevin Godley album *Consequences* he was raring to go at breakfast, when they were still in bed, and sloshed by lunchtime, when the musical duo got up after a late night in the studio.

By the end of the 1970s Cook's decline contrasted sharply with Dudley Moore's surprising ascent. His erstwhile partner's unlikely sex-symbol film career had taken off with the romcom *10*, and after the failure of *The Hound of the Baskervilles*, the arguments during Derek and Clive and the bitter US tour it did not look like they would work again. Cook's marriage to Judy was on the rocks and his addiction to drink and drugs was worse than ever. He may have only recently turned forty, but his was more than a mere midlife crisis.

Yet there was fight in him still. In 1979 Cook joined Alcoholics Anonymous, acknowledging that he had a problem, and in June made a memorable appearance on the second night of Amnesty International's *Secret Policeman's Ball* concerts in London. A story in the press after the first night had asked what had happened to comedy's bite. Cook took the comment to heart and spent the afternoon writing a bang-up-to-the-minute sketch, proving that while form might be transient, talent never goes away. Against all expectations he delivered a blisteringly funny send-up of judicial bias. The trial of Liberal leader Jeremy Thorpe for incitement and conspiracy to murder had just taken place, with the judge strongly advising the jury to go away and bring in a not guilty verdict. Cook brilliantly ridiculed the judge's reverence for the accused Liberal leader and lack of support for the man who claimed to be Thorpe's former lover, Norman Scott. Just before Cook went on, he asked the other comedians backstage if they knew any good euphemisms for homosexual, and Billy Connolly provided him with a Glaswegian epithet. Cook went on and during his comic summing-up described 'Norma St John Scott' as 'a self-confessed player of the pink oboe'. The sketch was such a hit it was even released as a record – 'Here Comes the Judge'. For someone who claimed that he was never a satirist, Cook's potshots at authority could still hit the bullseye – pointing out that even in the late twentieth century the Establishment still closed ranks.

But Cook was also busy flexing his frivolity muscles, appearing on the BBC series *Pro-Celebrity Golf*. When racing driver James Hunt brought his dog, Cook trumped him by bringing along his pet goldfish Abe Ginsberg, placing the bowl by the tee.[47] Golf and pranks seemed to go side by side. At one tournament in Malaga he infringed the rules by carrying two golf bags, although only one held clubs. The other contained booze. In 1984 he was enjoying a golfing weekend in Spain with Ian Botham and Patrick Mower but the police were called when he allegedly punched a German tourist. Sometimes he would get into trouble even when golf was not

---

47 During one tournament he had his revenge on Ted Dexter for the beating during their schooldays at Radley all those years ago by turning up as a transvestite World War I pilot to put him off his stroke.

involved. At Ronnie Wood's wedding on New Year's Day in 1985 he made advances towards Jo Wood and got into the wrong car.

Cook tried to cut down, but by 1981 he was drinking heavily again. He had had his own crack at American screen fame, co-starring in the sitcom *The Two of Us*, in which he played a butler, but it had been axed. He was lonely in America and had to live with Dudley Moore's continuing film success. After *10* Moore had had another hit with *Arthur*, about a badly behaved, privileged English alcoholic. Rumours hinted that the character might have been partially based on Cook.

His alcoholism overshadowed a comparable addiction to sex. He used to visit the same prostitutes as Dudley and ask them who was best. As well as those what-happens-on-the-road-stays-on-the-road infidelities he also visited sex clubs and when he was back in England for a while hung out at Stocks, the mansion run by Victor Lownes, Hugh Hefner's flamboyant representative in the UK. Cook would spend his time there surrounded by Playboy bunnies, and one doesn't need to stretch one's imagination too far to envisage the scene. He once went to an orgy in Muswell Hill. It was a long way from Beverly Hills.

Life in Hampstead without Judy was chaotic. Drink and drugs abounded and Peter's behaviour was erratic. He once emptied a rubbish bin over a Rolls-Royce parked outside his house. He was a passionate supporter of the 1980s rave drug Ecstasy, which filled everyone who took it with indiscrimate love for humanity. He once said to his old friend William Donaldson, 'You'd even like Richard Ingrams if you tried Ecstasy.'[48] It did have its downside though: 'The trouble with E though,

---

48 Thompson, p.412.

is that you do want to fuck everything – I started looking at the Corby trouser press in a different light.'[49] William Donaldson's theory was that Cook took drugs to avoid boredom. With his career slipping away and no real financial worries, ennui was a constant spectre on the horizon.

The mid-1980s drifted by in an alcoholic haze, floating on a sea of triple vodkas for breakfast. In 1986 he drove his new Honda into the back of a police car and was fined £200. He was not even fifty but had put on weight due to endless days and long nights on the sofa interrupted by occasional rounds of golf, powered by swigs from cans of Bacardi and Coke. 'I do fifty eyebrow-raises a day,' he replied when challenged on his exercise regime.

Occasionally there was a glimmer of his glorious past. Cook reunited with Dudley Moore on Joan Rivers' British talk show in 1986, but it was a bright moment in a misjudged career move. Cook had signed up to be Rivers' regular sidekick, which meant he would do a spot of banter and then be relegated to the end of the sofa while the guests hogged the limelight. Even when Dudley came on and he was shunted back up, there was a sense that Moore was the star and Cook was chipping in. It was only when the two got into character riffing on being sexually harrassed by Jane Russell and Greta Garbo ('I had to poke her off with a broomstick') that the old magic returned. Other editions were more awkward. On one show camp astrologer Russell Grant was being interviewed by Rivers while Bernard Manning sat in the green room watching onscreen and waiting his turn. 'What's that poof doing on television with professionals out of work?' blasted

---

49 Ibid., p.447.

Manning. After the show another guest, Rupert Everett, wanted to thump Manning, while Cook stood behind him, jokily saying, 'Hold me back. Hold me back.'

There was clearly still a subversive twinkle in Cook's eye that could not be dimmed by booze. In late 1986 his beloved magazine *Private Eye*, which had been flying the flag for satire since the 1960s, lost a court case against publishing tycoon Robert Maxwell. During the case Cook's contribution was to take editor Ian Hislop out for lunch and wave his chequebook at Robert Maxwell in the courtroom. As part of his victory, Maxwell was going to have the *Eye* removed from WH Smiths and replaced with his own version, *Not Private Eye*. Cook wanted to see the rival publication so sent over a case of whiskey to the people putting it together at Maxwell's HQ around the corner from Fleet Street. Cook then went there himself with some friends, charmed his way into Maxwell's suite, ordered champagne, invited *Mirror* photographers up to take photos and drew on the windows with crayons. Oh and called up Robert Maxwell in New York to tell him what he was up to. Maxwell promptly called security, who went to remove Cook but ended up joining the party . . .

In 1989 he married his third wife, Lin, and she did her best to sort his life out. There were good times as well as bad. Sometimes together. After the launch party for the video release of *Derek and Clive Get the Horn* in 1993 Cook invited various members of the Rolling Stones and various ex-Pythons back to his house for a post-party party. Cook was in his element as host, but also so drunk that at one point he set fire to his trousers and had to jump into his pond to put the flames out. Humour was always his default setting. Barry Humphries said, 'One felt sometimes that Peter was not going to stop being funny for a minute in case you got a little bit too close to him.'

But these highlights on- and offscreen became fewer as Cook got older. Years of abuse were starting to catch up with him. Flickers of the old genius – a famous appearance playing all the guests on an edition of the Channel 4 chat show *Clive Anderson Talks Back* and a Radio 3 verbal ramble with Chris Morris entitled 'Why Bother?' – became increasingly rare. When he divorced Judy he cut a pathetic figure, admitting in court that he was addicted to cocaine, gambling and pornography.

I encountered Cook twice. In the early 1980s I regularly used to see him walking down Hampstead High Street in the early hours of the morning. I was working as a dustman during the summer holidays, I imagined him returning from some glamorous all-night party. In reality he had probably been up all night watching obscure sports and game shows and was just popping out for more fags or, according to a *Sunday Times* 'Life in the Day' article, up early to speculate on the yen on the Tokyo stock market or call the manager of his jojoba farm in California. ('Jojoba is the secret of Eternal Beauty, so I think it's a good long-term speculation.') In 1993 I interviewed him over breakfast in the basement of the Everyman cinema round the corner from his home in Perrin's Walk. He had a big fry-up and a drink that looked suspiciously like a Bloody Mary, and was an amiable but slightly shambling figure in casual slacks and non-ironic socks and sandals. He was somewhat bitter about being trumped by others. There was no nastiness about Dudley, but he was convinced that Johnny Rotten had copied his deadpan vocal drawl. Fair comment in 1977, but still to be going on about the Sex Pistol in 1993 seemed a bit much. We popped back to his house at one point and the lounge, dominated by a large television, was a terrible mess. The coffee table was covered in piles of newspapers and remote controls; there were glasses everywhere. The only thing that seemed organised was his set of golf clubs by the front door in case he fancied a different kind of round.

I remember where I was when I heard that Peter Cook had died. I was on the M62 heading to Manchester to interview comedian Caroline Aherne, or Caroline Hook as she was then, because at the time she was married to hard-partying New Order bassist Peter Hook. Not surprisingly my ears did a double take when I heard the news. Did they say Cook or Hook? It was 9 January 1995, and he had suffered a gastrointestinal haemorrhage, his liver ruined by decades of drink. His last words were not recorded, but maybe he had left his own self-mocking epitaph a few years earlier: 'I might have some regrets . . . but I can't remember what they are.' Like Bruce, Cook shone brightly, maybe too brightly, only to be brought down by the weight of his own genius.

7

Turned Out Nice Again? From T'rific to Not Feeling So Well

Mike Reid, Malcolm Hardee, Jo Brand and Arthur Smith . . .

There is joke theft and then there is real theft. The kind that can get you banged up for a stretch. There is also a long tradition of comedians who have had serious brushes with the law. We have already seen two examples who trampled all over the thin blue line between legal and illegal. It is no surprise that Lenny Bruce tried a few cons in his time. It was a little more surprising to discover that Tommy Cooper did a spot of ducking and diving.

Then there are examples of blatant dishonesty used to get a foot in the showbusiness door. Peter Sellers managed to create his own hype by ringing up producers and agents, pretending to be someone else and recommending an exciting new talent called Peter Sellers. The trick worked and his career got a boost. Bob Monkhouse found an opening at the BBC in 1948 during National Service by faking a letter from his psychiatrist saying that Monkhouse was obsessed about acquiring a professional examination of his broadcasting ability so could this please be arranged so that his therapy could continue. He landed a try-out and never looked back.

Crime does not always pay and sometimes it ends in tragedy. The late writer Frank Muir penned a radio sitcom called *Heigh Ho* for a war veteran, Peter Waring, aka Commander Peter Roderick-Mainwaring, DSO, RN. Waring had apparently left the navy due to injuring his arm in the war and became a comedian. The series was not a big success and worse was to come. It turned out that Waring had not been a commander or invalided out of the navy at all. His arm injury had been caused by a scald from a hot-water pipe on a cross-Channel ferry. A year after his brief shot at fame Waring was found hanged in his cell in Pentonville Prison. He had been sentenced to nine months' imprisonment on charges of false pretences.

For some though, comedy does work out as a way of going straight – a means of escape without digging a tunnel or getting a file hidden in a cake. Without comedy they really could have gone down for a long stretch. A notable example of this is gravel-voiced Mike Reid, who was a stalwart stand-up comedian of the giant-bow-tie variety long before he won a nation of soapy hearts as dodgy Frank Butcher in *EastEnders*. But long before Reid was a star, he had been giving the police the runaround.

Mike Reid was born in Hackney, east London on 19 January 1940. As a kid during hard times he did anything to make money, rarely bothering to question whether it was legal. He finally confessed all in his auto-biography, *T'rific*. He would nick bottles of drink then have the nerve to claim back the deposit on the empties. He painted the big old pennies and tried to pass them off as half-crowns. He lost his virginity at ten, was nicking cars from eleven and breaking into jewellery stores not long after. At thirteen he had an affair with his mate's mum and her seventeen-year-old lodger. When he wasn't thieving he was usually with women. In the house with his parents upstairs, in the garden behind the shed. In his cousin's bedroom. Round at his Uncle Fred's.

He left school at fifteen and only went back to nick the lead off the roofs. Eventually his mother said she couldn't handle him and he was sent to an approved school in Wales. Oh, did I mention that he did a spot of poaching in Norfolk, catching birds by leaving out whiskey-soaked corn? Oh, and then there was joining the Merchant Navy at seventeen. In New Zealand a Maori woman and a Spanish woman fought over him. The Maori won but he had the Spanish woman later too.

Back in London Reid was part of a scam collecting scaffolding from building sites and selling it for scrap before graduating to hijacking lorries with the assistance of bent drivers who would hand over the keys – after clearing out the stock Reid's gang would smash the lock to make it look like a legitimate robbery. Safes were stolen too. But during this period Reid also started performing, doing gags and a bit of singing. Still in his early twenties, he even had his own club in Wardour Street, but corrupt police and gangsters asking for protection money put him off. He was also settling down with his young wife Shirley, and maybe the life of a villain was no longer for him. There were still lapses though. A jewel theft here, a blag there. One time it looked like Reid had been fitted up for a motorbike theft and was going to do time, but the resourceful Shirley, who was his second wife, turned up in court with a cushion up her dress, pretending to be eight months pregnant. It was corny but the judge was fooled and Reid got off with a fine. It didn't always work though. A spell in Brixton Prison was the reality check he needed. The world of the Krays and the Richardson gang did not seem quite so alluring.

Even when he was innocent Reid was always nervous of the Old Bill. One time when he thought he was going to be done for the theft of a coat and wallet he simply did a runner from his home in Wanstead and jumped on the first train from Liverpool Street, which happened to be going to Grimsby. Once there he signed up for a job on a fishing trawler going to Iceland. He was away for a month and hated it, getting into fights with the crew and freezing his nuts off, but at least when he returned he was able to clear his name and get back to ordinary life.

Reid realised he had to go straight and tried to find a way into show-business. He landed a gig as a cruise ship entertainments officer, though he really wanted to perform. And then he got his break in style. After eventually becoming cruise director – with a nice sideline in kickbacks from shops he recommended to tourists – the boat docked at Puerto Rico, where he and his fellow officers were taken to a club. Just as the show was about to start Reid was asked if he would compère for the night, which meant introducing a couple of acts passing through called Dean Martin and Frank Sinatra. He was delighted with the experience and was impressed with the Rat Pack twosome – particularly Martin, who performed seamlessly despite draining tumbler after tumbler of neat bourbon between numbers. Reid had his own favourite tipple – Remy Martin – and received so much in thank yous from shops that he had recommended that he had to ditch case after case overboard when the ship got home.

Eventually things fell into place. On holiday at Butlins in Minehead he decided to enter the holiday camp talent competition. Before he knew it his gruff-toned cocky cockney patter had got him through the heats and he was appearing in the final at the London Palladium, where he came second. Oleaginous compère Hughie Green wanted Reid to appear on his TV show *Opportunity Knocks*, but Reid had other ideas. He had heard about a new show, *The Comedians*. He used his charm to get through to the producer on the phone, who was so impressed by his spiel that he booked him. It was 1971 and Reid was going to be a star at last, but before the show hit the screens there was another TV incident that recalled the life he wanted to leave behind. His stepson came round one night and offered him a television, assuring Mike that it was legitimate. Inevitably it wasn't, and when the original thief grassed his stepson up, the coppers were round. Despite Reid's protestations of innocence he was fined for receiving. Luckily this all happened before *The Comedians* was transmitted or he might not have made the cut. But this was a difficult period. On the one hand he was becoming a household name, on the other his life felt like an episode of *The Sweeney*. He constantly expected a Ford Granada to sweep around the corner and John Thaw and Dennis Waterman to leap out.

In the end he was a success, breaking through in the fast-paced clips show alongside the likes of Bernard Manning, Frank Carson and Colin Crompton. Reid stood out as one of the few southerners on the show and because of his catchphrase, 'T'rific!' His patter wasn't breathtakingly new – he could be as light-fingered as ever when it came to material but he had a way of reshaping stories and making them fresh. Live bookings started to come in, and Reid moved his family to Nottingham, a central base which meant he could get to the northern club circuit as easily as he could get to London. But it didn't last. Reid was unhappy and moved his family back to London. It was a dark time for someone who tended to keep a firm lid on his emotions. Stand-up comedy helped him to get through it, as Reid recalled in his autobiography: 'I had to stick on the clown's face to hide what was inside for longer than I care to remember.'[50] As with entertainers going right back to Joseph Grimaldi mourning the death of his wife and baby, Reid realised the audience wasn't interested in his personal problems: 'They're not here to see me with a face like a donkey's dick.' Comedy is all about giving pleasure, even if the cost is giving greater pain to oneself.

Despite his success it was hard to shake off the past completely. On a holiday in Spain he got into a fight in a bar. His opponent had connections with London villains and wanted to sort the matter out in the traditional fashion. Back in London Reid got wind of the connections but had lost none of his early nerve. He went to see the gang in their pub. Fronting them out worked, and the matter was forgotten.

More unforgettable was his job as presenter of kids' quiz show *Runaround*, which he landed in 1975. The producers wanted to make the show educational as well as entertaining so they had guests who were interviewed before the quiz competition. The first show featured an elephant, a herd of sheep and a couple of motorcycle police. The elephant relieved himself onstage as elephants tend to do when there are cameras pointing at them; the sheep left their droppings everywhere, and the two policemen collided with each other as they rode off. Reid was so

---

50 Mike Reid with Peter Gerrard, *T'rific – Mike Reid: The Autobiography*, Partridge.

exasperated he swore and had to apologise to the children. Not a great start.

Success brought other problems. Reid was not the greatest businessman in the world, and while he was making a mint a lot of it was disappearing faster than he could say his other catchphrase, 'Wallop.' He invested in greyhounds but was ripped off. He had bad luck with horses. He crashed a brand-new Lotus outside his house the first time he took it out. And when he invested in property things went totally pear-shaped. He bought a club in Spain but could not make it pay. The chef (possibly descended from the staff at Fred Karno's Karsino) invoiced for expensive meat, cooked cheap cuts and pocketed the difference; and while the place was full, the tourists had paid their travel company for their night out so Reid barely covered his costs. Eventually, due to red tape and money issues, he lost the club and in the process a lot of other assets at knock-down prices too. He had property in America, a boat and a Lincoln Continental, which were all sold for a song. Worse still, by the time Reid returned to England having sorted out the mess, television stand-up was thinner on the ground. Comedy was changing in the early 1980s and like Monkhouse, Howerd, Hill and the others before him, Reid's mug did not quite fit any more.

So he supplemented his club work with little scraps of acting, which in 1987 eventually turned into his stint as Frank Butcher in *EastEnders*, Things should have had a happy ending, but while Frank was portrayed towards the end as having a breakdown onscreen, Mike in real life was not far behind. He may have looked more resilient than your average insecure, self-obsessed stand-up, but he had been bottling things up for so long they had to come out at some point, and when his son Mark died at the age of twenty-four it was too much. Mark had been diagnosed as schizophrenic, and while he had had periods of normality, the blue mist would descend for no particular reason and he would fly into destructive rages, attacking his mother Shirley and smashing up his car. No one knows exactly what happened, but one day when he was seventeen he shot and killed his friend Ian. In court the verdict was death by misadventure. The tragedy shattered everyone. Mark attempted to take his own life by swallowing weedkiller and cutting himself. Eventually, just when it looked as if he was settling down, he poured barbecue fuel over himself and set it alight. He died just as Mike and Shirley arrived at the hospital. Two nights later Reid had to do a gig. He behaved as if nothing had happened but inside he was destroyed. On the way to another gig he had to hit himself in the leg with a golf club as he arrived at the venue to create a pain to distract him from the agony of Mark's death. Then four months later his granddaughter, Mark's daughter Kirsty Anne, was a victim of cot death. Reid was devastated for a second time. He only got over it by working harder than ever and also developing a love of gardening. Pulling up weeds and planting flowers helped him to rebuild his life more than any therapist could. A villa in Spain purchased from former Spurs and Wales footballer Mike England helped too. Just landing at Malaga lifted the depression that kept returning.

Reid had left *EastEnders* in 1994 because of the depressing storylines, and when he returned full-time in 1998 one of his conditions was that the writers avoided these for him. It did not work out quite as planned. He killed Tiffany, and his wife Peggy had to fight breast cancer. He finally left in 2000, but still popped back to Albert Square before dying suddenly of a heart attack on 29 July 2007 in Marbella. Reid was only sixty-four but had lived a few lives: criminal, family entertainer, soap star. He had also shown that however tough a comedian might seem on the outside, however much they are laughing, somewhere there will be pain.

Tributes flooded in from fellow comedians and *EastEnders* stars. Reid was gone but not forgotten. He even made another TV appearance – in 2008 in the ITV reality series *The Baron*. Competing against Malcolm McLaren and Suzanne Shaw, the previous year Reid had been elected Baron of Troup by the residents of the small town of Gardenstown near Banff in north-east Scotland. Reid was triumphant and genuinely moved. Not many comedians acquire a genuine if powerless posthumous aristocratic title. Even fewer who carried a shotgun and rubbed shoulders with the Krays.

Mike Reid is not the only London comic-cum-overgrown-wide-boy who has juggled being banged up with gags. The alternative comedy world spawned its own lawless legend in Malcolm Hardee, who lived a colourful life on and off the stage and in his own way died a death that was as tragic and also as poetically fitting as that of Tommy Cooper. At times Hardee's life and work seemed to merge into each other. As long as you were not a victim of one of his crimes his entire life could be seen as one long comedy performance.

Malcolm Hardee's parents were together when he was born in Lewisham on 5 January 1950, but he was still placed in an orphanage. His mother suffered from tuberculosis and it was not considered normal for a father to bring up a baby then, so off Malcolm went to Ware in Hertfordshire. He did not see his mother again until she came to collect him when he was nearly two years old.

His father wasn't much in evidence either; he was a lighterman who worked long hours and didn't have much contact with Malcolm as a toddler. Although Malcolm inherited his father's love of the Thames, the bigger influence was his two grandmothers. His paternal grandmother was eccentric and used to take young Malcolm to the Cafe Royal in Regent Street; his maternal grandmother was more down to earth and preferred bingo and Ramsgate. Malcolm probably erred towards a quick game of chance and a seaside resort too.

Hardee grew up at a time when money was scarce and yet life was strangely idyllic. It has been calculated by those that calculate these sorts of things that being born in England between 1948 and 1950 was truly to win the bingo of life. The country would be on the cusp of shouting 'House!' just as you reached maturity, and in the meantime as a child there was plenty of fun to be had larking about on bombsites. And not a health and safety officer to be seen.

A lighterman's wages were pretty good and the money all went on having fun. The Hardee household was lively and boisterous. One day they had a neighbour round for tea while Hardee's father was dying the carpet. When the neighbour discovered his wife had just gone into labour Malcolm's dad would not let him step on the wet carpet to leave so he had to climb out of a window twenty feet from the ground.

As a young boy Malcolm Hardee was, according to his frank but maybe not entirely accurate autobiography, *I Stole Freddie Mercury's Birthday Cake*, pretty well behaved and bright. He would have got a scholarship to the local public school, St Dunstan's, if his parents had not made the wrong impression at his interview; instead he went to the posh grammar school, Colfe's. But by the age of fourteen he had changed.

One suggestion is that he was punished for a misdemeanour he was not involved in, so teenage logic told him he might as well get stuck in. A member of his family subscribes to the Frankie Howerd theory of personal development and suggests maybe he banged his head when he toppled from a ledge. Whatever the reason, the teenage Hardee fell in with a bad lot. Actually that is not strictly correct. As he put it succinctly, 'I was the bad lot.' Formal education played second fiddle to nicking bikes, bunking into strip clubs, messing about on the Underground and stealing Coke from the local Coca-Cola factory, for which he got a conditional discharge. He was eventually expelled from Colfe's for setting off railway-line detonators during assembly and ended up at the rougher Sedgehill Comprehensive. When he arrived it was usually on a stolen scooter, and he was soon expelled from Sedgehill too for being disruptive.

It should be noted that, despite the myth that Oxbridge churns out all the great wits of modern times, there is a tradition of comedians not faring so well in the educational system. From Charlie Chaplin and his fellow Victorian vaudevillians leaving school early to the present day, comedians often have a subversive streak which is perfect for their career but not so good for schooling. Although he eventually got a Masters Degree, Frank Skinner was expelled from school after doing a roaring black-market trade in reselling dinner tickets. Barry Cryer was even more enterprising. Not only did he do the dinner-ticket trick long before Skinner, but he also sold a short cut to the cross-country course for tuppence before going straight.

Hardee's crimes, however, became increasingly audacious. One day while playing in a derelict pub he knocked some bricks out of a wall and discovered a way through to the fishing tackle shop next door. Hardee helped himself. He also indulged in a spot of arson. He set fire to a Sunday school piano because he wanted to see 'holy smoke' and claimed to have burned down the Lewisham Rex Cinema by setting light to the screen.[51] It certainly isn't there any more. He may not have been doing well academically, but by the age of fifteen he had mastered the art of breaking and entering, stealing a banjo from a house and then later breaking into the pawn shop where he had swapped it for money and helping himself to more musical goodies. At least his dishonesty was bringing out his artistic temperament.

Hardee definitely had the performing gene even before he was a performer. At a 'Happening' at Goldsmith's College where both Spike Milligan and Pink Floyd were appearing – there is no record of this line-up, but Hardee remembered it this way – he took his clothes off and wandered across the stage. But it was 1967 so no one really cared or noticed, but for dedicated students of Hardee's later career as a testicle-revealing raconteur this was a seminal moment. Maybe there was something in the south-east London water. Spike Milligan had of course also spent formative time on the Catford/Bromley borders.

It was only a matter of time before Hardee's antics got him into deeper hot water, and in 1968 he was sentenced to three months in a detention centre for breaking into the record department of John Menzies. On his release he got off the train in Blackheath directly opposite the shop, which had an advert in the window for the post of shop manager. Hardee walked in and landed the job. He eventually got bored

---

51 Malcolm Hardee with John Fleming, *I Stole Freddie Mercury's Birthday Cake*, Fourth Estate, 1996, p.21.

with the routine, stole a car and drove to Cornwall, where he was put in prison for three months. On his release he stole another to get back to south London.

Eventually things got a bit more serious after a bungled burglary on a house near Tonbridge in Kent. Hardee had gone down there for a party, but got the wrong weekend so helped himself, but as he was about to load up the stolen Ford Consul the owner arrived and chased him with an axe. This time it was borstal, Gaynes Hall, a former RAF camp near Bedford. Inevitably, he decided to escape. Taken on a monastic retreat, he borrowed a monk's robes and did a runner up to Leeds, where he was finally caught. On his release in January 1971 he landed a job as sports organiser and entertainer at Groom's holiday camp in Great Yarmouth around the same time that Mike Reid was making a splash at Butlin's. Both were now in showbusiness of sorts.

But Hardee's criminal activities continued. Burglaries, cheque frauds and car theft followed: not even a suspended prison sentence and time on remand in Wandsworth put him off. Jewellery, car radios, even a photographic enlarger were all fair game. Eventually he got three years for theft in Exeter, increased because he tried to escape on the way to Totnes Magistrate's Court. Another helping of porridge in Exeter Prison for cheque fraud started to make Hardee think it was time to go straight. Well, as straight as a committed anarchist could manage. As he noted sometime later, 'Prison is like mime and juggling. A tragic waste of time.'

In 1977, after a bit of theatre and some minicabbing, Hardee teamed up with Martin Soan in *The Greatest Show on Legs*. They toured seaside resorts doing Punch and Judy for children and a more adult version for grown-ups. This was a couple of years before alternative comedy, but, partly by accident, Hardee claims to have coined the term – this was how their show was billed at Salcombe in Devon in 1978. Hardee and Soan's shows were slapdash and silly – the rake-thin Soan and Hardee in his jam-jar glasses like a bargain-basement Eric Morecambe making a truly odd couple – and not quite the finished article yet.

As alternative comedy took off as a recognised phenomenon at the end of the 1970s, however, Hardee slotted neatly into the movement. Hardee's all-purpose catchphrase 'Oi, oi' was friendly but also had something of punk's flinty nihilism about it. *The Greatest Show on Legs* finally made its mark at the Comedy Store with its balloon dance in which Hardee and Soan and sometimes a third friend hid their privates behind ever-deflating balloons. Hardee had the idea after the furore about the nudity in *Romans in Britain* at the National Theatre. Anti-smut campaigner Mary Whitehouse had been outraged by the play, and when they heard she liked the cha-cha Hardee and Soan decided to combine nudity with her favourite tunes, and a cult was born.

Hardee's success got him invited to some big parties, prompting a return to his previous career. *The Greatest Show on Legs* was asked to perform at Freddie Mercury's fortieth birthday party at the Xenon in Piccadilly. Except that they weren't allowed to perform in the end because, according to Hardee, someone objected to their act. So they were paid off but missed out on the VIP party. As he was leaving Hardee saw Mercury's lavish birthday cake in the corridor and decided to pop it in the car. It was a big cake though – in the shape of a Rolls-Royce, number plate FM 1 – and when he got it home he couldn't get it into the house without removing a window. The next day there was a knock at the door. Mercury's people were furious. The cake had cost £4,000. Hardee decided the best option was to donate it to charity so out came the window again and they dropped it off at an old people's home. Just in time. A detective later arrived and combed the living-room carpet for crumbs. For once though he got away with it, at least until he confessed all in his autobiography.[52]

Like many of the greatest comedians Hardee seemed to dance to the beat of a different drum. He wasn't immoral or amoral, he simply had a morality entirely of his own making. An incident at the 1982 Edinburgh Fringe Festival exemplifies how he could take matters into his own hands. He was performing in a tent, and in the next marquee American performance artist Eric Bogosian was doing his solo show. A section in which Bogosian mimed to heavy metal music was driving Hardee mad, so he decided to pay the American a visit mid-show on a tractor that he was using for a daredevil jumping stunt. He invited his audience too. 'Look, we'll go and see Eric. All of us. He'll like it. He's a bit of a laugh. He's an anarchist.' Oh, and Hardee was naked. Hardee's version of what followed suggests that Bogosian was furious at the interruption and later went backstage, attacked the tractor and tried to punch Hardee, except by this time he was dressed and Soan was naked so he took it out on Soan by mistake.[53]

Hardee could hardly be said to cut a dash – you could usually tell what he had had for breakfast by scanning his lapels – but he was very popular with women. He had a relationship with then aspiring comedian

---

52 Ibid., p.114.
53 Ibid., p121.

Jo Brand and on their first date he drove through a red light at the Elephant and Castle and was arrested. In fact Hardee claimed it was him who suggested she had a crack at stand-up.

Eventually Hardee decided to open his own club and found suitably chaotic premises at the Mitre Pub just by the southern exit of the Blackwall Tunnel. The latter-day Lord of Misrule finally had his own fiefdom. Once again the comedy ley lines seemed to link up. Spike Milligan was said to have appeared here in the 1950s – according to Hardee at least, who was never backwards when it came to self-publicity. Some of his most notorious antics at the club, however, were spontaneous. He once urinated on a audience member's head and famously did an impression of President de Gaulle by placing spectacles on his penis. He claimed that the latter was inspired by local lad Milligan, who had known someone who used to do a similar thing in the army. Hardee was a unique compère. While quietly supportive of new acts, giving breaks to the likes of Vic Reeves, Harry Enfield and Simon Day, onstage he would play up the part of the ultimate mean-spirited link man, introducing turns by saying something on the lines of, 'The next act is probably a bit shit.'

It was no surprise the audience took their cue from their charismatic host and echoed this streak of cruelty. Some of stand-up's greatest heckles occurred at the Tunnel Club. Often acts barely needed to speak to incur the wrath of the audience. Jim Tavaré once came onstage and said, 'Good evening, ladies and gentlemen. My name is Jim Tavaré and I'm a schizophrenic.' To which one wag responded, 'Why don't you both fuck off then.'

Despite no longer being a career criminal Hardee still got into trouble. On tour with Vic Reeves at the Copthorne Hotel in Newcastle, he decided to play a trick on his chum Simon Day and surprise him at his hotel window wearing nothing but socks and a leather coat. Hardee crawled along a ledge outside the building but could not attract Day's attention so crawled back to be greeted in his room by armed Special Branch officers. This was the height of the IRA bombing campaign, not long after Prime Minister Margaret Thatcher's hotel had been blown up in Brighton. It turned out that as well as the Reeves and Mortimer party, Michael Heseltine was staying at the Copthorne. Security was understandably tight, and the police were on the lookout for anything out of the ordinary. Malcolm certainly fitted the bill.

Hardee never made it as a star – although if you are observant you can spot him in the background of an episode of *The Black Adder* – but he probably didn't care. He preferred to do things his way. In the 1990s in Edinburgh he took some Ecstasy, felt funny, thought he was going to have a heart attack and had to call an ambulance. The paramedics glanced at Hardee and said, 'You should be old enough to know better.' They may have been less concerned about his drug use and more concerned that he was sporting luminous testicles. Did I mention that his testicles were his pride and joy and also something of a showbiz calling card? He claimed they were the biggest in the business.

I had a few dealings with Hardee over the years and they were never less than interesting. I was constantly amazed that he ever made any money or managed to run any kind of business. When I saw him shambling around his club, I found it hard to believe he had ever made an honest living out of comedy (and if some of the rumours about him are true, 'honest' is the last adjective you'd apply to Malcolm). But there was no doubt that he was an inspirational force of nature, mapping out his own idiosyncratic route through life.

He certainly loved comedy and was always keen to launch new clubs. After the Tunnel closed down he opened Up the Creek in the heart of Greenwich. When he sold his stake in that he opened a new venue. At the time I was writing about comedy for the London *Evening Standard* and one afternoon – probably morning for him – I got a call from Malcolm asking me to list his club's opening night. I apologised, explained he'd missed the deadline, asked him to send the details in and said I'd list it the following week. Unfortunately the letter I received didn't include the full details, so I still couldn't list it until the week after that, when Malcolm phoned me with the full line-up. Third time lucky, I was determined to give this London legend's latest venture a massive plug. The newspaper came out, and I got a call from Malcolm. I was expecting some gratitude for the free publicity; instead I got an apology: 'Sorry, Bruce. The gig's not happening now. We've had to close the club. The venue didn't have an entertainment licence.' Typical Malcolm.

Then at the start of February 2005 I received a text: 'Have you heard about Malcolm?' He had gone missing. I wondered what his latest stunt was. Selling the Millennium Dome? Refloating the *Cutty Sark*? Sinking HMS *Belfast*? Sadly it was water- and Greenwich-related. It was thought that Malcolm had been in a dinghy rowing back to the *Sea Sovereign*, the boat he lived on in Surrey Quays when he fell in and drowned, though the coroner at his post-mortem suggested he had fallen from the quayside. The Thames had always been important to him, and now it had taken him back. He had drowned on 31 January.

Rumours were rife about his death. There was talk that the reason he sank so quickly was because he had just had a big win on a fruit machine and the coins had weighed him down. Another story said that he was found with a beer bottle clutched in his right hand. The full truth will never be known, but what we do know is that Hardee was a one-off. When I attended his funeral in Greenwich, St Alfege's Church was packed to the rafters with the comedy glitterati. Jo Brand, Stewart Lee and Arthur Smith (who said, 'Everything about Malcolm, apart from his stand-up act, was original') and Malcolm's son Frank were among those who gave readings, Jools Holland played the piano, and the coffin, with a jaunty sailor's cap on top, was carried past the mourners to the tune of 'Return to Sender'.

The curious thing about Malcolm is that, unlike virtually every other comedian in this book, he does not seem to have had a dark side. I asked people who knew him, and although he was not the kind of comedian who was always 'on', he always seemed cheerful. One of his friends told me that as far as he knew Malcolm had never had therapy. This was no surprise. People like Malcolm never resort to therapy; they hope that a drink, a shag or a good night's sleep will sort them out. It was only occasionally towards the end that maybe he could be a little low, not answering emails as quickly as usual or returning phone calls. If Hardee teaches us anything, it is that if you want to lead a successful life start out as an unsuccessful criminal. Things can only get better.

Malcolm Hardee's friend Jo Brand would have presumably steered clear of him if he had been no fun. You may have noticed that there are few women in this book. This is not because they are less troubled, not because they are better behaved or indulge in less scurrilous behaviour. There are simply less women in the comedy pool. Brand is one of the most colourful female figures in contemporary comedy so perhaps it is

Tommy Cooper: Big feet, big personality.
The hard-grafting magician could never resist coming up with a trick when there was an audience, but the pressure to be funny took its toll in the end.

Public faces, private vices. Tony Hancock and Hattie Jacques, seen here during the glory days of *Educating Archie*, brought smiles to millions while their private lives were messy.

Frocky Horror Show: It is easy to see why Benny Hill started to cast dolly birds in his TV shows – he didn't quite make the pin-up grade himself.

ankie Howerd: Having become
radio superstar, the master of the
aspish aside branched out into
ovies with less success. Seen
re with Dorothy Bromiley who
rred with him in *A Touch of*
e Sun (1956) which failed to
t the movie screens alight.

Bob Monkhouse:
The quick-fire comic
claimed that Diana Dors'
husband Dennis Hamilton
threatened to slit his eyeballs.

Lenny Bruce: The outspoken American truth-speaker was a sensation at Peter Cook's Establishment club. So much so that when he was invited to return for a second residency the Home Secretary got involved in keeping him out of the country.

Master of his Domain.
A rare glimpse of Peter Cook at the peak of his powers,
holding court at his Establishment club in Soho in 1961.

The Greatest Show on Legs: The late Malcolm Hardee's life was one long comedy sketch. Perhaps his finest five minutes came when he danced onstage clad in nothing but a balloon. From left to right: Keith Chegwin, Malcolm Hardee, Steve Bowditch, Martin Soan.

Phil Hartman:
You may remember him from *Saturday Night Live*, but Hartman, alias *The Simpsons'* Troy McClure, finally made the front pages when he was shot dead by his wife.

am Kinison:
Not so much a stand-up,
more a purveyor of
primal scream therapy
with added punchlines.

Russell Brand: The man who changed modern comedy also tried to change the world by protesting at a May Day rally in 2002 without his trousers. There's a joke about a bobby's helmet waiting in the wings, if anyone cares to make it.

no surprise that she was drawn to Hardee. When I first interviewed Brand in the early 1990s she told me that her favourite pastime when not performing was Scrabble. That was only half the story. Brand's own story could teach men a thing or two.

Very little on the comedy circuit has disturbed Brand because she has seen far worse as a psychiatric nurse: violent families, paranoid schizophrenics self-harming, a large naked man sitting on the floor with matches between his toes during therapy sessions while another patient sings 'Oh What a Beautiful Morning'. After that being told to fuck off while trying to perform is nothing. Brand has seen it all and is tough enough to have dealt with it all. As she once told *The Times*, 'I always found people with mental illnesses were much more creative in their abuse, and in a way much more hurtful – because they would focus in unwittingly on your Achilles heel. They delivered this gloriously creative and imaginative stream of insults which, as a stand-up, you don't hear. You just get the standard "You're fat," "You're ugly," whatever.' Some hecklers are creative though. If it is hard enough putting up with men shouting, 'Get your tits out,' Brand has also dealt with 'Don't get your tits out.'

Brand has noted that there is sometimes a thin line between comedy and psychiatric disorder. Often some early upset has driven a comic on – the early death of a parent, perhaps. Looking further back, maybe the trauma of war as a young combatant (Harry Secombe, Spike Milligan, Michael Bentine, et al.). She has even suggested to certain comedians that they seek professional help. In fact there are particular qualities in comedy which match up almost perfectly with conditions seen in mental illness.

Brand also talks of patients being 'labile' – loose tongued – constantly exhibiting extraordinary energy and pouring out a stream of words like some of the greatest comedians. And take all those grumpy old men on the circuit and on television. Some would probably be diagnosed as not just fed up with automated checkouts in supermarkets or budget airlines, but actually depressed. She has had her own loose-tongued moments, but usually due to PMT. At a gig in Glasgow she was getting a hard time from the audience so just upped the ante by saying, 'Who the fuck won Culloden?' The only thing you can do after that is duck. It is no surprise that she sometimes describes the stage not as a place for the expression of ideas but as the 'firing line'. Yet comedians need that attention. Even the shyest comedians somehow craves the audience. As philosopher Henri Bergson wrote on the subject of comedy, laughter is 'in need of an echo'. The late Linda Smith put it equally well with her closing line to her audience: 'You are the difference between a performance and an affliction.'

Comedians are often extreme people. Whatever they do, they tend to do it to excess whether it is perform or in the case of Eddie Izzard, run huge distances for charity. Greg Whyte, who helped to train Eddie Izzard when he ran forty-three marathons in fifty-one days was blown away by his determination to succeed which was stronger than the drive of many professional athletes. Izzard has gone on record as saying that his record-breaking run was a way of trying to get back the love that he lost out on when his mother died when he was a child. 'If I do enough things, maybe she'll come back,' said Izzard in the 2010 documentary *Believe*. Surely Bob Monkhouse's obsessive quest for laughter was partly an attempt to claw back the love he never got from a mother who was cold towards him? Actor Simon Russell Beale once said that all performers are trying to please their mother or father, and that seems to be part of the case with Izzard, who appears to drive himself on to incredible physical feats. I ran four miles with Izzard between Leicester and Market Harborough. That was enough for me.

Jo Brand's own pivotal moment came in her teens. She was born on 23 July 1957 in south London to Ron and Joyce, who soon moved out to Kent. Ron was a structural engineer, and the family had a comfortable life, with Brand sandwiched between two boys. She was a bright student and all was well until the family moved to Hastings. Brand wanted to stay at her old school. She went off the rails and decided that drugs, drink and dangerous boyfriends were more attractive than academia. In her autobiography she suggests that part of the problem was her shyness. Like a number of comedians she is considerably less outgoing offstage. 'It's not me onstage. It's someone else, a version of me. A confident, cleverer, funnier version of me.'[54] The authority of being onstage with a microphone enables Brand – and many other stand-ups – to behave in a way they would never consider behaving in real life.

In Hastings she found her 'bad lot', smoking, drinking and hanging around on the seafront. It did not help that at home her father was prone to mood swings – he may have suffered from depression, thinks Brand – and had a tendency to fly off the handle without much prompting. She recalls him really exploding one night when he discovered that Brand had been to see *Last Tango in Paris* with some dubious hippy friends. After waiting for her outside the cinema and having a blazing row, he gathered all of her clothes that offended him, mainly Laura Ashley skirts and T-shirts, piled them in the garden and set them on fire.

Alcohol was always Brand's vice, although she once took acid and spent an evening talking to a poster of Bob Dylan. Her parents naturally didn't approve of her boyfriends. When her father first met her hippy boyfriend Dave he ended up thumping him. She left home at seventeen, staying on at school part-time to do her A levels. Brand's late adolescence was dominated by drink rather than the pursuit of exam excellence. One night she got drunk with a candle by the side of her bed and was woken by the smell of burning. She poured a jug of water on the flames and went back to sleep, then woke again when the burning smell returned, at which point the mattress went up in flames. Luckily a sober neighbour dialled 999 and the blaze was put out.

Getting around meant learning to drive, which was a challenge. Brand was so nervous when she took her driving test she took a Valium beforehand and ended up too relaxed. So relaxed, in fact, that she drove into a pothole. Somehow she passed, and when she went to study nursing at Brunel University in west London she seems to have become her social group's designated driver. One night after driving from Uxbridge to Exeter to see an Anthony Minghella play she skidded across a soaked M4 and was lucky to survive. Her friends were unaware of the near-miss, being asleep in the back at the time.

While training to be a nurse she experienced a couple of darkly absurd incidents that summed up the kind of things that could happen in her profession. One night a male nurse made an aggressive pass at her and a couple of patients – suffering from depression and anxiety respectively – had to come to her aid. Another time she was leaving the car park when a man tapped at her car window. She wound it down only for him to poke his penis through. She should have wound it up again quickly, but it was too stiff. The window, that is. So she just drove off.

In 1986 Brand decided that she would like to have a bash at stand-up comedy. She ploughed through her five minutes anaesthetised by alcohol and decided she liked it. At first she did gags about Freud, but they didn't go too well, but when she started to do gags about herself and her weight things clicked: 'I went to a health farm. Ended up eating my bedroom.' The audience made that vital connection with the performer. She still enjoyed drinking though. On the way to a gig in Devon with fellow comedian Nick Hancock she realised they were ahead of schedule so decided to stop for a drink in every pub they passed once they reached the county line. They stopped at around twelve and were so drunk at the gig Hancock threw his shoes into the crowd while Brand at first refused to go on, eventually doing a very bad set.

For a while Brand continued to work as a psychiatric nurse in south London, but her two worlds were starting to collide. At a show at the Institute of Contemporary Arts there was a naked man at the gig talking into a mobile phone. Other people thought he was an art installation and left him to it; Brand recognised him as a previous patient. One night she had a gig in Nottingham with Bob Mills, Johnny Immaterial and Mandy Knight. Everything went fine, but she had borrowed the car from a friend who had MS and the controls were specially adapted. On the way back they stopped at Scratchwood Services on the M1. Having driven into the lorry park by mistake they were trying to get out when Brand spotted a juggernaut backing towards them. Not being familiar with the controls she couldn't find the horn and frantically tried to alert the lorry with the windscreen wipers instead. The front of the car was smashed in and Brand had to ring her friend to tell her. They had to lurch all the way back to south London – but not before having a full fry-up.

Eventually by the late 1980s Brand had to choose between psychiatric nursing and stand-up. The problem was that she was starting to appear on television. The last thing she needed was patients walking up to her and saying they had seen her on the box. It would be hard to tell if they were delusional or fans of Channel 4's *Friday Night Live*. Psychiatric nursing's loss was comedy's gain.

Malcolm Hardee's kindred comedy spirit Arthur Smith is still going strong, but he has had a closer brush with death than most of his stand-up peers. A life of alcohol-fuelled hedonism finally caught up with him in middle age when he found himself in intensive care. If this was a movie, the screen would go blurry now and we would flash back to discover how this carefree comedy troubadour got here.

Arthur Smith was born Brian Smith in Bermondsey on 27 November 1954. Aged twenty-eight, he had to change his name to Arthur when he joined Equity because there already was a Brian Smith. He initially opted for Captain Wanker, but that was ignored. Arthur Smith it was to be. Smith grew up in south London not far from Hardee. He was a few years younger and a bit better behaved. As a schoolboy he recalls being far too shy to get involved with girls even though he was thirteen in 1967, the summer of love: 'For me it was the summer of staying in to wank and study cricket averages.'[55]

As a student at the University of East Anglia Smith was moderately militant and only turned to petty crime out of a mix of financial necessity and ideology. He once shoplifted a Cornish pasty and some milk,

---

55 Arthur Smith, *My Name Is Daphne Fairfax*, Arrow, 2010, p.52.

convinced by political discussions that all property was theft. The police looked kindly on him when they discovered that Arthur's father Syd was a former copper, and let him off.

Smith started performing for fun and to meet women, later on adding the more philosophical explanation that it was a way of 'avoiding the tragedy of existence'. He first went up to the Edinburgh Fringe Festival in 1977, with four ambitions on his mind: 'I'll get drunk, I'll get laid, I'll get spotted, I'll get paid.' It was an era when there was little stand-up in Edinburgh, and Smith had few comedy role models so did an impersonation of Max Miller. It seemed to go down pretty well and he continued to return to Edinburgh, becoming a Fringe legend.

As the new wave of comedy swept across the UK in the early 1980s it pulled Smith along in its wake and he started to appear on television. This was the era of the Falklands War with Thatcherism rampant and Smith was an ardent left-winger. Low-level stardom gave him access to some casual sex but he refused to sleep with anyone he knew was a Conservative voter. One could write a PhD thesis on how liberal-minded comedians who wriggle like a maggot on a pin when faced with the prospect of sleeping with someone who does not conform to their own ideology. There is a picture of Frank Skinner in his first memoir, taken during the run of his excellent ITV chat show and featuring Tara Palmer-Tompkinson perched both precariously and seductively on his knee. Skinner's caption reads, 'Yes, I would. But only as an act of class warfare.'

But Smith was single and took plenty of advantage of the sexual opportunities on offer, looking back nostalgically on some selected highlights in later years: 'the French stripper, the RSC actress, on the centre spot at Stamford Bridge, university lecturer, human rights lawyer, single mum, artist.[56] Life in the 1980s was good. His stint fronting TV stand-up show *Paramount City* may not have been a smash, but he was a regular face on the box, a regular voice on the radio and rapidly becoming a live institution north of the border.

Smith's late-night tours of Edinburgh during the Festival became the stuff of legend. In 1989 he led 200 fans round to a small prison at the back of Edinburgh Castle and claimed that Nelson Mandela was there and they wouldn't leave until he was released. The guard was a good sport and got them to move on by saying, 'We'll be letting him out the side door further up the road.' In 1990 he ended the tour under the window of the flat of comedian/impressionist John Thomson, who entertained the nocturnal audience by lurking in the shadows doing his best James Bond voice and pretending he was Sean Connery. The police were quite often involved. In 2000 Smith's chum Simon Munnery was handcuffed and taken away, mistaken for Smith, who had previously been spotted wearing just his pants and shouting through a megaphone.

Yet even Smith, who seemed defiantly happy-go-lucky behind the Sid James wrinkles, was not immune to depression, particularly as he approached middle age. At one point he went to the A & E department of St George's Hospital in London in the middle of the night asking for sleeping pills. The response was an eerie echo of the remark made variously to Grimaldi and Grock. The doctor looked at Smith, thought for a moment and then said, 'Wasn't that you on *Have I Got News For You* last week?' How could a famous TV comedian with a quip for every occasion possibly be suffering from depression? Smith even tried Prozac

---

56 Ibid., p.262.

but was put off by the possible side effects: 'headache, nervousness, sleeplessness, muscle tremor, anxiety, nausea, diarrhoea, sweating, itching, poor sexual performance'. It was enough to make you depressed.

Life has a perverse way of sorting itself out. The booze-inspired anarchy came to an end in 2001, when Smith was rushed to hospital suffering from acute necrotising pancreatitis. His lifestyle had taken its toll and his pancreas was giving up the ghost. Smith hovered between life and death for a while, but then an amazing thing happened. He was told that if he drank again the alcohol might kill him. He really had to stop. Yet he still seemed to be funny when he performed. And to his great relief he still seemed to be very good company when he was offstage. The revelries and merriment could continue for this genial jester.

Shortly afterwards he got married and settled down, but he didn't particularly slow down. Life has been one long comedy gig for Smith. As with Malcolm Hardee – though maybe with less dramatic conse-quences – everything he does becomes a comedy event. I remember bumping into him at a very muddy Glastonbury one year. I explained that I had been flooded out, and he said that as he was about to go home I could borrow his tent. It seemed a very generous offer until I found out the tent was actually the BBC's and not his to lend out. Another year at the Hay Festival on a variant of his Edinburgh walk-abouts he paid my two daughters a fiver to run to a large tree and back again.

In 2010 I finally ticked off an ambition and appeared in an Edinburgh Fringe show myself thanks to Arthur. Where Malcolm Hardee scams tended to be dishonest – he once got Arthur to smuggle a bogus five-star review of his show into the *Scotsman* using the byline of a respected critic – Smith's publicity-generating scams tend to be more playful. That year he challenged critics to appear onstage with him. Juggling fish. I practised every morning with satsumas and then had an idea. What if I used fish cakes? But Arthur said it had to be fresh fish and he would supply them. The trouble with spontaneous wheezes like this is that they tend to be a little *fluid*. And, sure enough, on the day I had a call saying that he couldn't get any fish in time, so instead I interviewed him onstage and he pretended to fall asleep, which he said was his usual response to listening to journalists.

That year I also met up with Arthur on his traditional Edinburgh tour at 3 a.m. Unless you are a spy or handing over a hostage, the Edinburgh Fringe must be the only place in the world where you can arrange to meet someone at 3 a.m. He was singing Bob Dylan songs with a tramp on the Royal Mile. Smith was slightly maudlin by then and shortly afterwards disappeared into the night like a comedy superhero, coming to save the day with pranks and then slipping quietly away, preferring credibility to full-blown celebrity status. He might be a professional grumpy old man on the BBC these days and the voice of probiotic yoghurt, but in comedy terms he is Mr Cult as well as Mr Yakult.

8

Anything You Can Do . . . The Americans Can Do Madder

US oddness from Andy Kaufman to Sam Kinison

Tuesday, 26 April 2011. I'm in a church near Islington, north London watching comedian Simon Munnery body-slam comedian Josie Long in a wrestling ring. The event is part of the decidedly literary London Word Festival, and others taking part include oddball musical comedian Isy Suttie and veteran alternative stand-up Helen Lederer. Meanwhile a lederhosen-wearing brass band plays pop hits in the background. Is it comedy? Sport? Art? A metaphor for the enduring battle of the sexes? Is it somehow asking the eternal question, why are we here?

Actually the reason we are here – in this church, not on this planet – can be explained in two words: Andy Kaufman. The event, devised by artist/curator Mel Brimfield, is a homage to Kaufman, the provocative American who did not just straddle the boundaries between comedy and performance art, he positively body-slammed them. In the 1970s he declared himself World Inter-Gender Wrestling Champion and invited female wrestlers to take his title from him in the ring. This was just one exploit in a career that broke all the rules of comedy. While, as we have seen, British comedians have been quick off the mark at pushing boundaries, Kaufman is in the front line when it comes to Americans taking comedy way beyond a joke.

Andrew Geoffrey Kaufman was born in Queens, New York on 17 January 1949 and grew up in Great Neck, Long Island. Great Neck is an upper-middle-class suburb known for its swell former residents Scott and Zelda Fitzgerald. In fact *The Great Gatsby* was written about a mile from the Kaufman home. Andrew's father Stanley sold jewellery; his mother Janice was a former teen fashion model; his grandfather Paul was a frustrated performer who entertained at children's parties with purposely messed-up magic tricks.

He was a solitary child with an imaginary friend called Dhrupick, and his parents were understandably concerned. Not greatly at first, but as Kaufman retreated into his fantasy world there was increasing cause for worry. By the age of four he was said to be performing to an invisible camera in the wall of his bedroom. According to his biographer Bill Zehme, Kaufman's audience for those early gigs was Dhrupick. When he was interested in something he became really interested in it. He once visited a sideshow, Hubert's Museum and Live Flea Circus, and found himself inexorably drawn to the freakish exhibits. He loved wrestling, particularly villain Buddy 'Nature Boy' Rogers, and used to stage surreal fights with himself in the school playground. Later he was an obsessive Elvis Presley fan. Legend has it he once hid in a cupboard for eight hours in the Las Vegas Hilton in the hope that Presley, who was performing there, would walk past.

As he grew up, this fantasy world continued. When he reached adolescence his parents sent him to psychiatrists, but he went further into his shell and in 1967 he was classified 4-F, a 'paranoid schizophrenic with psychotic tendencies', an achievement of which he was reportedly proud. What he needed was an outlet for his strange personality. He found it in live performance.

When Kaufman left home and went to college in Boston, he studied TV production and created his own children's show. (What is it with American funny men connecting with their inner child by making kids' TV? Lenny Bruce had *Fleetfoot*; Kaufman had a puppet-based campus show.) His unbalanced, unhinged approach to the world was clearly taking shape, taking inspiration from Kerouac and the beat poets' spontaneous confrontational street theatre. The only thing that seemed to calm him down was Transcendental Meditation, which he felt expanded his consciousness – though if there was one person who did not need his consciousness expanding it was Andy Kaufman. In 1971 he attended a retreat with Maharishi Mahesh Yogi in Majorca. He asked the Maharishi about the connection between madness and comedy and received a Zen-like answer which would help to define and delineate his work: 'Oddness, according to his holiness, was simply a tool with which to create contrasts for an audience . . . the comedian's craft, he said, was akin to building two walls side by side and leaving a space in between. The mere presence of those two walls then creates a contrast based on an awareness of the space.'[57]

By the early 1970s Kaufman was doing his unconventional act in conventional clubs such as New York's Catch a Rising Star. He would get into a sleeping bag onstage and sometimes actually doze off. He did

---

57 Bill Zehme, *Lost in the Funhouse: The Life and Mind of Andy Kaufman*, Fourth Estate, 2000, p.122.

not seem to try to make friends with his audience or seek their approval, but worked on the very edges of what was normally perceived as funny. Kaufman didn't consider himself a stand-up comedian or an actor, more a performance artist. For a while artist/musician Laurie Anderson worked as his straight woman, but I doubt if they could have ever given Cannon and Ball a run for their money. Kaufman would come on and put on a record which played the jaunty theme from the children's show *Mighty Mouse*. He would stand stock still and rigid and silent, except when he mimed the chorus line 'Here I come to save the day!' before going silent again. It was disturbing and weird, but on a good night would bring the house down. He would also do impressions in the guise of his character known as Foreign Man, who claimed to be from Caspiar, a fictional island in the Caspian Sea ('it sunk'). Whether it was former President Richard Nixon or Archie Bunker from the sitcom *All in the Family*, the voices would all come out in the same cracked broken English that Foreign Man spoke. But then he would shock everyone by doing a quiff-perfect impression of his beloved Elvis, throwing his jacket into the crowd before retrieving it and leaving the stage with a 'T'ank you veddy much!'

Comedy fans did not always get it as he went from idiot to Elvis, but when they did they really got it. Kaufman started to build up a regular following on the circuit and people would actively seek him out. Gradually he developed another character, fat, lubricious, angry lounge singer Tony Clifton. As Clifton he was transformed – you could barely tell this was Kaufman at all. On his debut the mock-monstrous Clifton poured a full glass of Chianti over Kaufman's friend Bob Zmuda's head. The audience was both outraged and transfixed, not knowing what was going on. By 1975 he had made it on to the first series of the ground-breaking ensemble

TV show *Saturday Night Live*, doing his lip-synching *Mighty Mouse* routine, and by 1976 he had relocated to Hollywood, appearing on television and headlining at the LA Improv. His act did not appeal to everyone. In fact his appearances divided the *Saturday Night Live* audience so much that in 1983 a Keep Andy/Dump Andy phone vote was taken to decide whether to retain his services. The vote went against him, which maybe was a victory of sorts for this master of the perverse.

Foreign Man had won him friends in influential places though, and in 1978 the character was used as the basis for his role of Latka Gravas in the hit sitcom *Taxi*. The producers had seen him do Foreign Man and wrote the part of the language-garbling alien specifically for Kaufman. Latka's backstory involved suffering from multiple personality disorder, which allowed Kaufman to assume various personalities. There was something truly dark going on here – a man diagnosed as schizophrenic appearing as a fictional character in a comedy programme slipping in and out of different personalities.

This mainstream fame led to problems whenever he did live shows. Fans expected to see lovable Latka, not some nutty gag-free performance art. Kaufman would lose his temper if the audience were impatient and ditch his act in favour of reading from *The Great Gatsby*. As the audience walked out he would offer to put a record on instead.

He tried to explain his philosophy in the *New York Times*:

I am not a comic, I have never told a joke . . . The comedian's promise is that he will go out there and make you laugh with him . . . My only promise is that I will try to entertain you as best I can. I can manipulate people's reactions. There are different kinds of laughter. Gut laughter is where you don't have a choice, you've got to laugh. Gut laughter doesn't come from the intellect. And it's much harder for me to evoke now, because I'm known. They say, 'Oh wow, Andy Kaufman, he's a really funny guy.' But I'm not trying to be funny. I just want to play with their heads.

Kaufman began using Tony Clifton to open his shows. The character was so deeply rooted that when the name of Kaufman was brought up in interviews with 'Clifton', the singer would lose his temper and claim that Kaufman was trying to ruin his career and make money out of him. His imaginary friend Dhrupick seems to have metamorphosed into Clifton, an enemy determined to bring him down. There seemed to be a wafer-thin line here between comedy and multiple personality disorder. Kaufman was not just Kaufman. He was another latter-day Lord of Misrule.

As he became more famous one gig was particularly memorable. At Carnegie Hall – the scene of Lenny Bruce's great triumph – on 26 April 1979 Kaufman performed with an elderly lady sitting at the side of the stage on a sofa. He explained that he had always promised his Grandma Pearl that if he ever made it she would get the best seat in the house, so he had flown her in from Florida for the night. After the performance his grandmother removed her hat and glasses to reveal that she was actually Robin Williams. Kaufman invited anyone who wanted to meet him for milk and cookies after the show and again at Staten Island Ferry in the morning, where he bought everyone ice cream. When he did invite a real old lady on the stage she pretended to have a heart attack and die so that Kaufman could don a Native American headdress, do a dance and revive her. Not even death was a taboo subject for his humour.

These subversive, genre-busting pranks simultaneously discombobu-lated, fascinated and repelled audiences. In one sketch on the ABC show *Fridays*, in which he was one of a group of diners who were all supposed to be stoned, he refused to say his lines and another comedian Michael Richards – who would have his own dark times with stand-up later when he controversially used the word 'nigger' in a comedy club – stormed off and chucked the cue cards at him, at which point Kaufman threw water over Richards. The co-producer ran onstage; there was a fight, and the show cut to a commercial. The whole thing was a pre-planned hoax, but it certainly looked genuine. There was a real frisson when Kaufman seemed to be on the verge of throwing a punch at his female co-star after she had hit him with a buttered bread roll.

Fakery seemed to be the guiding philosophy behind this trickster, which may be why he had a soft spot for wrestling, particularly the theatricality of kayfabe, the staged element of the sport, which was always rumoured to be scripted and closer to theatre than spontaneous sport. Gradually Kaufman started to feature bouts on his shows but ended up with a broken neck after a brawl with real wrestler Jerry Lawler on *Late Night With David Letterman*. This, however, turned out to be another very convincing hoax, though he did actually end up fighting Lawler in the ring in Memphis.

Kaufman's interest in wrestling in general and lady wrestlers in partic-ular developed into an overwhelming obsession. His friend and TV producer Bob Zmuda recalled how Andy liked to arrange wrestling fights between skimpily clad women in his apartment, so perhaps it was no surprise when he made headlines and outraged feminists by declaring himself the World Inter-Gender Wrestling Champion, offering $1,000 to any woman who could pin him down. After there were no takers he increased his offer – not with more money but an additional offer to marry any woman that pinned him and could shave his head. A quarter of a century later London would stage its own version.

When Kaufman joined the cast of *Taxi* he also signed a deal to make his biggest TV show yet, *Andy's Funhouse*. This broke all the rules of comedy and light entertainment, then just as you thought you had grasped the new rules it had created just for itself it went and broke those too just for good measure. Everything Kaufman did came with a twist. When he did a chat-show segment in *Funhouse* his desk was way too high, making the guests crane their necks to communicate with him. If comedy is all about cognitive dissonance – the contrast between the expected and the unexpected – Kaufman was the master. There was the 'Has-Been Corner', with ex-child-star Gail Slobodkin singing. Plus some conga and some Elvis. Sometimes the screen filled with static as if the viewers' televisions were not working. It was perhaps no surprise that the bosses at ABC did not want to air it. It eventually went out in 1979, but you could understand their confusion. A foreign man in a sitcom about a taxi firm? Sure. A comedy show with no jokes? Are you crazy? Ludwig Wittgenstein once said a serious and philosophical work could be written that would consist entirely of jokes. Kaufman managed to produce a comedic work that had no jokes in it whatsoever.

He was still a hit in *Taxi* though. In fact Kaufman had so much clout for a while that he was able to engineer a bizarre post-modern scenario in which Tony Clifton appeared in *Taxi* too. Kaufman stayed as Clifton on the set as well as on the screen. He was accompanied by hookers, drank and smoked, and argued with the production team about his lines. Eventually, and perhaps unsurprisingly, he was fired, being forcibly removed from the set.

From this peak, however, Kaufman's career could go no further. He still worked and was still a success after *Taxi*, but his approach to comedy was so disturbing it was hard to keep coming up with new ideas that would shock his audiences. Then it looked like he had come up with the greatest gag of all. On 16 May 1984 Kaufman died of kidney failure. He was only thirty-five years old. He had been suffering from a rare form of lung cancer since 1983 and had tried umpteen treatments including an all-fruit diet, psychic surgery and radiotherapy. Nothing worked, but for a while, though appearing thin, he did not reveal publicly how ill he was, which led to persistent rumours that the master prankster had pulled the ultimate prank and faked his own death.[58] One of the reasons Kaufman's death seemed unbelievable was that Tony Clifton continued to gig, but it was assumed that it was Kaufman's long-time chum Bob Zmuda. There was no surprise punch-line to this routine.

Andy Kaufman was a comedy one-off, but he emerged at a time when American stand-up was going through a massive boom. And along with the boom came the inevitable bad behaviour, when raging hormones and raging egos got together. But while Kaufman's antics on the outer limits may have been connected to both art and mental illness, the

---

58 The same mixture of denial and wish-fulfilment would be mooted when Malcolm Hardee died in 2005. His death was such a surprise, friends thought he would soon pitch up at his own wake in the Trafalgar Tavern overlooking the Thames in Greenwich.

scurrilous antics of much of the American comedy scene around this time had more to do with the effect of narcotics.

In the 1970s and 1980s, the rock-and-roll drug cocaine became the narcotic of choice among comedians, who were being treated like rock stars. Dressing rooms and hotel rooms floated on a cloud of Colombian marching powder. As comedians played bigger and bigger venues during the boom years and made more and more money, dealers popped up to help them to spend it. As comedian Robin Williams said, 'Cocaine is God's way of telling you you are making too much money.' And Robin Williams – whose act at its peak seemed like one perpetual display of attention deficit hyperactivity disorder but with better punchlines – certainly knew about drugs. In America cocaine use had been rife in comedy circles at a time when Tommy Cooper was happy with a bottle of whiskey. John Belushi had long been an inveterate cocaine user and on 5 March 1982 was found dead in his hotel room at the age of thirty-three, killed by a combination of cocaine and heroin.

Richard Pryor, whose life seemed to be one long routine-inspiring scandal, nearly died when he was freebasing cocaine and set himself on fire. On 9 June 1980, while drinking 151 proof rum, he poured it over himself and set it alight. He was taken to hospital suffering from burns to over half his body. He had always been a painfully truthful storyteller so had no option but to discuss the incident in his set once he had recovered. In his show *Live on Sunset Strip* he talked candidly and comically about the incident: 'You all did some nasty-ass jokes on my ass too.' Pryor strikes a match and waves it about. 'What's that? Richard Pryor running down the street . . . I say, God, thank you for not burning my dick.' At least he could see the bright side to his near-death experience.

As for Robin Williams, his act was so manic when he wasn't stoned I dread to think what it would have been like if he had just snorted cocaine. He was part of the hell-raising Hollywood scene but survived to tell the tale and, like Pryor, got some great material out of it. In *Live at the Met* in 1986 he recalled those crazy days on 'the devil's drug' – 'anything that makes me paranoid and impotent – give me more of that . . . It's not free, it costs you your house. It should be called home-basing.'

For Williams, who was always 'on', cocaine returned him to a sense of normality. 'Cocaine for me,' Williams told *People* magazine in 1988, 'was a place to hide. Most people get hyper on coke. It slowed me down. Sometimes it made me paranoid and impotent, but mostly it just made me withdrawn. And I was so crazy back then – working all day, partying most of the night – I needed an excuse not to talk. I needed quiet times and I used coke to get them.' John Belushi's death and the birth of his son Zachary in 1983 were wake-up calls that told Williams to slow down and stop partying so hard. He quit, going cold turkey by just saying no. In 2006 he checked himself into a rehabilitation clinic in Newberg, Oregon to sort out his drinking issues, but those mad, bad days now seem a very long time ago.

The American comedy circuit has thrown up some scandal in its time, but who would have thought that the greatest cartoon show of all time, *The Simpsons*, would be touched by the dark side of comedy? Yet it had to change due to one of the most bizarre comedy-related tragedies of the last two decades. Phil Hartman, born on 24 September 1948, was a Canada-born actor who made it big in America, getting his first big break with Paul Reubens' Pee-Wee Herman character. He regularly appeared on Reubens' show *Pee-wee's Playhouse* and co-wrote the movie *Pee-wee's Big Adventure*, appearing as salty sea dog Captain Carl. Eventually Hartman would end up on *The Simpsons* before his life was cut cruelly short.

Hartman grew up in a big family and in interviews suggested that he got the performing bug because it was a way of getting his parents' attention. By his twenties he was making people laugh on a full-time basis. As a live performer Hartman was member of the Los Angeles-based improvisational sketch group the Groundlings, where he worked with Reubens. Other Groundlings alumni include Will Ferrell, Lisa Kudrow and Jennifer Coolidge. Hartman graduated from there to television, working on *Saturday Night Live* in the early 1980s. In eight seasons he did over seventy voices, becoming famous for his Bill Clinton impression.

Hartman was, by all accounts, a very easy-going guy, never big on ego or nerves in a world of big ego and nerves. He also had a way of calming those around him. Co-performer Adam Sandler dubbed him 'the glue' because he held *Saturday Night Live* together. He was a consummate team player, which was just what the show needed to complement its stars. For a while it looked as if Hartman might be the next big breakout star of *SNL* – he was due to front his own variety show – but then in 1995 he went to NBC sitcom *NewsRadio* as radio news anchor Bill McNeal.

But Hartman actually became more famous for his voice. He voiced various *Simpsons* characters including Lionel Hutz and, most famously, Troy McClure, the down-on-his-luck movie star best known for his catchphrase 'Hi, I'm Troy McClure. You may remember me from . . .' who married Marge's older sister Selma to keep rumours of a sexual scandal at bay.

He originally did *The Simpsons* as a one-off but liked the experience and the writers enjoyed writing for him so became more regular. He enjoyed doing Troy McClure so much he did him off camera to keep the audience entertained when *NewsRadio* was being filmed: 'It's the one thing that I do in my life that's almost a vocation. I do it for the pure love of it,' he told the *Houston Chronicle*. Voiceover work also left him time to pursue other projects. He appeared in movies such as *Sgt. Bilko* with Steve Martin and on TV in *Seinfeld* and *3rd Rock from the Sun*. He described the characters he played as 'the jerky guy' or 'the weasel parade', seedy or nasty, villainous characters that contrasted sharply with his own personality. Hartman looked like he had the perfect life. Success, wealth and no hassle being recognised in Walmart.

Real life, however, has a nasty habit of being more complex. Hartman married his third wife, Brynn Omdahl in 1987. On the evening on 27 May 1998 Brynn returned home after an Italian meal with a colleague at the Buca di Beppo restaurant on Ventura Boulevard, and there was a heated argument. One of the tensions in their relationship was that his career was going better than hers. Hartman had tried to be reasonable and had even talked about giving up comedy to support Brynn. He went to bed and at 3 a.m. his wife entered the room where he was asleep in his purple T-shirt and boxer shorts with cartoon dachshunds purchased from Gap and shot him twice in the head and once in the side with a

.38 calibre handgun. Their two children were asleep elsewhere in the house.

After going to a friend's house over the road and confessing, Hartman's wife returned to the house. By the time the police arrived, Brynn had locked herself in the bathroom and committed suicide by shooting herself in the head.

Hartman's body was cremated and his ashes scattered over Santa Catalina Island's Emerald Bay. Tributes flooded in from the comedy world. *Simpsons* creator Matt Groening called Hartman a master. Recording of *The Simpsons* was cancelled on the night of his death, as was a performance by the Groundlings. *NewsRadio* paid tribute by saying that his character had died of sudden heart attack and filmed an episode which involved the other characters reminiscing about him. As for the future of Troy McLure, it was decided that Hartman was irreplaceable and he no longer appears. It is one of those horrible ironies that for Hartman's first-ever film role, in 1980's *The Gong Show Movie*, he was billed as 'Man at airport with gun'.

The comedy world was understandably shocked. As the community tried to make sense of the event, it was suggested that Brynn had suffered from the side effects of a certain antidepressant. Her executor, brother Gregory Omdahl, filed a wrongful death law suit and the manufacturer settled the case out of court.

Pee-wee Herman's creator Paul Reubens has had problems of his own. In 1991 he was arrested after allegedly exposing himself in an adult cinema in Sarasota, Florida. His career as a children's entertainer seemed in jeopardy. He entered a plea of no contest to the charge of indecent exposure to keep the publicity down while maintaining his innocence.

He was sentenced to community service and afterwards chose to keep a low profile for a while. It was joked that he did not have a manager any more; Pee-wee was handling himself. He has however made a come-back in recent years. There was a Broadway show, and there is even talk of an adult Pee-wee movie.

Sometimes life has a way of kicking you in the face. Not once, but a few times. Sam Kinison was born in Yakima, Washington on 8 December 1953. He came from a family of Pentecostal preachers and that was what he started to do too. He married young and for a short period had his own church in Chicago. However, when the marriage ended he became a stand-up comedian and drew on the same fire and brimstone, hell and damnation capital-letter delivery to make his name as one of the angriest, most passionate performers in the USA. With, undoubtedly, one of the darkest streaks imaginable.

Even as a comedian, religion was constantly on his mind. It was as if he was exorcising himself every night as he paced around the stage, sweating buckets in his trademark overcoat.

It all goes back to Jesus . . . He's got to be up in heaven freaking out at all the interpretations of the things they SAY he said. He didn't even KNOW he was the son of God. As soon as he was born, as soon as he could speak the language, his mother said, 'You're the son of God. When you were born the angels came, and the stars stood in one place, the wise men brought gifts, and the whole world's been waiting for you to come and do great things.' [as baby Jesus] 'Really? Me? Are you sure?' [back to normal voice] Everybody but Joseph. Joseph's walking around going, [very suspicious] 'Yeah, you had better be the son of God, I'll tell you that. You had BETTER be him, little mister. And you better be the ONLY son of God.'

Kinison was no matinee idol. Short, with thinning long hair in his twenties, the handsome department was out of stock when he got there. His material was often about how hard his life was and particularly how badly women treated him. Every time he thought he had found the right one, he explained, she turned out to be just as bad as all the others. 'People go, "Aren't you worried about hell?" No. No, because I WAS MARRIED FOR TWO FUCKIN' YEARS. HELL WOULD BE LIKE CLUB MED. HELL WOULD BE LIKE A FUCKIN' RESORT!!'

Kinison usually delivered his pay-offs directly into the face of a member of his flock, sorry, audience. When I think back to his performances I don't think of any of his dark-hued gags, I think of one long continuous hoarse howl of anguish. It was like Edvard Munch made comedy flesh. When he got his big break on *Late Night with David Letterman*, the host warned his audience, 'Brace yourselves.' He toned his act down for television and cut out the swearing, but still occasionally got censored. On the *Tonight Show* he took a leaf out of Andy Kaufman's book and seemed to be doing a straight version of Elvis Presley's 'Are You Lonesome Tonight?' but when he reached the monologue in the middle he reverted to the familiar Kinison rant. But the gospel according to Sam Kinison was never misogynistic. The trouble was that lines such as 'I don't condone wife-beating. I understand it' were open to misinterpretation. But Kinison's anger came from the heart.

Disillusioned with the Church, he upset believers by calling Jesus the only saviour who could use his own hand as a whistle. He seemed to have an axe to grind but Kinison did not hide his past – the licence plate on his car was EX REV. His short-tempered style attracted rock fans, particularly followers of heavy-metal bands, as did his appetite for drugs and alcohol. He indulged in 'various vices', as if making up for lost time. As he told DJ Howard Stern, 'I have lived a carnal life. My view of life is "If you're going to miss heaven, why miss it by two inches? Miss it!" I don't have to go through the thing of paying for it in the next life. I know I'm screwed in the next life.' Billy Idol and Steve Tyler from Aerosmith were among the stars who appeared in the video for his novelty single, a cover of the Troggs' 'Wild Thing', while Kinison repaid the compliment, appearing in the video for Bon Jovi's single, 'Bad Medicine'. Meanwhile, he started to move into the mainstream, even having a cameo as an unlikely guardian angel in an episode of the sitcom *Married With Children*.

As the 1990s dawned, Kinison's career was doing well but he was still a long way from a regular prime-time vehicle. Like Bill Hicks, whom he influenced in terms of both style and content, he was very much an outsider looking in. And he got into trouble when his audience of young adolescent men took his outrageous remarks about Aids and women at face value. He did not want to alienate his original fans, but he was changing. His private life finally seemed to be sorting itself out. He gave up cocaine after he thought he was having a heart attack and while he was no saint he no longer lived the full-frontal rock-and-roll lifestyle. He talked about going to Alcoholics Anonymous in Malibu: 'It was like going to church, except Ozzy Osbourne was there.' Even if there were a few lapses – 'Folks, I've been straight for seventeen days . . . not all in a row.'

– he was on the right track. And after two divorces, on 5 April 1992 he married his girlfriend, Malika Souiri. He had once joked, 'If I get married again, I want a guy there with a drum to do rimshots during the vows.' But this time it seemed serious. Kinison was cleaning up his act.

Five days after the wedding ceremony, Kinison was dead. Driving his white Pontiac Trans Am on Route 95, he was hit by a pickup truck driven by a seventeen-year-old who had been drinking. He was buried in Tulsa, Oklahoma with a simple epitaph on his stone: 'In another time and place he would have been called prophet.' But he had already written his own haunting epitaph with a joke about drunk drivers: 'Child killer? Attempted manslaughter? We don't want to drink and drive, but there's no other way to get home.'

9

No Alternative – You Can't See the Join

From Rik Mayall to Frank Skinner

When the Sex Pistols caused a seismic rumpus in the autumn of 1976 the ripples affected everything in Britain from trousers to hair to television. It took a while for it to change comedy but, sure enough, in May 1979, neatly coinciding with the arrival of Margaret Thatcher as prime minister, the Comedy Store opened in Soho. A new generation of comedians was about to sweep away the old guard. How much things would truly change is another question entirely.

It might have been a happy coincidence as well as something in the water, but the ethos of alternative comedy seemed to echo the ethos of punk rock. It was all about sticking two fingers up at the Establishment and doing it yourself. Not following the style of the old wave, just doing it your way. On the other hand, the creators of the Comedy Store, Don Ward and Peter Rosengard, were distinctly old school. Insurance salesman Rosengard had been inspired by a visit to a comedy club in Los Angeles, while Ward had been a comedian since the early days of Cliff Richard and had latterly been running a strip club. And as for the early stand-up acts, few of them were doing it for political reasons; many were ex-drama students who went into comedy just to get that precious Equity card which meant they could get respectable acting work.

The first generation of alternative comedians was, however, genuinely exciting. Rik Mayall and Adrian Edmondson might not have hidden their Manchester University drama degrees very efficiently, but alongside their fondness for Samuel Beckett they had a wonderfully anarchic streak and a love of slapstick that had its roots in Chaplin and Keaton. Alexei Sayle offered a more right-on neo-Marxist-surrealist version of cabaret. Keith Allen was a force of nature, doing whatever came into his head with little regard for the consequences. While working backstage during a Max Bygraves show he got so fed up with Bygraves he joined the line of dancing girls completely naked. Allen was told he would never work in the theatre again, but as with Val Parnell and Max Miller it had little effect. Allen would graduate from comedy to straight acting, finding time along the way to produce various children, including chip off the old bolshie block, Lily.

Gradually the comedy new wave was discovered and embraced by the mainstream. In 1982 on its opening night Channel Four aired *The Comic Strip Presents . . . Five Go Mad in Dorset*, in which Mayall, Edmondson and co. parodied spiffing old Enid Blyton japes. In the same year on BBC2 *The Young Ones* made its debut. The student house-share sitcom mucked around with narrative, featured bands such as Madness and Motörhead and had at its core some wonderfully hyperkinetic perfor-mances from Mayall and Edmondson as Rik and Vyvyan, plus Planer as hippy Nigel and Christopher Ryan as wide-boy Mike. Success seemed pretty straightforward. And a new comedy establishment was born. One that could behave just as badly as the old comedy establishment.

The story that really laid bare the potential for excess of modern comedy featured the unlikely figure of Angus Deayton, the one-time straight man for Rowan Atkinson, who became a huge star in his own right as the host of *Have I Got News For You*. Deayton hit the headlines in May 2002. After twelve years as host of *Have I Got News For You*, where he was said to be paid £50,000 per episode, a story appeared in the *News of the World* that he had spent time with a prostitute and had snorted cocaine through rolled-up twenty-pound notes at the Park Lane Hilton. This would be embarrassing for anyone, but Deayton was being paid a lavish wage funded by TV licence-payers and was the anchor on a show that skewered others who behaved like this. He should have been above reproach, like Caesar's wife. Instead, stories suggested he was behaving like Caligula.

At first it looked like Deayton would be able to weather the storm. The first show recorded after the story broke got great ratings and he tried to shrug it all off with a little light self-deprecation: 'Good evening and welcome to *Have I Got News For You*, and this week's loser is presenting it.' But panellists Ian Hislop and Paul Merton mercilessly mocked him. Hislop held up a copy of a red top and read a quote from the woman who had kissed and told: '"He made me groan all night" – what were you doing, reading the autocue?' Merton then trumped him by pulling open his grey tracksuit top to reveal a T-shirt emblazoned with the front page of the *News of the World* featuring Deayton's face and the headline TV DEAYTON'S DRUGS ROMP WITH VICE GIRL. 'The words, pot, kettle, smug, git, good and kicking all come to mind,' said Merton.

Yet Deayton continued to front the show and was back in the autumn. But then in October the tabloids ran another story about a previous incident of alleged bad behaviour, which was old but arguably even more damaging. The joke wasn't really funny any more. The BBC now said that his position had become 'untenable', and he was asked to resign. A few years later, on his chat show, Michael Parkinson asked Paul Merton if he had stabbed Angus in the back. Merton replied, 'No, I stabbed him in the front.' It looked as if Deayton's career might be over, but after a period in broadcasting purdah he has been able to return to the screens on a regular basis. The real problem was not his behaviour, but the show he hosted. Other less scandal-fixated satirical shows were not a problem. In fact his colourful past probably helped him to land the job of hosting the irreverent British Comedy Awards when regular host Jonathan Ross dropped out because of his part in the Sachsgate controversy.

The funny thing is that personally I blame a colleague at *Time Out* magazine back then for inadvertently contributing to Deayton's troubles. Fellow critic Tina Ogle had dubbed Deayton 'TV's Mr Sex' in the magazine, and the nickname had caught on. Deayton seemed an unlikely sex symbol – which made the stories even more sensational and newsworthy. This was not another Premier League footballer playing away; this was an outwardly buttoned-up comedian who underneath was a seething mass of sexual energy.

In the 1980s and 1990s the worlds of old and new comedy came together. The lines were being blurred. Political correctness did not seem quite so important any more. It would eventually get to the stage where jokes about women, rape and the disabled could be told as long as they came complete with ironic quote marks. The goal posts seemed to be moving, or rather the old ones were being quietly re-erected. And back came the same type of bad behaviour. But is it any wonder that the comedians ended up reverting to type? The new breed of comedians might have written their material themselves and had a left-wing-ish stance, compared to the old wave, who used writers and often admired Margaret Thatcher, but underneath they were just as riddled with insecurity, just as prone to anxiety, depression and addictions. The aforementioned Merton, a devoted fan of Tony Hancock, spent time in the Maudsley Psychiatric Hospital in south London. Jack Dee has admitted to having problems with alcohol and going to Alcoholics Anonymous before he ever had a serious attempt at comedy. Before he was a stand-up he managed a restaurant in Covent Garden, and when he put the takings in the safe at the end of the night he would sometimes be so drunk the only way he could remember he had done so was to headbutt the safe as he locked it. That way if he saw a fresh bruise he knew the money was secure. The misdemeanours of the modern funny man were positively legion.

Comedians really did seem to be behaving like rock stars, which was somehow inevitable. There had long been a connection between comedy and rock and roll. Michael McIntyre's father Ray Cameron opened for the Rolling Stones back in 1965. Deadpan monologuist Norman Lovett supported The Clash. Keith Allen supported Dexys Midnight Runners. Tommy Cooper had that ominous fez-shaking gig warming up for The Police. Music hall legend Max Wall opened for Ian Dury and recalled that he 'died like a louse in a Russian beard'. And of course there were all those bands who had bootleg tapes of Derek and Clive on their tour bus long before it was legitimately released. But comedians had always played second fiddle to musicians. That was about to change in the 1990s.

It was Janet Street-Porter who came up with the notion that comedy was the new rock and roll in 1993. David Baddiel and Robert Newman had been trundling along nicely. They had a few BBC programmes under their belts and a few catchphrases that teenagers could lob at each other on the bus to school. Then somehow, thanks to comedy timing if you like, thanks to good management, thanks to an uncanny impression of The Cure, they were superstars.

Their most famous catchphrase, 'That's you, that is,' originated in a sketch in which two fusty rival history professors become increasingly puerile and abusive. The duo's own moment of history came on 10 December 1993 when they became the first stand-up comedians to appear at Wembley Arena.[59] These days any comedian of note takes it for granted that they can fill Wembley. On the night that Baddiel and Newman played there was a rumour, perhaps started by envious promoters, that although they sold all the available tickets the capacity was smaller than usual. And even if it was full to the brim, one night at the 12,500-capacity Wembley Arena is a dribble in the Pacific compared to the runs the likes of Peter Kay, Lee Evans and Michael McIntyre have had at the 14,000-capacity O2 Arena in London's Docklands. Peter Kay did so many nights at the O2 in 2010 and 2011 he should have been paying his Council Tax there.

But the link between comedy and rock and roll had been forged, both onstage and off. These two highly intelligent Cambridge graduates fell for the trappings of the superstar lifestyle, from dry ice to groupies. 'Whilst obviously rock star will always be the top job for bedpost

---

59 If we are going to be pedantic, the first comedian to appear at Wembley Arena was Sean Lock, who was the support act on the night. I seem to recall two things about that night apart from Baddiel and Newman. The *Daily Telegraph's* theatre critic got rather tetchy because the gig did not start bang on the scheduled time and Sean Lock wore a rather fetching safari-style ensemble.

notching, comedian isn't far behind,' wrote Baddiel in *The Times* in 2005. By the end, however, they had fallen prey to that other double act cliché, of barely speaking to each other when not working together. They were travelling separately, using separate dressing rooms and not really having any extended contact apart from the show.

Soon after Wembley the duo stopped working together. Newman went off to write dense novels with labyrinthine plots and long words and become political. Baddiel went off and also wrote thoughtful novels, but retained his street credibility by working with Frank Skinner. Together the latter twosome became unexpected figureheads of the new lad movement, recording 'Three Lions', England's Euro 96 anthem.

Baddiel is an intriguing figure, cannily marrying high and low culture, happy to talk about his interest in pornography and also in *Anna Karenina*. He has an enviable confidence in whatever he does. Particularly fascinating in that somehow this trailblazer for a new kind of pop culturally aware comedy hooked up with Frank Skinner, a brilliant comedian but one utterly rooted in the traditional. If Baddiel and Newman were the Odd Couple, something of a marriage of convenience rather than thrown together by true love, Baddiel and Skinner were an even odder couple, the north London public-school-educated Jew and the West Midlands Catholic, united by a shared interest in comedy and smutty videos. It seemed to work though. Skinner moved into Baddiel's flat when his relationship broke up and he was still there years later.

Yet both Skinner and Baddiel have something else in common: an almost pathological urge to be honest onstage. Exposure is often where they find the best gags. Baddiel has talked candidly about his encounters with groupies, and once when the duo were doing their unscripted show *Baddiel and Skinner Unplanned* a man in the audience mentioned that he knew a lady footballer who had once had a one-night stand with Skinner. Skinner recalled the night – he has a fabulous gift for remembering details – because after sex they had had an illuminating discussion about footballing tactics and the changing nature of the game. When Skinner was then told that she had become a lesbian he said he wasn't surprised. Partly because, he mock-boasted, she probably thought no man could top his performance, and partly because afterwards when they had the traditional post-shag smoke, he lit a cigarette and she pulled out a pipe.

Skinner has talked extensively about himself in not one but two bestselling autobiographies. He describes himself as 'a nondescript bloke from a working class family in West Bromwich who got lucky'.[60] Skinner – born Christopher Collins on 28 January 1957 – is a rare thing: the funny bloke in the pub who actually turns out to be funny onstage too. He is one of the most naturally gifted stand-up comedians of recent years (Denby Dale's Daniel Kitson is better but prefers to keep under the television radar), with a laser-guided rapid-fire wit and a quip for every occasion. But it was not until he hit thirty that he had a crack at it professionally, after a woman asked him what was it like to be that age and on the scrapheap. Within a decade the man who grew up in a small house in Oldbury with an outside toilet would be having sex in the toilets after a tribute gig to Peter Cook and then end up singing 'It's All Over Now' with Ronnie Wood and Bill Wyman.

He had come a long way. As he wrote in his autobiography as a

---

60 Frank Skinner, *Frank Skinner*, Arrow, p.215.

teenager Skinner lost his virginity to a black-haired prostitute who 'looked like Cher's six-month-old corpse' in the Balsall Heath area of Birmingham for the princely sum of a fiver. Though Cher probably doesn't have 'Corky' tattooed on her thigh. She was wearing so much denim, Skinner recalled, he was worried it would feel like having sex with a member of Status Quo.[61]

Skinner's twenties rattled by in a haze of no-future jobs, further education and heavy drinking. One night, for example, he stayed over at a friend's house and wet the bed. When he got up he went straight to the kitchen, pulled a bottle of ouzo out of the fridge and settled himself by taking a swig. Then he tried to convince his friend's wife that he had been so hot that the damp patch was sweat. During the punk era he caught as many bands as possible, but if they came on late he was often too drunk to appreciate them. He slept through Generation X twice at Barbarella's in 1977. After the first show he woke up at 8 a.m. on the grass next to a major roundabout.

It was not all punk rock though. Kenny Ball and his Jazzmen appeared at the local pub one Sunday lunchtime and Skinner stole the limelight by dancing in front of them with his pants down. Kenny Ball was not necessarily the turning point, but Skinner knew he had to address the drinking. He was boozing so much he once got drunk just so that he could join the library. It got to the stage where he could not function without a drink, whatever the time of day, whatever the occasion. Fortunately fate lent a hand. On 24 September 1986 he stopped drinking completely. He was suffering from flu and simply didn't start again. He

---

61 Ibid., p.215.

clearly has an iron resolve, particularly given that he compares giving up alcohol to giving up breathing. As he reflected on his BBC2 series *Opinionated* in 2010, at least he can now remember what he did last night: 'Nothing!'

Around the same time as he gave up alcohol Skinner tried his hand at stand-up comedy. He had been reading about Lenny Bruce and, inspired by Bruce's quest for truth, Skinner went for the same policy, talking about his life and what was on his mind. Around this time he also reconnected with his Catholic faith. There was clearly a change brewing. Slowly but surely, Skinner's career took off. The gigs were exhilarating and the perks were good too. One night he was out in Moseley when an unusually attractive woman approached him and said that she had seen him perform at his regular residency at the Ivy Bush and thought he was brilliant. They promptly spent the night together. That had never happened when he was working in a factory. A few years later he got laid in the changing rooms at Bloomingdales in New York. That hadn't happened in his factory days either.

Skinner has never seemed like someone crippled by anxieties, but he had two main worries when he gigged back then: 'Will I get a laugh and will I get a shag afterwards?' Yet even today Skinner suggests that there is more to the Black Country lad than meets the eye. He has always struck me as one of the easiest people to talk to, someone who loves to get stuck into a conversation, and yet he calls himself a 'weirdo loner'. He is obsessive about crafting his live sets and studiously avoids reading his reviews. If someone else mentions seeing a review he is paralysed by curiosity – did they notice it because it was particularly negative or because it was particularly positive? Even comedians like Skinner who seem to have the lightest of touches can be riddled with insecurity over their performances.

He may have started late but he quickly made up for lost time. A visit to the Edinburgh Fringe Festival, where like a David Attenborough of laughs he experienced other comedians in their natural habitat, inspired him. He spent all of his savings booking a venue there for the following year, which meant developing his act. Compèring shows and doing new material every week sharpened his wits, and in 1991 he won Edinburgh's prestigious Perrier Award. After the party had died down – and he had given away his bottle of champagne to a member of the audience who had been heckling him all night – he went up Arthur's Seat, the 700-foot-high slab of volcanic rock just outside the city, and had wild outdoor celebratory sex.

As a successful comedian, Skinner's opportunities for sex increased exponentially. As he was the first to admit in the first instalment of his autobiography, 'Sometimes I find myself on tour when I'm single. In these circumstances I feel duty bound to, how can I put this, fuck anything that moves.'[62] For Skinner one of the attractive by-products of celebrity was winning the 'casual-sex lottery'. One woman in black PVC was covered with piercings. 'I'm often attracted towards older men,' she said. 'Yeah, and magnets,' replied Skinner.[63]

It's funny how the more comedy changes, the more it stays the same. When Skinner won the Perrier Award some critics castigated him for being a throwback to the pre-alternative age. The *Guardian* suggested he was 'the nearest thing to Bernard Manning to win the

---

62 Ibid., p.351.
63 Ibid., p.352.

Perrier'. There has always been something of the old school about our Frank, and when he decided to go back on the road in 2007 he wanted to put some music into his shows. Searching for inspiration, he wondered what George Formby would be singing about if he was gigging in the noughties. Formby used to do cheeky satirical songs about Hitler, calling him a windbag, who would he be skewering if he was around today? Skinner bought a ukulele, learned to play it and did his best George Formby impression[64] as he sang songs about the latest threat to global peace, Osama Bin Laden.

Skinner's comeback tour was a resounding success, but one which marked a change in his life. He was over fifty, and the things that had pre-occupied him as a young man no longer dominated his waking hours. He was still fairly fixated on sex – making gags about the niche market for granny porn, and how getting your shirt tangled in a woman's rear during doggy-style sex was like getting a piece of A4 in a printer jam – but as I write Skinner is in a settled relationship. The groupies and casual sex are a thing of the past. Likewise with David Baddiel, he might talk with a hint of wistful nostalgia about his old life on the road, but it is firmly in the past now. He would rather write novels that get compared to Saul Bellow and his beloved John Updike. Baddiel is still very funny and clearly still wants to be judged as funny, but he also wants more. For some a laugh is everything. For others there comes a point when it is not enough. Robert Newman reached that point quite a few years ago. He still surfaces on the stand-up circuit,

---

64 In 2010 Harry Hill had less luck when he wanted to pay tribute to George Formby by releasing a Smiths medley in Formby style. Johnny Marr of the Smiths, who usually has a very easy-going sense of humour reportedly, declined to give Hill permission.

but these days has the air of a troubadour and the agenda of a political campaigner. He can still find room for a gag, but the days when Newman could be frivolous about despotic world leaders seem to be behind him: 'I sent a letter to General Pinochet and he wrote back. And we've become pen pals.'

Baddiel and Newman and Skinner, however, were just the overture. If comedy was about to turn into the new rock and roll, they were just the John the Baptists. The real messiah was a few years away. While David and Rob were warming up for Wembley, and Frank was gearing up for Edinburgh, Russell Brand was still bracing himself for a metaphorical rap on the knuckles from his teachers in Essex. The future comedy conquerer, who would eventually take stand-up to an entirely new level and in the process change the way British comedy is perceived at home and around the world, had been naughty again . . .

10

Rock and Roll

Russell Brand – the laughing cavalier

The school report. Sometimes it can say so much about a person's future without even realising it. On 26 April 1990 Russell Brand's PE teacher Mr Rider spoke volumes when he passed judgment on the teenage tearaway in class 4KY – as in the petroleum jelly – at Grays School in Essex: 'Sometimes he gives the impression that rules do not apply to him.' The future superstar was only fourteen at the time, but a pattern had been established for the transgressive, boundary-demolishing behaviour that would land Brand in rehab, in fights and in headlines, but also create a truly unique performer. Russell would rather stand out than fit in.

As Brand once said himself, 'Without fame my whole persona doesn't make sense. Without fame my haircut just looks like mental illness.'[65] Yet this latter-day libertine (by his own admission) was acting outrageously long before the press hung on his every Wildean witticism and

---

65 Russell Brand, *Booky Wook 2 – This Time It's Personal*, HarperCollins, 2010, p.130.

the paparazzi hung on his every appearance on the red carpet. His blend of rock-and-roll flash, linguistic flourish and refusal to self-edit makes him unique. Arthur Askey probably had it about right when he said, 'Every generation's the same, a load of crap and a few brilliant people.' Comedy may not see Russell Brand's like again for some time.

The root of Brand's exceptionally bad behaviour may lurk in his family background. His biological parents Barbara and Ron argued and separated when he was six months old. In those early years Ron had less contact with Russell than Barbara. There is something of a pattern here. Ron's father died when he was seven so he was short of a role model too. When young Russell did spend time at his father's home in Brentwood Ron would often neglect him. He 'diddled birds' next door or simply read the papers. Meanwhile his mother doted on Russell and he learned to enjoy the company of women through her, which is not to say his father was not an influence too. He rather liked the idea of being like his dad and diddling birds.

In fact by the time Brand reached Mr Rider's class there were two things that preoccupied him: comedy and women. Staying with his dad he would watch his father's collection of pornographic video cassettes, but he also started to consume comedy voraciously – *Blackadder*, *Fawlty Towers*, even shows from way before he was born such as the work of Peter Cook, Dudley Moore and Tony Hancock. He was an enormous fan of Cook, who, he later said, achieved everything he wanted by his early twenties and then became bored with life but remains 'a beautiful debonair genius'[66]. He read about the troubled soul of Tony Hancock

---

66 Ibid., p.216.

and sensed a kindred spirit. Like Hancock, the wannabe Left Bank intellectual in his bedsit in East Cheam, Brand felt out of place in Essex. Grays by name, grey by nature.

His mother had a hysterectomy when he was around six after being diagnosed with uterine cancer. It was a traumatic period, Brand's very own Rosebud moment. A new stepfather, Colin, arrived on the scene, and Brand moved to a new school. The cancer returned in various forms but each time his mother defeated it. This was the sort of potentially cataclysmic event that would cast a shadow over anyone's embryonic psychological make-up. It was no surprise that he was depressed. At thirteen Brand was self-harming, at fourteen he was bulimic, at fifteen he became a vegetarian, inspired to forsake meat by his beloved Morrissey. He also wanted to be noticed. Brand was an accomplished show-off, but it was only when a drama teacher suggested he audition for the school production of *Bugsy Malone* that he saw a way of harnessing this drive. From that early role as Fat Sam he was determined to get what he wanted at any cost. For Brand his mother's illness was the turning point. It was like a cosmic loss of innocence. It led to him being constantly aware of the inevitability of death and the development of a determination to live in the moment whatever the consequences. The famous Latin phrase *Carpe diem* means 'seize the day'. No one in comedy history would ever *carpe* the fuck out of the *diem* quite like Russell Brand.

Fast-forward nearly twenty years and we can see evidence of this in his audition for his Hollywood breakthrough as rock star Aldous Snow in *Forgetting Sarah Marshall*. Brand was asked to improvise a scene with his co-star where he had to persuade her to spend the afternoon horse riding rather than in their hotel room. Brand was attentive to the instructions and on his best behaviour, but once the cameras rolled he improvised a familiar riff that was as much about his fundamental philosophy as about the part he wanted to be cast in: 'When you look back at your life you're not going to go "Curse the day I went horse-riding with that glamorous young man" are you? It'll be a good experience – you are not going to regret it.' Brand's entire life has been one long seized day. Doing what grabs you in the moment. And it seems to have worked for him. By the way, he got the part.

Brand's transgressive tendencies were given free rein in his teens. He knew what he wanted to do and once he had made his mind up just went ahead and did it. He left school at sixteen and soon left home too, going to the Italia Conti stage school. But he left there within a year due to his persistent bad behaviour and emerging appetite for drugs. He was growing up fast. His father took him to Bangkok when he was seventeen and after some tentative fumblings Russell got the hang of sex. Back in London his bedroom antics were soon getting him into all sorts of trouble. One night he got drunk and went back with a woman but after a trip to the toilets lost his way and woke up in the morning in a bed full of refugee children and their grandmother.[67]

After Italia Conti he landed a place at the prestigious Drama Centre in Chalk Farm, just north of the bustle of Camden Town. He was an impressive student when he focused on the work, but his behaviour still left something to be desired. During one evening when the third years performed a revue for the newcomers at the Enterprise pub, he overdid the vodka, smashed a glass on his head, cut himself and passed out. A

---

67 Russell Brand, *My Booky Wook*, Hodder, 2008, p.174.

kind friend took him back to their flat where he tried to have sex with a woman who also lived there and ended up urinating on the sofa.

Drama school appealed to his eccentric sensibilities and gave him licence to explore himself – for a month he had a white mouse called Elvis living in his hair – but his increasingly erratic behaviour was too disruptive and he ended up being thrown out during a production of *Volpone* for shoplifting. It was now that he decided to concentrate on stand-up comedy rather than acting, and once he hit upon the idea he realised it was perfect for him. To be a great comedian you need to have an eye for the absurd and you always need to be watching the world. Brand, always the voyeur, felt uniquely qualified: 'I'm always observing, always outside.'[68]

His comedy career started hesitantly – short gigs in tiny pubs to tiny audiences, then slightly longer sets. For a while he worked in a double act with Karl Theobald, a friend from drama school who later went on to become a successful comic actor in his own right. During this time I received a handwritten letter from Theobald and Brand asking for my support. A few years later I met Brand and said I could not remember if it was him or Karl who wrote the letter. Without hesitation Brand said it was him. He was the pushy half of the partnership, trying to get journalists to see them, prepared, as in most situations, to go that bit further.

In early 2000 Brand had the first hint of success but, as he was destined to do on numerous occasions in the future, was quick to press the self-destruct button. He reached the final of the Hackney Empire New Act of the Year competition and it looked like things were taking off. Previous finalists included David Baddiel, Eddie Izzard, Harry Hill

---

68 Ibid., p.210.

and Harry Enfield. Agents and promoters would come to the show in search of new talent, and just putting in a promising performance could kick-start a career. On the night, however, Brand was more preoccupied with his on-off Spanish lover Amanda. They had a blazing row and then, much to compère Arthur Smith's chagrin, got drunk and made love in his dressing room while he was introducing the acts onstage. Brand failed to win, but Karen Koren, promoter of the Gilded Balloon in Edinburgh, saw something there and booked him to do a show at her venue in the summer. As ever his charm and unerring ability to win people over cancelled out his erratic talent for drug-enhanced career immolation.

Brand and Edinburgh were made for each other: the perfect Bacchanalia for the latter-day Dionysian, the anarchic festival and the anarchic comedian. And of course he excelled himself. With days and nights to fill between shows he turned the arts festival into a veritable shagathon, while employing children that he encountered in the street to do his flyering[69] for him like a gang of Dickensian ragamuffins. Unfortunately even the Gilded Balloon, which liked to indulge new talent, drew the line at using unpaid underage child labour, and Brand was told to get rid of them. There was also the problem of them removing equipment from the Gilded Balloon offices, something that Brand had not put in their job description. And not just the odd pencil. It was a first for the Edinburgh Fringe, which thought it had seen everything, but maybe not such a first for comedy. Joseph Grimaldi's father Giuseppe, had been around when impoverished circus children were stealing lead off church roofs.

---

69 The noble art of handing out flyers advertising forthcoming gigs.

On the plus side, however, one review said Brand had "'star of the future" tattooed beneath his Calvin Kleins'. His success in Edinburgh gave him his first big television break, landing a job on MTV presenting *Dancefloor Chart*. This was synergy made flesh. It was also handy that MTV's studios were in Camden Town, where he could easily score a ten pound bag of heroin from one of the many dealers that plied their trade on the streets nearby. The job involved presenting music from assorted nightclubs, which also meant that he could avail himself of the women in the clubs. He enjoyed the narcotics and the sex and unsurprisingly took to the job like the star of the future he clearly felt he was. He would put prostitutes and lap dancers on his long-suffering publicist's gold credit card and he used the MTV account with a courier firm to have everything delivered to his flat, from his mum to lap dancers to drugs.

Sigmund Freud suggested that men go onstage to win the love of beautiful women. If they had the confidence and looks to ensnare one without going to all that trouble of performing they certainly would. This certainly explains the high proportion of troglodytes, goblins and gargoyles on the comedy circuit. Brand was the exception – drop-dead handsome and sexy. Combine that with a devil-may-care sense of humour and you've got a pretty indestructible babe magnet. Stardom won Brand added attention from women, but it didn't stop him from getting into trouble. One sexual indiscretion led to him finding himself stuck outside his front door without a key. Or any clothes. Luckily his flat was above a bar, so he went in and managed to get a locksmith to visit and a pair of ill-fitting chef's trousers. Maybe he should have put a lock on Brand's trousers.

Even at his most wayward, Brand had a way of winning people over. Having got drunk in the business-class lounge before boarding an aeroplane, he was asked to leave an Iberian Airlines flight because he had his feet up on the seat in front. After trying to get the economy-class passengers to support him against the system, he eventually got off – sobering up enough to remember he had some heroin in his anus and not wanting to cause so much trouble it would prompt a full-body search. Yet despite all this, the security woman booked him a hotel for the night and gave him a hug before sending him on his way.

At this stage in his life success had not prompted Brand to forsake his pursuit of the extraordinary. If anything it was making him spiral further out of control, giving him licence to misbehave and create his own world. Reality finally intruded on 12 September 2001. The day after the Twin Towers tragedy Brand pitched up for work to host the pop show *Select* with his drug dealer Gritty and Gritty's eight-year-old son Edwin in tow and after smoking some crack in the disabled toilets he decided to introduce Gritty to the special guest that day, Kylie Minogue. Sorry, did I mention that Brand had decided to come into work dressed in a camouflage combat jacket, a false beard and a tea towel attached to his head by a shoelace, doing a passable impersonation of Osama bin Laden? He was sacked a couple of days later.

Brand was still performing as a stand-up comedian. As a fan of situationism – a post-Marxist quasi-revolutionary ideology which helped to inspire Malcolm McLaren when he managed the shock-creating, headline-making Sex Pistols – he was determined to make his gigs into real spectacles at any cost. He would walk onstage and cut up pigs' heads, release locusts or smash dead mice, rats or baby birds with a hammer and throw the bits into the audience, asking people why they were disgusted; all he had done was rearrange some atoms. The stand-up situationist wanted to make a statement and shake people out of their complacency. He usually just made a mess.

And then there was the self-harm, which is what he was up to when I first stumbled upon him at the Edinburgh Festival late at night in the summer of 2002. I'd seen Iggy Pop cutting his chest onstage during songs, but I'd never seen a comedian doing a similar thing between gags with a broken bottle. There was something disturbingly riveting about Brand's performance. It was about 2 a.m. Half the audience was repelled by his behaviour, half was compelled by it. The more the hecklers yelled at him to get off, the more blood he defiantly smeared over his body. This was a long way from Marie Lloyd doing a lewd song.

At a gig at the Astoria in London he inserted a Barbie doll into his bottom as a protest against consumerism. 'It seemed like a good idea at the time,' he told *Playboy*. It also seemed as if this was a man having a mental meltdown onstage, going way beyond the normal limits of entertainment. Never in the history of comedy had self-destructiveness and comedy rubbed shoulders like this. Not even Lenny Bruce at his most twisted had behaved in this way. Yet somehow Brand was able to harness his deep-seated need for the extreme. Anyone less talented would have become unemployable, but the television industry knew that Brand had something, they just had to find the right vehicle for it. Now defunct satellite channel UK Play had a bash with *RE:Brand*, in which they allowed him to push the documentary genre to snapping point with a series that took the word 'immersive' about as literally as one can.

Each week Brand challenged one of society's taboos. One week he lived with a homeless man, James, which entailed sharing a bath with him – truly immersive – while in another episode Brand tried to establish whether sexual orientation was innate by wanking off a man called Gary in a pub toilet. Brand persevered, ever the professional, but didn't enjoy the encounter. He later recalled in his live show that Gary had pubic hair like 'furious Shredded Wheat'. Brand decided that he was definitely heterosexual, and just to confirm it went off with a couple of lap dancers in a limousine afterwards. In other shows he befriended a member of the BNP, fought his own dad in a boxing match and lived with a prostitute in Norwich. At the London May Day anti-globalisation rally in 2002 he stripped off in front of Eros and was arrested then de-arrested by the police so went and stripped off again on top of a van, finally being charged with indecent exposure. Brand was taking the feckless attitude of beat generation writers like Jack Kerouac, the drink-fuelled spirit of Charles Bukowski and the gonzo journalism of Hunter S. Thompson and applying them to the comedy format.

Brand's heroin addiction did not stop him from getting work, it just stopped him from keeping it. By his own admission, around this period he was 'carrying on like a nutter'. It was about this time that he landed a part in *Cruise of the Gods*, a one-off BBC comedy about a sci-fi convention filmed on a real-life cruise liner travelling around the Mediterranean and starring Steve Coogan, Rob Brydon and the up-and-coming David Walliams and James Corden. Brand had a small role which was about to get a lot smaller. One night in Istanbul he left the boat, picked up a prostitute in a brothel and nearly got into a fight when he asked for a refund after the sex did not work out as planned. Then in Athens he found a lap-dancing club more to his liking and kept going back for more until he left and got into an argument with one of the bouncers. Eventually he was sent home, Brand later recalling in the first volume of his autobiography the producer saying he had never experienced anyone quite like him.

Things could not really get much worse; in fact they were about to get better. He landed a new agent and was taken under the wing of Chip Somers, founder of a treatment centre called Focus 12. While in rehab Brand was able to take stock of his career. He was watching television one night in December 2002 and saw Jimmy Carr on a programme paying tribute to Peter Cook. Brand recalled that he had started out around the same time as Carr, but while Carr was on the BBC, Brand was in rehab. It was all very well behaving like he was a Jack Nicholson-sized film icon but he hadn't reached those giddy heights yet. He needed to get some perspective and channel his urges in a positive direction. Tony Hancock's melancholic streak had led to his eventual suicide. Brand did not want to go down that path.

Focus 12 helped to sort out Brand's drug addictions, and with his new agent assuring commissioning editors of his reliability as well as his genius Brand was able to start working again. This was a transitional period, as he started to metamorphose into the Russell Brand we know today. His hair was long but straight; it had not yet spiralled out of control into his trademark goth cavalier look. He did not wear much jewellery and favoured jeans and T-shirts which emphasised his skinny frame and he was yet to grow his facial hair.

Despite being off the drugs he was still in regular pursuit of the opposite sex, maintaining a veritable harem while presenting *Big Brother* spin-off *Efourum*. He was still gigging regularly and starting to pick up favourable reviews. His shows had now become painful but comical confessionals, homing in on the funny side of his lifestyle, which at times sounded like a bad Carry On film directed by Mike Leigh. In his comedy set 'Better Now' he recalled how he had been invited to an orgy in a Hackney council block but it failed to live up to expectations. The flat was bleak and in the middle the plumber turned up – not as if in some kind of porn-film role-play scenario, but to fix the washing machine. (Comedy did its bit to imitate life when Brand made a cameo appearance in *Little Britain*'s 2006 all-star Comic Relief show at the Hammersmith Apollo, in which he played a plumber who pulled off his overalls to reveal he was wearing bra, stockings and suspenders.)

Brand needed to calm down. In 2005 – on April Fool's Day – he checked into the KeyStone clinic in Philadelphia, 'the winky-nick', to address his sex addiction. The treatment might not have turned him into a born-again virgin, but somehow he managed to get some perspective on his behaviour, learning to understand it. He was able to see why he needed to have sex after a gig. Other performers drink, others take drugs. Brand did not have those options any longer, but women were still widely available to him after every live show. His appearances on *Big Brother*'s reality TV spin-off show, now rebranded *Big Brother's Big Mouth*, had attracted a whole new audience, tantalised by his off-the-cuff riffing and obsession with his 'ballbags'.

Frank Skinner once wrote, 'When good looks come through the door comedy goes out the window,'[70] but Brand exploded that myth as well as plenty more. He proved that good looks and comedy are actually a surprisingly unstoppable combination. I was attending Brand's shows

---

70 Frank Skinner, *Frank Skinner*, Arrow, 2002, p.65.

regularly by now, and the audience was very different to run-of-the-mill comedy crowds. Women in high heels, low-cut tops, peroxide hair and French manicures are not the normal stand-up comedy constituency, but they were making an exception for Brand, leaving notes for him onstage, hanging around long after the gigs were over. Comedy nerds normally want their videos not their breasts signed. There had always been comedy groupies – 'gag hags' – but this was different. Something special was happening with Brand. On his *Scandalous* tour, his security team would compete to see who could bring the most women backstage.

By 2006 Brand was off the drugs but not off the sex, which was his preferred method of winding down after a gig: 'the moment of climax is like pulling a rip-cord which helps me to parachute down to earth'.[71] Performing live onstage is a strange phenomenon, whether it is in front of sixteen people in a pub or 14,000 people at the O2 Arena. Without having done it, it is hard to understand what one goes through and how one comes back down from it. Brand had always craved attention and now he was getting it in spades.

He was skilfully rehabilitating himself with the determination and focus of a reborn zealot, exorcising as many demons as he could and as fast as he could. He did yoga, meditated, did anything to take his mind off the temptations that had been his downfall in the past. He could not risk going anywhere near drugs – he had a 'sack on sight of substance abuse' clause in his TV contract – but he could not resist saying the unsayable. He even landed a new series, *1 Leicester Square*, on his nemesis MTV. When Tom Cruise was a guest he told the *Top*

---

71 Russell Brand, *Booky Wook 2: This Time It's Personal*, HarperCollins, 2010, p.10.

Gun star he shouldn't sit on the floor or he would get piles. I interviewed Brand around this time and asked him what it was like to be a phenomenon. He seemed surprised to be described that way, but there was no other word for him. Brand was different to any other comedian I had ever come across, in the flesh, on video, or while studying the history of comedy. No one was ever quite so raw, so unedited. Or so nakedly ambitious. He was making the transition from cult to mainstream to global domination, but making it on his terms and offering something to everyone. The broadsheets embraced him because he name-dropped Jean Baudrillard, J. G. Ballard and talked about Michael Foucault's theories on Victorian sexual repression, while the *Sun* made him 'Shagger of the Year'.

Success gave Brand the opportunity to revisit old haunts in a new context. In the summer of 2006 Brand appeared at the Edinburgh Festival again, but not this time in a small, sparsely populated shoebox, but for four big nights in the 1,000-seater Edinburgh International Conference Centre. I remember having a drink in the Gilded Balloon loft bar one night when Brand walked in. Edinburgh is a down-to-earth place where performers mingle comfortably with the public. This was the first time I had ever seen anyone at the Festival with what could be described as an entourage. Dressed in black and towering over everyone else in the bar, silver jewellery jangling, hair teased to towering proportions, he certainly seemed like a star.

Fame also gave him the chance to interview Rolling Stone Keith Richards in Cologne, though Brand ended up spending longer in the company of prostitutes in a brothel than with the legendary axeman. With a male friend he had a threesome, but as with other similarly overcrowded encounters made a point of stressing there was nothing gay about it: 'Our threesomes were all conducted in a manly bonding way, like a fishing trip – but a fishing trip where two pals simultaneously have sex with their catch.' Life was rarely simple with Brand. On a trip across America retracing the footsteps of *On the Road* writer Jack Kerouac he had a woman installed in a hotel and when he brought another back had to book into a different room to keep them apart. Life imitated a Whitehall farce as he shuttled between rooms keeping them both happy.

As his film career took off though, this seemed to mark the end of his swashbuckling era, some kind of last hurrah for his overworked ballbags. Brand was asked to present the Video Music Awards and there he first met his wife-to-be Katy Perry. He was clearly smitten. For once he went home alone to his rented house in the Hollywood hills, previously occupied by Bette Davies. There he indulged in his second-favourite pastime, googling himself, and finding out that calling President George Bush a 'retard and cowboy fella' had certainly helped to make him a household name in America. What were a few mad death threats if his remarks helped to make Brand a bigger star than ever? He returned to England and decided to keep a low profile for a while, just doing his Radio 2 show and maybe getting someone in like Jonathan Ross in as a guest . . .

Brand didn't just date ordinary women, this comedy Caligula dated rather exotic women such as Voluptua, or rather Georgina Baillie, from the burlesque group the Satanic Sluts. During a gathering back at Brand's house *Fawlty Towers* came on the television and Georgina said she was the granddaughter of seventy-eight-year-old actor Andrew Sachs, who played Manuel. Brand was inevitably fascinated, his mental Rolodex flicking back to those days watching classic BBC comedy videos while his dad diddled women in the bedroom. It was an odd interlude, perhaps even odder than the Saturday when the Satanic Sluts and Brand's mother sat around the dinner table.

The subject had already come up on Brand's radio show and then the following week Andrew Sachs was due to be a guest on the phones. When he didn't answer, someone, Brand suggests it might have been the producer Gareth, suggested leaving an answerphone message. 'And so began perhaps the most significant minute of broadcasting in the BBC's history.'[72]

Russell Brand overstates the case, but he has a point. Broadcasting has not been the same since Sachsgate. In fact comedy has not been the same since Sachsgate. It has been forced to clean up its act and placed under a microscope. Sachsgate was a perfect storm with a few conspiracy theories thrown in.

1) Newspapers were in decline and needed an outrageous story to boost their circulations: Brand's bad-boy reputation neatly fitted the bill.

2) The *Daily Mail* had been critical of the licence-funded BBC for a long time. This was a nice stick with which to beat the corporation.

3) In the age of the Internet and email, one no longer needs to rely on a few angry colonels in Tunbridge Wells making merry with their green ink. In a matter of days one can have thousands of

---

72 Ibid., p.252.

people joining a campaign, many of whom haven't even heard the offending broadcast.

And so a prerecorded show was broadcast on 18 October 2008 in which Russell Brand improvised a song about Georgina Baillie including the line 'It was consensual and she wasn't menstrual' and Jonathan Ross shouted 'He fucked your granddaughter' during four messages left on the answerphone of Andrew Sachs. The *Mail on Sunday* ran a story about the calls on 26 October. There had originally been only two complaints – and not about the particular content of the answerphone messages – but things soon snowballed. MPs including Prime Minister Gordon Brown criticised them, saying they were 'inappropriate and unacceptable'. Ross was suspended for twelve weeks without pay, and Brand and Lesley Douglas, controller of Radio 2, resigned. After an Ofcom investigation the BBC was fined £150,000. Brand and Ross both sent written apologies to Sachs, which he accepted, and the BBC also issued an apology, but the matter was far from closed.

'The English are a people who have no interest in a work of art until they are told it is immoral,' said Brand later, quoting Oscar Wilde. Rumour had it, however, that if only he had kept his counsel the furore might not have been so great. Although while presenting his show on Saturday 25 October he took the opportunity to apologise on air to Andrew Sachs, he was also critical of the *Mail* prompting the paper to get even more angry with him.

The decision to broadcast the answerphone messages meant that henceforth comedy on the BBC would be monitored far more closely. Some programmes would be prerecorded to avoid any risk of causing offence. Anything remotely controversial would have to be cleared before broadcast. BBC broadcasts suddenly became sterile and cowardly in equal measure. I recall hearing Frank Skinner being interviewed on the radio around this time and when he used the word 'bitch' in quote marks, to refer to it being used elsewhere, the presenter immediately apologised. Sachsgate prompted a moral clampdown the likes of which had never been seen before. The clean-up comedy brigade seemed to be going over programmes with a forensic enthusiasm Quincy MD would have envied. Salem had nothing on the comedy witch-hunt. When *Mock the Week*'s resident folk devil Frankie Boyle suggested – in an already previously seen episode – 'I'm now so old my pussy is haunted' when asked for things the Queen would never say in her Christmas broadcast the press went into overdrive, and comedians who had ever said anything remotely satirical about the Establishment had to take cover.[73]

Even though it was decided that Boyle's joke did not breach editorial guidelines there was a fear in the stand-up world that comedy on television would be neutered. In fact at the time there was not a great deal of stand-up on the box, but that was about to change. With Jonathan Ross's BBC1 chat show off air the BBC had to find a suitable light entertainment replacement, and they came up with the stand-up series *Live at the Apollo*. The fourth series of this reasonably successful show had already been scheduled for Monday nights, but moved to Fridays it had a higher profile. And the very first show, on 28 November 2008, featured someone who was the very antithesis of Russell Brand. Michael McIntyre was clean-cut and middle

---

73 In one of current affairs television's more absurd moments, BBC2 *Newsnight* presenter Emily Maitlis had to say 'I'm now so sorry my pussy is haunted' when she quizzed Director General Mark Thompson on the subject during a news item.

class, rarely used rude words, and made jokes about the awkwardness of having your hair cut, the embarrassment of choosing wine in restaurants and the odd domestic flotsam men keep in their drawers.

McIntyre was a big hit very quickly. He was perfect for an age when television wanted comedians who did not scare the horses. He soon landed his own series, *Michael McIntyre's Comedy Roadshow*, putting more comedians on the television, generating more interest in stand-up comedy and spawning more shows on other channels. Stand-up comedy was suddenly big business, with family-friendly names such as Jason Manford, John Bishop and Rhod Gilbert breaking into the big time. They were all very funny, but somehow you could never see them sticking a Barbie doll up their bums or cutting their chests open with a broken bottle. It looked as if maybe the age of the extreme comedian was over. Killed by Russell Brand.

Brand had other things on his mind, however. He had a film career on the horizon and flew off to appear in an adaptation of *The Tempest*, in which he was cast, appropriately, as the jester Trinculo. From one storm to another. For Brand the shoot was business as usual. There was something about his mental chemistry which meant that he was often only a whisker away from an inappropriate gesture. He used to talk in his act about meeting the Queen when he appeared at the Royal Variety Performance in 2007 and constantly having a little demon niggling away in the back of his mind saying 'Grab her fucking tit' – a very long way from Tommy Cooper asking her if he could have her FA Cup final ticket. His tendency to live in the moment was like a version of Tourette's syndrome. Leaving the *Tempest* shoot in Hawaii he had to rush for a flight. As he ran out of his dressing room, his co-star Dame Helen Mirren called out to him and invited him over to say goodbye. Brand did not know what kind of gesture to make but was certain he had to make one. He realised he was still clutching the yellow underpants that he had been wearing and had just removed. 'Please accept them as a token of my erection, I mean affection,' he said as he handed them over.[74]

Brand was clearly evolving though. Women still trooped in and out of his hotel rooms and house but the thrill was not quite the same. Where once he had felt like a 'charging locomotive' now there was an increasing sense of futility to the chase. After a while even the novelty of having a hotel room featuring a shower with a pole for writhing around wears off. One of the few exciting encounters around this time occurred when he had two women back at his house in separate rooms. At one point he thought a ménage à trois had kicked off when he felt someone licking his behind, but when he looked round it turned out to be the pet bulldog of one of the women. On the bright side though, even dogs clearly found Brand irresistible.

Brand's Video Music Awards appearance might have been controversial, but it must have gone down well with the organisers because they asked him back in 2009. This time the show was memorable for all the right reasons. During rehearsals at New York's Radio City Music Hall he met Katy Perry again. She playfully lobbed a bottle of water at him and it hit him on the head. Maybe it knocked some sense into him, or knocked some randiness out, but he was smitten. At midnight on New Year's Eve 2009 Brand proposed to her. His womanising was over. He really would have to be on his best behaviour now.

---

74 Brand, *My Booky Wook*, p.271.

11

Time for Bed . . .

'Had a good week? Glad someone has.'

Sachsgate changed comedy as we know it in this country, serendipitously putting it right on the entertainment front line. Television looked for safer stand-up, and the success of *Live at the Apollo* helped to spawn *Michael McIntyre's Comedy Roadshow*. Soon every channel had to have its version with its own twist. Channel 4 had *Stand Up For the Week*, aimed at a younger audience. ITV had *Comedy Rocks*, which mixed the new wave with bands and pier-end old-school jokesmiths such as Joe Pasquale. Digital channel Dave had *One Night Stand* in which comedians did gigs in their home towns. It was a veritable once-in-a-generation comedy gold rush.

Suddenly comedians and their material were being devoured by the small screen. New blood was constantly needed to feed the beast. Comedians so new to stand-up they had barely done one Edinburgh Festival show were beamed into millions of homes on a Saturday night. Stalwarts who had plied their trade on the circuit for years hoping that one day they might maybe, if they were lucky, get a quick slot on a Radio 4 panel show suddenly had major exposure. The likes of Stephen

K. Amos, Milton Jones and Micky Flanagan – all very good but not what you would call iconic superstar material – were selling out 4,000-seater rock venues such as the Hammersmith Apollo. Meanwhile Jason Manford and John Bishop were packing out arenas. DVD sales went through the roof. Comedy had, to put it bluntly, gone stark raving mental.

No one in their right minds had expected comedy to get this big. There was a touching moment at the end of the Channel 4 *Comedy Gala* at London's O2 Arena in May 2010 which summed the boom up for me. Lee Evans had headlined the show in front of a sold-out 14,000-strong crowd, and at the end of his act Jack Dee came on and presented the rubber-faced loon with a specially created lifetime achievement award. If the award seemed a trifle cynical, the conversation between them was genuinely touching, as Dee talked about the fact that when they started out playing to one man and his dog a quarter of a century before they may have had ambitions, but they never thought in their wildest dreams it would come to this. There may even have been a couple of moist eyes. I couldn't be sure because my seat was in a different postcode, but I'm pretty confident there wasn't a peeled onion in sight.

But there was a downside to the laugh-quake. Sachsgate had inadvertently made comedy more popular than ever, which was a good thing, but it had also made broadcasters more scared than ever of taking risks, which was a bad thing. Apart from Channel 4's roundly condemned Frankie Boyle shockathon *Tramadol Nights* and BBC2's roundly praised *Stewart Lee's Comedy Vehicle*, comedy was now flattened out into identikit comedians in well-cut suits on shiny floors doing their best, least-likely-to-scare-the-horses ten minutes. Even Jimmy Carr, who had made his name with a distinctive brand of one-liners which often upset the political-correctness brigade, was considered a safe enough pair of hands to have a large role on the BBC's *Comic Relief Night* in 2011.[75] Stand-up comedy is best when it has an air of disruption, a sense of the unexpected. That had all but evaporated.

There are odd pockets of disturbance here and there, but they are few and far between. There is Dr Brown, an anarchic confrontational clown who has been known to hit members of his audience as well as throw olives at them and smother them in baby oil. And Kim Noble, whose background is in art and who suffers from depression, summons up the spirit of Andy Kaufman in his bleakly comic multimedia shows. Sometimes in a Noble show you don't know whether to watch or look away. This is comedy that makes you flinch. In his last show, *Kim Noble Will Die*, he threw out one member of the audience mid-show, but did give them a microwave oven as they left. He also stated that he would be committing suicide after the run was over. He didn't, but some of his behaviour remains deeply disorientating. After he did the show in Edinburgh in 2009 the audience was instructed to meet him in a deserted flat in the middle of the night. There we spoke to his mother on a mobile phone before being taken in to see Noble, who quietly explained that he felt he owed us all a personal apology because he had decided not to end it all.

Comedy since the first modern boom in 1979 had been growing up.

---

75 Jimmy Carr is a true modern comedy enigma. Someone hooked on humour. He is forever making jokes – not for nothing was one of his tours called Gag Reflex (a typically brilliant title neatly encapsulating his skill as a punsmith), and colleagues suggest that although he is always amicable he is hardly a party animal. He has also, says one colleague, 'never been known to dance'.

Time for Bed . . .

We had had Rik Mayall and Adrian Edmondson screaming like a couple of toddlers whose rattles had fallen out of their prams, Baddiel and Newman being sulky and pop-obsessed like a pair of pouty adolescents. Had alternative comedy now reached maturity, had a couple of kids itself and moved to the suburbs? It certainly felt like it when the C4 Comedy Gala returned to the O2 Arena in May 2011. Twenty-one comedy acts – headed by the usual suspects, Evans, McIntyre, Bishop, Manford, Jack Dee – rolled on and off the stage like a comedy conveyor belt, but few were distinctive enough in the short time they had onstage to make a real impact. In fact Sean Lock told virtually the only topical gag of the night, combining two subjects then dominating the headlines – the ash cloud caused by an Icelandic volcano and the superinjunction taken out by a Welsh footballer whose name had just been widely revealed in the press. 'Do you know where the ash cloud comes from? It comes from Ryan Giggs burning every newspaper he can get his hands on.' It got a massive laugh, proving that even mainstream audiences like their banter to have a bit of bite.

So stand-up was in danger of growing up, getting boring and turning out comedians like vacuum-packed sausages. There was no threat in comedy any more. If a goose happened to wander onstage while Michael McIntyre was recording his Comedy Roadshow he was more likely to ask one of the security staff to remove it than say boo to it. Comedians did not just look like bank managers in their suits; they were starting to behave like civil servants, and behind the scenes they seemed to be behaving themselves too. They had wives and young families, and in their routines painted pictures of cosy domesticity. Michael McIntyre joked about having to choose between his children

257

when they ran in opposite directions in the park. John Bishop had separated from his wife for a while, but they got back together when he had started doing stand-up and he had lots of material about his teenage sons' typically sulky behaviour. There didn't seem to be much of a dark side to comedy any more. I've met Michael McIntyre a number of times and he certainly has his insecurities, but he is not in the Hancock league or the Milligan ball park. Good for him, maybe not so good for his comedy.

But you cannot change human nature. Comedians are comedians and just because they don't wear the same style of suit as George Formby doesn't mean they aren't prone to the same temptations. In fact, in the last few years the comedy scene has moved so fast and comedians have rocketed to the top so quickly it is perhaps no surprise if sometimes they suffer from the bends. Comedians are still going to push the bad behaviour boat out at some point. As Shakespeare wrote in *The Tempest*, 'Misery acquaints a man with strange bedfellows.' Or in Jason Manford's case, being bored when on the road acquaints a man with a string of Twitter followers.

The case of Jason Manford and Twitter sums up the fact that comedians will never stop misbehaving, they will simply find new ways to misbehave. The genial northern comic had been doing stand-up for a decade before he was the proverbial overnight success in 2010. I interviewed him in the early summer when he was promoting his forthcoming tour entitled *I'm Turning Into My Dad*. Events, however, moved very fast for Manford, which was typical of the way stand-up was being absorbed by the mainstream. Before the interview was even printed it was out of date when it was announced that he was replacing

Adrian Chiles as the co-host of BBC1 prime-time magazine the *One Show* in July.

This was a direction that I hadn't expected Manford to take. He was a supremely confident quick-witted storyteller with a terrific ear for a memorable phrase, but how would he cope with the gear changes of a show that could be doing a light-hearted report on tortoises one minute and a harrowing story about cancer the next. In the event Jason did well, but after only a few months in the high-profile hot seat he left the job, after being embroiled in a very modern scandal, taking in the Internet, Skype and Twitter. Not things Max Miller ever had to worry about.

In November 2010 it was reported that he had been sending suggestive messages on Twitter to a female fan. Manford said, 'I don't drink or do drugs, so it's not like I've those to blame – just my own stupidity.' Manford responded quickly, resigning from the *One Show* on 18 November to concentrate on 'family and tour commitments'. He and his wife Catherine tried to draw a line under the revelations by appearing together at the Mother and Baby Awards at the London Hilton, which he was hosting. But this did not nip the story in the bud; instead it grew. It was revealed that he had been tweeting as well as chatting on Skype with around twelve women.

Manford dealt with the matter fantastically well, in the way only a comedian with his sort of skill could. He made a gag out of it. Shortly after the headlines he resumed his UK tour, now retitled *It's Off On Tour We Go*, possibly to avoid further embarrassment for his dad. At the Hammersmith Apollo he decided that the best approach was to get it over with. 'You dirty bastard,' boomed a voice from the upper circle, before he even reached the microphone. 'Had a good week? Glad someone has . . . Nothing you can say,' he told his audience, 'can possibly embarrass me more than last week, when seven million people caught me wanking.' Pause for supportive applause. 'It's bad enough when your mum walks in.' From that point Manford had the audience's sympathy. Never mind superinjunctions, that is how to deal with gossip.

And so what comes around has a habit of going around. Comedians will always misbehave. There will always be scandal. It is only the names and the technology that change. And sometimes even the names barely change. Back in 1907 Willie Hammerstein caused uproar with his Sober Sue scam in which he lured in top-class comedians to try to get a woman to smile. The stunt was great for his business. Just over a century later stories appeared in the UK press about the opening in London of a branch of a New York club called The Box. This was intended to be the cabaret and burlesque nightspot to top all cabaret and burlesque night-spots. The New York branch was already legendary. Lady Gaga performed there; Lindsay Lohan and Jude Law were seen there. The man responsible for opening The Box? Simon Hammerstein, Willie's great-grandson. And the venue he chose? The Raymond Revuebar, previously the home of the Comedy Store, where Rik Mayall, Adrian Edmondson, Dawn French, Jennifer Saunders and many more had their big breaks.

List of Illustrations

Plate Section 2

14. Tommy Cooper © Popperfoto / Getty Images
15. Tony Hancock and Hattie Jacques © Popperfoto / Getty Images
16. Benny Hill © Popperfoto / Getty Images
17. Frankie Howerd and Dorothy Bromiley © Popperfoto / Getty Images
18. Bob Monkhouse © Popperfoto / Getty Images
19. Lenny Bruce © John Lindsay / AP / Press Association
20. Peter Cook © Time & Life Pictures / Getty Images
21. Malcolm Hardee © ITV / Rex Features
22. Phil Hartman © Hulton Archive / Getty Images
23. Sam Kinison © Hulton Archive / Getty Images
24. Russell Brand © Mark St George / Rex Features

Bibliography

Keith Allen, *Grow Up* (Ebury)

Kenneth Anger, *Hollywood Babylon* (Delta)

Christopher Beeching, *The Heaviest of Swells* (DCG Publications)

Michael Bentine, *The Long Banana Skin* (Granada)

Edmund Bergler, *Laughter and the Sense of Humour* (Intercontinental Medical Book Corp)

Henri Bergson, *Laughter: An Essay on the Meaning of the Comic* (Arc Manor)

Kevin Booth with Michael Bertin, *Bill Hicks: Agent of Evolution* (Harper Collins)

Mark Borkowski, *The Fame Formula* (Sidgwick and Jackson)

Jo Brand, *Look Back In Hunger* (Headline Review)

Russell Brand, *My Booky Wook* (Hodder)

Russell Brand, *Booky Wook 2 – This Time It's Personal* (HarperCollins)

Gyles Brandreth, *The Funniest Man on Earth: The Story of Dan Leno* (Hamish Hamilton)

David Bret, *George Formby: A Troubled Genius* (Robson)

Louise Brooks, *Lulu in Hollywood* (Alfred A. Knopf)

Lenny Bruce, *How To Talk Dirty And Influence People* (Panther)

Jimmy Carr and Lucy Greeves, *The Naked Jape* (Penguin)

Charlie Chaplin, *Charlie Chaplin: My Autobiography* (Penguin)

Julian Clary, *A Young Man's Passage* (Ebury)

David Cohen and Ben Greenwood, *The Buskers: A History of Street Entertainment* (David and Charles)

Judy Cook with Angela Levin, *Loving Peter – My Life with Peter Cook and Dudley Moore* (Platkus)

William Cook, *Ha Bloody Ha: Comedians Talking* (Fourth Estate)

William Cook, *Morecambe and Wise Untold* (HarperCollins)

William Cook (ed.), *Tragically I was an Only Twin: The Complete Peter Cook* (Arrow)

William Cook, *The Comedy Store* (Little Brown)

John Cohen (ed.), *The Essential Lenny Bruce* (Panther)

Barry Cryer, *Pigs Can Fly* (Orion)

Barry Cryer, *You Won't Believe This But . . .* (Virgin)

James Curtis, *W. C. Fields: A Biography* (Backstage)

Jack Dee, *Thanks for Nothing* (Doubleday)

Charles Dickens, Memoirs of Joseph Grimaldi (MacGibbon and Key)

Jim Driver (ed.), *Funny Talk* (The Do-Not Press)

John M. East, *Max Miller: The Cheeky Chappie* (WH Allen)

Jimmy Edwards, *Six of the Best* (Robson Books)

Lawrence J. Epstein, *The Haunted Smile* (Public Affairs)

Peter Evans, *Peter Sellers: The Man Behind The Mask* (New English Library)

Jean Ferguson, *She Knows You Know! The Hylda Baker Story* (Breedon Books)

John Fisher, *Tommy Cooper* (Harper)

John Fisher, *Tony Hancock: The Definitive Biography* (Harper)

Bibliography

Seymour and Rhoda Fisher, *Pretend the World is Funny and Forever: A Psychoanalysis of Comedians, Clowns and Actors* (Hillsdale New Jersey: Lawrence Erlbaum Assocs)

Sigmund Freud, *Jokes and their Relation to the Unconscious* (Vintage)

Stephen Fry, *The Fry Chronicles* (Michael Joseph)

Albert Goldman from the journalism of Lawrence Schiller, *Ladies and Gentlemen – Lenny Bruce!* (Random House)

Cliff Goodwin, *Sid James* (Virgin)

Thomas Goodwin, *Sketches and Impressions: Musical, Theatrical and Social* (GP Putnam)

Lita Grey Chaplin and Jeffrey Vance, *Wife of the Life of the Party* (Scarecrow)

Fred Lawrence Guiles, *Stan: Life of Stan Laurel* (Scarborough House)

William Hall, *Titter Ye Not: The Life Of Frankie Howerd* (HarperCollins)

Malcolm Hardee with John Fleming, *I Stole Freddie Mercury's Birthday Cake* (Fourth Estate)

Frankie Howerd, *On The Way I Lost It* (Star)

Bill Hicks, Foreword by John Lahr, *Love All The People* (Constable)

Oliver James, Britain on the Couch (Arrow)

Edward Joffe, *Hancock's Last Stand* (Methuen)

Dennis Kirkland with Hilary Bonner, *Benny - The True Story* (Hodder)

John Lahr (ed.), *The Orton Diaries* (Methuen)

Danny La Rue, *From Drags to Riches* (Penguin)

Stewart Lee, *How I Escaped My Certain Fate* (Faber and Faber)

Stewart Lee, *Perfect Fool* (Fourth Estate)

Roger Lewis, *Charles Hawtrey: The Man Who Was Private Widdle* (Faber and Faber)

265

Roger Lewis, *The Life and Death of Peter Sellers* (Arrow)

Mark Lewisohn, *Funny Peculiar: The True Story of Benny Hill* (Pan)

Philip Martin Williams and David L. Williams, *The Theatrical World of Arthur Twist: The Early Career of Frank Randle* (History On Your Doorstep)

Philip Martin Williams, *Wired to the Moon* (History On Your Doorstep)

Graham McCann, *Bounder – The Life of Terry-Thomas* (Aurum)

Graham McCann, *Frankie Howerd Stand-up Comic* (Harper Perennial)

Graham McCann, *Spike and Co* (Hodder and Stoughton)

Andrew McConnell Stott, *The Pantomime Life of Joseph Grimaldi* (Canongate)

David McGillivray, *Doing Rude Things* (Sun Tavern Fields)

Michael McIntyre, *Life and Laughing* (Michael Joseph)

Andy Medhurst, *National Joke: Popular Comedy and English Cultural Identity* (Routledge)

Members of the Lord's Taverners' Company, *Theatrical Digs: Tales From The Green Room* (David and Charles)

Bob Monkhouse, *Crying With Laughter* (Arrow)

Sheridan Morley, *Theatre's Strangest Acts: Extraordinary but True Tales from Theatre's Colourful History* (Robson Books)

Patrick Newley, *The Amazing Mrs Shufflewick: The Life of Rex Jameson* (3rd Age Press)

Barry Paris, *Louise Brooks* (Mandarin)

Barbra Paskin, *Dudley Moore: The Authorised Biography* (Pan)

Nicholas Parsons, *The Straight Man – My Life in Comedy* (Weidenfeld and Nicholson)

Richard Pryor with Todd Gold, *Richard Pryor: Pryor Convictions and Other Life Sentences* (Revolver)

Bibliography

Mike Reid with Peter Gerrard, *T'rific – Mike Reid: The Autobiography* (Partridge)

Ken Robinson with Lou Aronica, *The Element: How Finding Your Passion Changes Everything* (Allen Lane)

Michael Sellers, *PS I Love You: Peter Sellers 1925–1980* (Fontana/Collins)

Dominic Shellard (ed.), *Kenneth Tynan: Theatre Writings* (Nick Hern Books)

Ed Sikov, *Mr Strangelove: A Biography of Peter Sellers* (Sidgwick and Jackson)

Frank Skinner, *Frank Skinner* (Arrow)

Frank Skinner, *Frank Skinner On The Road* (Century)

Arthur Smith, *My Name Is Daphne Fairfax* (Arrow)

Matthew Sweet, *Shepperton Babylon* (Faber and Faber)

Robert Taylor Lewis, *W. C. Fields: His Follies and Fortunes*

Harry Thompson, *Peter Cook: A Biography* (Hodder and Stoughton)

Mary Tich and Richard Findlater, *Little Tich: Giant of the Music Hall* (Elm Tree)

Barry Took, *Star Turns: Mischievous World of Benny Hill and Frankie Howerd* (Weidenfeld and Nicolson)

Sheila Van Damm, *We Never Closed: The Windmill Story* (Robert Hale)

Stephen Wagg (ed.), *Because I Tell A Joke Or Two: Comedy, Politics and Social Difference* (Routledge, 1996)

Max Wall, *Fool on the Hill* (Quartet)

Stephen M. Weissman, *Chaplin: A Life* (Arcade)

Kenneth Williams, *Just Williams: An Autobiography* (HarperCollins)

Kenneth Williams, *The Kenneth Williams Diaries* (Harper Collins)

Roger Wilmut and Peter Rosengard, *Didn't You Kill My Mother-in-Law* (Methuen)

Roger Wilmut, *From Fringe To Flying Circus* (Book Club Associates)

Bob Woodward: *Wired – The Short Life and Fast Times of John Belashi* (Faber & Faber)

Bill Zehme, *Lost in the Funhouse* (Fourth Estate)

Bob Zmuda with Matthew Scott Hansen, *Andy Kaufman Revealed* (Ebury)

Brother Sam: The Short, Spectacular Life of Sam Kinison (William Morrow)

Many publications were out of print or hard to obtain and my thanks go to the British Library for giving me access to their catalogue.

As well as books, newspapers were essential. *The Times, Sunday Times, Guardian, Independent, Daily Telegraph, Sunday Telegraph, Observer, Sun, Daily Mirror* and London *Evening Standard* were an invaluable source of information, as was the *New York Times, Rolling Stone, Playboy* and *Entertainment Weekly*.

I am also indebted to the ever-expanding number of websites that populate cyberspace. Particularly www.chortle.co.uk, www.sabotage times.com (Andrew Collins' profile of Benny Hill was a vital starting point in his chapter), www.brightlightsfilm.com, www.franksreelreviews. com and www.samkinison.org.

John Fisher's TV series *Heroes of Comedy* was both enjoyable and educational. The same can equally be said for BBC4's *The History of Light Entertainment* and *The Secret Life of Bob Monkhouse*.

If I have missed anyone out please inform my publisher and I shall endeavour to include you in future editions.

Index